History of Christ United Methodist Church

MEMPHIS, TENNESSEE
1955–2002

*"Study to shew thyself approved unto God,
a workman that needeth not to be ashamed,
rightly dividing the word of truth."*

—II Timothy 2:15 KJV

History of Christ United Methodist Church

MEMPHIS, TENNESSEE
1955–2002

VOLUME III
Dr. Maxie D. Dunnam
1982–1994

Harry A. Johnson Jr.

Providence House Publishers
PROVIDENCE PUBLISHING CORPORATION
FRANKLIN, TENNESSEE

Copyright 2003 by Harry A. Johnson Jr.

All rights reserved. Written permission must be secured from the publisher to use or reproduce any part of this book, except for brief quotations in critical reviews or articles.

Printed in the United States of America

07   06   05   04   03   1   2   3   4   5

Library of Congress Catalog Card Number: 2003103876

ISBN: 1-57736-278-0

Cover design by Lindrel Moates

Cover illustration by R. Brown

Excerpts from *The Book of Discipline of the United Methodist Church* © 1960, 1968, 2000 The United Methodist Publishing House. Nashville, Tenn.: The United Methodist Publishing House. Used by permission.

Unless otherwise marked, Scripture quotations are from the Revised Standard Version of the Bible, copyright 1952 [2nd edition, 1971] by the Division of Christian Education of the National Council of the Churches of Christ in the United States of America. Used by permission. All rights reserved.

Scripture quotations marked "KJV" are taken from the Holy Bible, King James Version, Cambridge, 1769.

Scripture quotations marked "NEB" are taken from New English Translation [computer file]: NET Bible. –electronic. –Dallas, TX: Biblical Studies Press, 1998. Used by permission. All rights reserved.

Not endorsed by the Executive Committee
of Christ United Methodist Church

PROVIDENCE HOUSE PUBLISHERS
an imprint of
Providence Publishing Corporation
238 Seaboard Lane • Franklin, Tennessee 37067
800-321-5692
www.providencepubcorp.com

DEDICATION

To all lay volunteers who have made Christ Methodist/United Methodist Church a vibrant and aggressive arm of the Lord Jesus Christ, for whom it was named.

There have been thousands of lay volunteers doing outstanding work that has made a lasting imprint on this church for all its forty-seven years. It is reasonable to assume that the dedication and the accomplishments of volunteers will continue to have a positive effect on all the ministries of Christ Church as long as it exists.

Many of these faithful volunteers have made major contributions performing unglamorous tasks that go unnoticed and unsung. These humble people doing unexciting but essential labors in His vineyard are the backbone of the programs of the church.

Literally thousands of members have given of themselves to teach our children Sunday after Sunday and in doing so are laying a foundation of solid rock on which to build the future of the church.

To the adults and children who participate in and plan the worship services, prepare for communion and see that the needed sacraments are on hand and that the banners are displayed properly, the people who collect the registration pads from the pew after each service, the ushers and greeters, the men who built the first playground on Saturdays, those who distribute food and clothes to the needy, the ones who physically labor to repair and build houses, those who teach Bible studies, work in the flower beds as volunteers, man the information desk, stuff envelopes, and the hundreds of others who do the menial tasks that are very humbling. There is no way to list all the things and all of the time sacrifices that individuals make because they love the Lord and His church.

May God bless every minute given in His name.

It's not the clothes we wear,
The cars we drive,
The houses we live in,
Or the color of our skin that determines what and who we are.

It's what we wear in our hearts—
The love of Jesus Christ that puts us in the brotherhood of Christians.

FINANCIAL CONTRIBUTORS TO HISTORY PUBLICATION

Dr. James F. Bigger Jr.
Mr. Earle Billings
Mrs. Dorothy Billings
Ms. Karen Brasfield
Mr. Ben Carpenter
Mrs. Lillie Carpenter
Mrs. Nell Cochran
Mrs. Charlie (Kate) Davenport
Mr. James A. Davenport
Mrs. Mary Davenport
Mrs. Rubye Davie
Mr. Frank Fisher
Mrs. Dorothy Fisher
Judge William H. D. Fones
Mrs. Albert (Alice) Fulmer
Mr. J. Albert Fulmer Jr.
Mr. William L. Hurdle
Mrs. Betty Hurdle
Mr. James C. Ingram Jr.
Mrs. June Ingram
Mr. Harry A. Johnson Jr.
Mrs. Penny Johnson
Mrs. Martha Anne Johnston
Mrs. D. Keith (Mary) Kelley
Mr. David L. Kelley
Mrs. Samuel (Eloise) Mays
Mr. Gordon A. Miles

Mrs. Tennie Miles
Dr. P. D. Miller
Mrs. Greene Miller
Mr. John A. Montgomery
Mr. Raymond E. Moore
Mrs. Virginia Nowlin
Mr. George R. Payne
Mrs. Lou Payne
Mrs. Helen Pipher
Mr. William Poole
Mrs. Elizabeth Poole
Mr. Henry Clay Shelton
Mrs. Harriet Shelton
Mr. Thomas Wade Smith
Mrs. Thomas W. (Nell Carolyn) Smith
Mrs. Alice B. Stolte
Mrs. John (Jane) Stone
Mrs. Jewell Sullivan
Mrs. J. A. (Mary) Summers
Mrs. Jane A. Taylor
Mr. Don Thomas
Mrs. Saralene Thomas
Mr. Jack Wright
Mrs. Martha Wright
Dr. James R. Wyatt
Mrs. Mary Kate Wyatt

CONTENTS

Acknowledgments	ix
Introduction	xi
Dr. Maxie D. Dunnam	1
Ministers of Christ United Methodist Church	16
The Administrative Board	17
History of Counseling and Family Life Center: 1984–1994	20
One Month in Dr. Dunnam's First Year at Christ Church	24
The Joel Committee	35
Archives History	47
The History of the Christ United Methodist Church Library: May 1985–December 1993	52
Lay Delegates to Annual Conference	54
Annual Conference:1986	56
Annual Conference:1991	58
The Church School	66
Missions: 1982–1993	67
The Board of Trustees	92
United Methodist Women: 1982–1994	106

History of Worship: 1982–1994	119
Recollections of Fourteen Years at Christ United Methodist Church	162
Appendix: The Official Boards, Commissions, and Committees	167
Index	236
About the Author	243

ACKNOWLEDGMENTS

Research

Barbara Melton
Worship

Glenn Ragland
Music

D. A. Noel
Land and Buildings

Linda McVean
Day School

Ben Carpenter
Church School

Preparation

Beth Sanders

Data Entry

Clara Downen

Rubye Carlile

Ervin H. (Buddy) Wright

Roylyn Parks

INTRODUCTION

Dr. Charles Grant spent all of his life in the Kentucky Conference before coming to Memphis to become the senior minister of Madison Heights Methodist Church and subsequently to Christ Methodist Church.

Harold Beaty had spent all of his life as a minister in the state of Georgia before coming to Christ Methodist Church as its senior minister.

Maxie Dunnam was born and raised in poverty in southern Mississippi. He then attended the Candler School of Theology at Emory University in Atlanta, Georgia, where he also served his first assignment as a minister to establish a new congregation. He and a friend took a semester off and toured Europe, which had a very broadening effect on Maxie's view of the world.

When he was ordained and had received his master's degree, he went back to his home conference to churches on the Gulf Coast.

Maxie's next move was to southern California where he was viewed as an ultraconservative; he had been thought to be a flaming liberal in Mississippi.

He developed churchwide friendships and began to write some of his well-accepted and still-used books. These led him to Nashville, Tennessee, to the Methodist Publishing House, where he became the world editor of *The Upper Room*.

Maxie became well known throughout the United Methodist and other denominations as well as the Catholic Church.

He continued to write his very readable and usable books and to serve the world Church.

Maxie came to Christ United Methodist Church knowing the religious leaders of the world and with a firsthand knowledge of the mission fields and their needs.

Maxie brought a broader view of the world and its needs to us. Maxie didn't change the direction of the church from its goals to serve God and the world, but he broadened its perception of these goals.

As with this history project, it is impossible to put everyone and everything that has shaped Christ Methodist Church into what it is today.

DR. MAXIE D. DUNNAM
Senior Minister, Christ United Methodist Church, 1982–1994

Maxie Dunnam was born on August 12, 1934, in dire poverty, near a country town called Deemer, in South Mississippi. Deemer doesn't even show up on a current map.

The five children loved to go barefoot and could hardly wait until spring. They only got one pair of shoes each year, which were brogans ordered by mail from Mr. Roebuck's mail-order catalog. Brogans were rough, heavy, high-topped shoes that never fit properly and were never comfortable.

His mother would not let them go barefoot until wild violets began to bloom. Every one of the children would begin to search the fields for the sight of the first violet blooming so they could run to their mother and take off their shoes.

The barefoot experiences in childhood prompted the name of one of his books *Barefoot Days of the Soul*, which includes the childhood story above.

I don't imagine that Maxie and his family fully realized there was a depression even though he was born during the depth of the Great Depression. When everyone around is living in similar circumstances, people don't notice that they are doing without. Word-of-mouth was the only means of communication, so one didn't know what was going on in the county, much less on the other side of the world. He was both economically and culturally deprived, but his parents were honest, hardworking, and committed Christians.

The children of those who grew up in these conditions cannot believe that electricity and indoor plumbing did not exist for them. Water came from a spring until Maxie's family was finally able to bore a well and bring water nearer to the house.

Their house was on a gravel road eight miles out of Richton, which in 1999 had a population of 1,047.

His mother worked hard to maintain their family during the worst of times. She was excitable, talked a lot, and was very loud. His father, Murdock (Mut), was a very quiet man with a native wisdom, which, if it had been coupled with a formal education, could well have made a brilliant man.

Maxie was shaped in a loving home, learning warmth and an expressed emotion from his mother and a noble honesty and genuineness from his father.

Maxie's religious life consisted mostly of hard-shell Baptist preachers and traveling evangelists preaching outdoors, from front porches of farmhouses, or in barns.

In 1946 when he was twelve, the family moved closer to the town of Richton where he came under the influence of Brother Grissam, the pastor of East Side Baptist Church. With the move to Richton, a town of about eight hundred, they were just a short walk up the hill to East Side Baptist Church, which was about three or four miles from town. Maxie and his father both joined the East Side Baptist Church in September. They had to be baptized in Thompson's Creek, which was pretty cold in September. They didn't want to wait until spring and it would be even colder in the depth of winter.

Maxie soon became involved in the youth groups at First Baptist Church, Richton, and the youth ministry of the Methodist church. The Methodist preacher was a young dynamic visionary who took the time to pay attention to Maxie, and Maxie spent a lot of time in the preacher's home. There he saw a model of Christian ministry that gave him a vision of what God can do with a committed Christian.

When Maxie was sixteen and a senior in high school, he began to feel God's call to preach. He went to college that summer and fall. He had not figured out what God wanted him to do, so he quit college and went to Mobile, Alabama, to live with his brother for three months where he worked selling women's shoes and finally making his decision to preach.

He was still a Baptist, but he didn't tell anyone about his call to preach until he settled the issue of church membership.

He read books about different denominations and sent a shock wave through Richton when he joined the Methodist Church and shortly announced his desire to be a candidate for the ministry. David McKeithen saw to it that Maxie received a local preacher's license and used Maxie to preach in a little country church with only ten or fifteen members.

He had only one year of college but teachers were scarce during the Korean War, so the superintendent of the country school invited him to teach the fourth and fifth grades and coach basketball, which he did for one year.

He then went back to Southern Mississippi College at Hattiesburg where he finished college with a bachelor of arts degree in 1955.

During his time in college he was assigned a Methodist charge which consisted of three churches the first year and four the second. "Uncle Walt" was the leader in one of these churches. He played the violin and his family sang to open every service. There were only about ten people in attendance.

Uncle Walt thought a preacher should just open the Bible and start preaching, with no notes. He would stay by Maxie until he opened the Bible and started preaching, then take his seat beside an open window. He would take a big chew of tobacco and then spit out the window all during the service.

Maxie took a friend out in the field to meet Uncle Walt one day. After their short visit Maxie and his friend walked away. Uncle Walt called Maxie back and told him that his wife had just left him and asked Maxie, an eighteen-year-old, to pray for him. It seemed a little odd for this much older man to ask his preacher

Maxie's parents, Cora and Murdock (Mut) Dunnam during better times after World War II.

Twins Lloyd and Lois (two years older than Maxie), Maxie, and their father.

Maxie (age ten or eleven), with his brothers Edgar and Lloyd standing beside their home near Richton, Perry County, Mississippi.

A friend, Lloyd, and Maxie (age thirteen).

Lloyd, Edgar, Maxie, and Murdock.

Maxie really looks like he wants to take that ball somewhere!

The whole Dunnam family: Lloyd, Edgar, Cora (seated), Lois, Irma, Maxie, and Murdock.

to pray for him when his preacher was only eighteen and hadn't been to seminary or been ordained to preach. It gave Maxie an early insight to what would be expected of him as a preacher.

An older preacher went to visit Uncle Walt and during the conversation Uncle Walt took his chewing tobacco out of his pocket. The preacher told him that God knew that he was going to take a chew of tobacco, so Uncle Walt stuck the tobacco back in his pocket and said, "I'll just fool the old man then."

In 1955 Maxie went to Atlanta and entered the Candler School of Theology at Emory University. He had no money so he had to work. The district superintendent in Atlanta wanted to organize a new Methodist church in southeast Atlanta. He chose two young theological students to do the groundwork. They were Maxie and Eldon Smith. He was a full-time student at Candler and pastor of this church that grew to three hundred before he graduated with a master of theology degree in 1958.

During his first year in seminary he began to find out that the world was much larger and more interesting than Perry County, Mississippi, so he and his good friend Buford Dickinson dropped out of seminary in the spring quarter of his first year and hitchhiked all over Europe. His inspiration for this trip came from his preaching professor, Dr. G. Ray Jordan, who wrote a book entitled, *You Can Preach*. Maxie took it to heart and preaching became his passion. He made the commitment to become the best preacher possible.

Interestingly, Dr. G. Ray Jordan wrote the foreword to Maxie's first book, a collection of meditations entitled *Channels of Challenge*. In that foreword Dr. Jordan said:

> Maxie Dunnam, the author of this book, is a young clergyman of superior ability and special talents. He's one of the most effective ministers of those who have studied at the Candler School of Theology in the 18 years I've

Ain't she sweet! Jerry, age four.

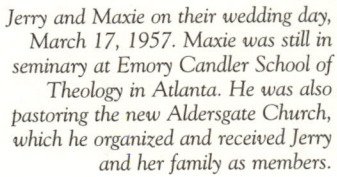

Jerry and Maxie on their wedding day, March 17, 1957. Maxie was still in seminary at Emory Candler School of Theology in Atlanta. He was also pastoring the new Aldersgate Church, which he organized and received Jerry and her family as members.

served as professor of preaching. His devoted interest in the pulpit ministry has directed him in practicing those disciplines that vitally concern his profession. His insight into truth, his ability to see the relevance of theology to life and his capacity to communicate the gospel—all these disclose marked ability. It was a personal privilege to teach him and it is a source of deep satisfaction to think of him as a friend.

Maxie married Jerry Morris on March 15, 1957, while he was still in seminary. Maxie met Jerry while on a date with her sister. They seemed to like each other's singing so they began their courtship which led to their marriage. A year and a half later they returned to his home conference in Mississippi. His appointment was to a small church in Gautier, a community near Pascagoula on the Gulf of Mexico.

Maxie took Jerry into a situation that was not altogether a happy one. The parsonage had a tacked-on bathroom and no furniture. In addition, eight of the church's leaders walked out when the district superintendent introduced Maxie as the replacement for "Pastor Willy" who was a shipyard worker by day.

A young man leaving Gautier to attend Mississippi State gave them his furniture. They were only in Gautier for one year, but it turned out to be a wonderful experience; even the eight leaders came back. While driving to Atlanta to visit Jerry's parents, they were in a terrible automobile accident.

The Dunnam family camping out in the mountains above Anaheim, California.

While Maxie was the pastor of Trinity Church in Gulfport, he and Jerry (pregnant with Kim) loved to get away in Maxie's pride and joy—the little red M. G. and go to Thompson's Creek as their hideaway.

Jerry and Maxie's three children, Kim, Kevin, and Kerry, pictured outside their home on Central Avenue in Memphis on their first Sunday at Christ Church in March 1982.

Kevin, Jerry, Kim, Maxie, and Kerry in San Clemente, California.

Maxie was hospitalized for a month with a fractured skull and a severed ear. The Christian Church Committees in Evergreen, Alabama, took Jerry in and cared for her and ministered to Maxie for a month. After six months in Gautier, Maxie started work on the establishment of a new church in Gulfport, Mississippi. Trinity Church in Gulfport is one of the outstanding congregations in Mississippi today.

A young contractor became a charter member and built all the buildings at this new church. This young man gave Maxie his first robe and his first typewriter. They have kept in touch. That young man became a very successful contractor and is now endowing a chair at Asbury Seminary.

In the Trinity congregation was a woman of prayer, over seventy years of age, and financially well off. She had lived all over the country and had become acquainted with great people like Frank Laubach, Tom Carruth, E. Stanley Jones, Louise Echolston, Estelle Carver, and an Eastern Orthodox nun named Sister Lelia. Nettie Beeson brought all of these people to Trinity Church to speak, where they made a profound impression on Maxie's life and he made a commitment to prayer in a way that he never had before.

The Civil Rights movement began to stir in the early sixties while they were in Gulfport. Maxie and four other Methodist ministers wrote a statement entitled *Born of Conviction* about the freedom of the pulpit and the maintaining of the public school system and not to organize private schools for the purpose of preserving segregation. In the context of today it was a mild statement, but it caused quite a stir then. A total of twenty-eight Methodist ministers signed it and presented it to the Mississippi Conference and, literally, "all Hell broke loose!" Many of these clergy were run from their churches and most left Mississippi. Maxie was not forced out of his congregation, but there was a lot of building tension. The Trinity congregation was made up of people stationed at Keesler Air Force Base and of civilians who had moved to the Gulf Coast from all over the nation. This cosmopolitan congregation sustained Maxie for five years. This church was the Cinderella congregation of the conference and successful in every way one could measure success. In the midst of this success Maxie began to feel emptiness in his life and even flirted with throwing in the towel.

Maxie's family, especially his mother, loved to play cards. After Maxie was ordained and preaching full time he went home to visit, and his mother gathered them around a table in the living room and they started playing cards. This was on a Sunday after they had been to church and had dinner. His mother was facing the front door and saw the local preacher approaching. With a shaking hand she ordered Maxie to hide the cards because the preacher was coming.

A man named Tom Carruth kept insisting that Maxie get to know Stanley Jones, the famous missionary evangelist in India, one of the great Christians of this century. His friend prevailed upon him to drive to Florida and attend an ashram (a Christian retreat) for a week, which was held by Stanley Jones. Maxie got so excited about what Stanley Jones was doing that he invited him to hold an ashram in Mississippi. He reserved the Methodist youth camp, but the leaders of Mississippi Methodism would not allow its use because they knew Stanley Jones would not hold any meeting which was not open to all races.

Bishop [James] Kennedy of southern California offered Maxie an opportunity to start a congregation in San Clemente so he and Jerry packed up and with their two daughters moved to California.

The San Clemente church started out in the Elks Lodge but grew to about five hundred with the full intention of being a 50/50 church—50 percent for self, 50 percent for missions. He accompanied Stanley Jones to the Scandinavian countries on an ashram and included a visit to East Germany.

An individual in San Clemente gave Maxie twenty-five hundred dollars to be spent on a mission trip. With a four-thousand-dollar-a-year salary, he borrowed another twenty-five hundred so Jerry could accompany him around the world to missions in India, Africa, Lebanon, Jordan, Israel, and Hong Kong.

Maxie had begun small prayer and Bible study groups back in Gulfport, and this ministry expanded as Maxie moved on to San Clemente and then to a thirteen-hundred-member church in Anaheim where he stayed for five years. The Anaheim church established a mission in Tijuana, Mexico, and a ministry to Hispanics in Orange County. He began a development of the relational understanding of theology along with an outstanding psychologist, Dr. Everett Shostrum, the author of *Man the Manipulator*. Dr. Shostrum, Maxie, and another preacher wrote a book entitled *The Manipulator in the Church*. This was an effort to bring the humanistic psychology movement into the church.

Maxie had four books published while in Anaheim, *The Manipulator in the Church, Dancing at My Funeral, Be Your Whole Self,* and *Direction and Destiny*.

Maxie was a part of the Faith at Work movement which was led by Episcopal clergyman Samuel Shumaker, Bruce Larson, and Keith Miller. Bruce wrote the introduction to Maxie's most autobiographical book, *Dancing at My Funeral*. "Maxie Dunnam is one of the architects of the new thing God is doing in our time. A pastor, a leader and a pioneer, he is helping many discover a fresh experience of God's Grace and man's potential."

Although Maxie can't dance very well, what he refers to in this book is to literally dance at the funeral of the past that has haunted him. The past for all of us should not be hidden but celebrated. He reminds us that our Lord said that the Kingdom is within us.

But about the title Maxie says:

> Am I dancing at my funeral? Yes! Funerals I know about. In rural Mississippi funerals were a part of our culture, like going to town on Saturday, fourth Sunday sings, summer revival, cakewalks and school socials and smoking rabbit tobacco behind the barn. Also as a minister, I've conducted hundreds of funerals. Most prefer the hell of a predictable situation rather than risk the joy of an unpredictable one. Funerals are about death; dancing is about life.

It is strange how God's design works in our lives. Maxie had shared in an evangelistic mission in Mexico where he met a young preacher from Texas who was the spiritual son of Ira Galloway, the general secretary of the Board of Evangelism of the United Methodist Church. *The Upper Room* was part of that board which became the Board of Discipleship. They began to seek a person to lead the new prayer movement. The young man from Texas told Ira Galloway about Maxie and that was the way God worked to bring Maxie to *The Upper Room*. Dr. Wilson Weldon, the world editor of *The Upper Room*, and Dr. Galloway invited Maxie to come to Nashville and *The Upper Room* to lead in this prayer

Dr. Maxie D. Dunnam

Maxie doing a little table cooking while on a trip to Europe.

Dr. Eddie Fox and his wife with Maxie in Germany while attending a meeting of the World Council—Jerry must have been the photographer.

Maxie looking like a relaxed Don Corleone at his favorite restaurant on an island retreat near Venice, Italy. Maxie didn't have a dime on him, the waiter took pity and gave Jerry and him a free cup of coffee while they waited for their ferry back to Venice.

movement. Maxie, Jerry, their two girls, and son, Kevin, born in San Clemente, packed up and moved to Nashville.

Shortly after going to Nashville he wrote another book, *Homesick for a Future*. In this he reflected that he became certain that the signs of the time, the counterculture, the intense interest in metaphysics, the occult, meditation, Eastern religions, the inward turn, and the religious concern of the present student generation, all testify to the express need—a meaningful life of prayer.

Although Protestants were saying little about spiritual formation at this time, the Catholic Church was big in this concern. Maxie and some of the staff experienced the Roman Catholic Chrysalis movement. He knew this had to be made available to Protestants, and so, the Emmaus movement was established. That movement has spread across the United States and around the world.

After four years of directing the prayer life movement, Maxie became world editor of *The Upper Room* and became a world Christian in the fullest sense of the word. In that position he traveled the world, leading conferences, promoting the work of *The Upper Room*, especially the *Daily Devotional Guide* which is in over fifty-three different languages. He had the opportunity of sharing with some of the great Christian leaders of the world like William Barclay, the great Bible commentator; James Stewart, the great Scottish theologian and preacher;

Lita Snowden, the New Zealand woman who has been one of the popular devotional writers of this century; Dr. Alexander Koon, the man who lived a martyr's life in Estonia and kept the Methodist Church alive during the days of Communist oppression; and Abel and Freida Hendricks, Christian leaders in South Africa who stood against apartheid.

Maxie feels that his *Workbook on Living Prayer* might be the most significant contribution that he has made to the Church. It was published shortly after he went to work at *The Upper Room* in 1974. It has sold over one million copies and is in print in four languages including Chinese. The twentieth anniversary edition was published in August 1994.

Because that workbook model was so effective, there followed six additional workbooks, *The Workbook of Intercessory Prayer, The Workbook on Being Alive in Christ, The Workbook of Coping as Christians, The Workbook of Spiritual Disciplines, The Workbook on the Christian Walk,* and *The Workbook on Christians Under Construction and in Recovery.*

The Upper Room expanded significantly in the area of spiritual formation and a new magazine for children called *Pockets* was launched. Jerry became a major illustrator for *Pockets* and was a writer of a special feature entitled "The Meeting Tree" which enabled children to address some of the crucial issues of life such as death, divorce, moving to a new city, and so on. Jerry did other work in graphic arts and illustration, designing covers of books such as *Blessed to be a Blessing* and Bishop [Edward] Tullis's book on Paul's letter to the Philippians.

There is no other position in the Methodist Church that provides more visibility than being the world editor of *The Upper Room*. The circulation of four million goes to Christians of all denominations all over the world, not just Methodists.

Maxie was invited by Dr. Douglas Steere, a Quaker, a professor of philosophy, and a world leader in the "Friends Movement" to become a part of the Ecumenical Institute of Spirituality. Dr. Steere had been invited by Pope John XXIII to be an observer at the Vatican Council. As a result he made a commitment to bring together twenty-two Roman Catholic and Protestant leaders to share personal spiritual experiences and to examine some of the pressing issues of the Christian faith. Maxie participated in this dialogue for eight years. He also was a conversationalist in a series of films on prayer and spirituality where he was able to share with Father John Powell, a professor at Loyola University in Chicago, and Anthony Bloom, a Russian Orthodox priest who was exiled from Russia and living in London. Relationships with Anthony Bloom, John Powell, Douglas Steere, Stanley Jones, and Tom Carruth are unrepeatable experiences that will forever shape who Maxie is and to some degree has determined his destiny.

Maxie has preached all over the nation and the world, delivered the notable *Denman Papers* in 1993, and spoke at the New Room, the first Methodist chapel built by Wesley in Bristol, England, at the celebration of the two-hundred-fiftieth anniversary of Methodism. He has spoken at Chitagwa in New York, and gave the Douglas Street lecture in christian philosophy and spiritual life at Dayview Association in Michigan in 1982. He gave the Lance Webb lectures on spiritual formation in Lake Bloomington, Illinois, in 1978 that stimulated his book, *Alive in Christ*. More than any other, that book captures the essence of Maxie's theology. He writes about the passion of his own life, to be conformed to Christ, to allow the indwelling Christ full expression. He defines spiritual formation as "that dynamic process of receiving through faith and appropriating through commitment, discipline and action, the loving Christ into our own life to the end that our own life will conform to and manifest the reality of Christ's presence in the world." He is committed to the renewal of the United Methodist Church for the recovery of our Wesleyan understanding of personal and social holiness, for an evangelical passion and zeal that wants to see the church reborn again into a transforming power in our culture. An honorary doctorate of divinity degree was bestowed upon Maxie in 1977 by Asbury Theological Seminary in Wilmore, Kentucky.

Bishop Tullis was the bishop of the Nashville area when Christ United Methodist Church of Memphis began looking for a senior minister after the death of Harold Beaty. Bishop Tullis was also chairman of the committee responsible for the work of *The Upper Room* where Maxie had been for ten years as world editor. After weeks of looking and interviews, Maxie came to Bishop Tullis's mind. After much thought and prayer he talked to Maxie about this strange notion. He and Jerry uprooted their family again and moved to Memphis. Maxie brought with him the world experience and view that he had gained at *The Upper Room*, in California, and even in Mississippi. In 1982, Dr. Maxie Dunnam was appointed to fill the vacancy at Christ Church. Dr. Dunnam stated in an article in the *Commercial Appeal* that he saw his new congregation as being in a unique position to become a dynamic force in the community. He said, "My primary task will be preaching. My primary gifts are preaching and teaching." The worldwide ministry of Christ Church expanded tremendously, especially in the area of world evangelism. The membership doubled during his twelve years, the budget quadrupled, the attendance tripled, and the buildings doubled in size. Christ Church became one of the flagship churches of United Methodism.

Jerry Dunnam and I had some different views on how to accomplish several things at Christ Church while I was chair of the Board of Trustees. I figured that the best way to resolve this was to take Jerry to lunch. I invited her to have lunch with me at Chickasaw Country Club. I picked her up at home on Central Avenue and we had a great time talking and eating and resolving our differences. She said that this was the first time ever that she had been invited by a man to have lunch without Maxie.

The next night Penny and I went to Chickasaw for dinner and our favorite waiter served us. I said, "Arthur, the lady that was with me at lunch yesterday is my preacher's wife." He said, "Mr. Harry, I didn't see you with no woman yesterday." Penny and I had a good laugh about that and so did Maxie and Jerry when I related it to them.

The thinker, the dreamer, or both, on one of his European trips. Maxie has probably dreamed of having this peace and quiet many times since then.

In 1984 Maxie, along with several laypersons, established the counseling center with Rev. Ed Horton as its first director and Jerry Johnston as secretary and only other employee. As this is written in 1998, the counseling center has eighteen full- and part-time employees.

Maxie served as chair of World Evangelism from 1986 to 1996 and chaired the Program Committee for the World Methodist Conference in Nairobi in 1986. He served on the Executive Committee of the World Methodist Council for ten years. Through his work on world evangelism, the connecting church's evangelistic effort has been launched and in eighteen months of that effort, thirty new churches were founded in eastern Europe following the fall of the Berlin Wall. Christ Church, Memphis, is responsible for the church in Pskov, Russia.

Maxie and I discussed the beginnings of the church and the function of the Steering Committee many times in his first few years at Christ Church. We (Penny and Harry A. Johnson Jr.) called and wrote all of the Steering Committee members and invited them and their spouses to a dinner at the Summit Club which we were pleased to host.

Everyone came except Mary and Howard Davenport, who had moved to Hot Springs, Arkansas, and entered a nursing home to be near their daughter. We received a long letter expressing their desire to attend the dinner and explaining their inability to do so. Howard also called.

We made a big mistake—we didn't record this dinner meeting on videotape. This was the only time the Steering Committee ever got together after Christ Church was organized. It was a nostalgic and exhilarating get together and we all enjoyed it.

A third worship service was added in 1991 at 9:45 A.M. on Sundays. This service is contemporary with a strong emphasis on praise and worship music. This service grew quickly to nearly one thousand in attendance, even using Wilson Chapel and a projection of the sermon on screen but with its own band and liturgies.

When Maxie is asked his opinion of dancing, his answer every time is, "Some can, some can't." Maxie wrote a book called, *Dancing at My Funeral*, but Jerry really likes to dance. Jerry and I danced at my daughter Janet's wedding reception, at a few other wedding receptions, anniversary parties, and a few times when we went to dinner at Chickasaw. Maxie would give it his best shot with

Maxie and Jerry flying in a private plane from Memphis to Louisiana and back each week to record a Bible study on video.

Jerry says goodbye to Maxie at Memphis International Airport, beginning her trip to Russia.

Penny, but never quite got the hang of it and didn't enjoy it very much. But Jerry gets a bang out of it.

In November 1993, a Saturday night service was started and patterned after the 9:45 service and attendance on Saturday night quickly grew to around five hundred.

In 1992 Christ Church made a dramatic move when they purchased a seven-hundred-thousand-dollar piece of property in Cordova for the establishment of a new Methodist church. This property did not prove to be what was needed so it was sold in 1996 and the proceeds (profit) on its sale went to the new Heartsong Church headed by Dr. Steve Stone. Steve served on the staff at Christ Church and carried approximately sixty members with him to begin the new church.

Between Maxie and Durelle Durham, *Perceptions* was started on radio and television five days a week. It was met with immediate and measurable success and accounted for over 60 percent of the visitors to the church. Maxie and his successor, Bill Bouknight, are household names all over the Memphis area because of *Perceptions*.

Maxie, Jerry, and their family experienced the strongest support possible by a Christian community. Maxie's writing ministry continued to be enhanced; his workbooks launched a publishing project called *The Communicator's Commentary*. Dr. Lloyd John Ogilvie, pastor of First Presbyterian Church, Hollywood, California, was the general editor of this series and he invited Maxie to write the volume on Paul's letters to the Galatians, Philippians, Colossians, and Philemon in the New Testament and a volume on Exodus in the Old Testament. In his introduction to the volume on Paul's letters, Dr. Ogilvie says, "Maxie Dunnam is a man in Christ, an exciting expositor of the Word, a Christian statesman and a faithful churchman."

After twelve years as the senior minister at Christ United Methodist Church in Memphis, Maxie and Jerry stunned the congregation in March of 1994 when they tearfully announced his resignation to become the president of Asbury Seminary in Wilmore, Kentucky. This time it was just Maxie and Jerry on the move, with a daughter in Ohio and leaving the other two children in Memphis.

It was to be another great adventure in faith that can possibly have the most profound and lasting impact on the church of any move they have made so far in their lives. So, another search was launched by Christ Church for its fourth senior minister.

There was a whale of a send-off for Maxie and Jerry in the sanctuary. Betty Moore was the chairperson, Kyle Rote the master of ceremonies, and Eddie Fox attended from Nashville as well as the wife of his best friend Jean (Mrs. Buford) Dickinson from Ohio. Kallen Esperian, the world famous opera star, sang "Amazing Grace," and Dr. Alvin Jackson, pastor of Mississippi Boulevard Christian Church, spoke.

This began another major career move for Maxie and Jerry and a nationwide search involving twelve bishops who helped our own Bishop Kenneth Carder find the person who appeared to be the best qualified to be Christ United Methodist Church's fourth senior minister in thirty-nine years.

Maxie's imprint on Christ Church is probably best illustrated by its continuing impact on world missions, for bringing the world to Christ Church with renowned Christian leaders to speak, and with *Perceptions* and his writings, which are used the world over. Maxie was on the board at Asbury Seminary in Wilmore, Kentucky, for twelve years and chaired that board for several years. In March

Jerry and Maxie in front of their home in Wilmore.

1994, he was chosen as the person to succeed Dr. [David] McKenna, a close friend of Maxie's, as the fifth president of Asbury. Asbury is well-endowed, having received $38.9 million from Ralph Waldo Beeson in 1990. This is the largest donation ever made to an institution of higher learning in Kentucky. There are about twelve hundred students from fifty denominations (predominantly Methodist) enrolled at Asbury.

Maxie and Jerry are living on a large tract of land in the north end of Wilmore in a mansion that was willed to the seminary. They chose this as their home instead of the traditional house used by former presidents.

There are beautiful places indoors and out for large receptions and it is much used. The kitchen, however, was a very small room and was a problem for the Asbury chef to serve the large (or small) receptions. The school decided in the fall of 1998 to build a new kitchen on the rear of the house. For several months Jerry had no kitchen (which suited her just fine). At Christmas 1998, they had all of their family plus some. There were about twelve or fifteen people over for a week, Jerry had only a refrigerator and a microwave oven, which she says is all anyone should need.

The new kitchen is a huge, bright, and wonderfully equipped room. The island in the center is about thirty-five to forty square feet. It has the most modern cooking equipment available. I asked Jerry what she was going to do with it. She said, "I've practiced what I'm going to show you." She picked her position between the island and a refrigerator and proceeded to demonstrate. She said, "Watch this! I can pivot and get food out of the refrigerator, pivot again and put it in the microwave. It's all quite simple!"

MINISTERS OF CHRIST UNITED METHODIST CHURCH

Senior Ministers

Dr. Charles W. Grant	1955–1969
Dr. J. Harold Beaty	1969–1981
Dr. Maxie D. Dunnam	1982–1994

Ministers

Rev. B. L. Gaddie	1956–1957
Rev. Marshall Morris	1958–1963
Rev. Howard W. Rash	1963–1988
Rev. Charles H. Lynn	1967–1969
Dr. Paul W. Clayton	1969–1974
Rev. Edward W. Walton	1970–1976
Rev. Albert M. Evans	1974–1977
Dr. Wayne Lamb	1976–1987
Rev. Robert H. Wood	1976–1979
Rev. Catherine Wood	1976–1979
Rev. Jerry F. Corlew	1978–1983
Rev. Pamela McDaniel	1979–1980
Rev. Earl A. Johnston	1983–1991
Rev. James L. Loftin	1983–
Rev. W. Edward Horton	1984–1985
Rev. Fred C. Morton	1986–1994
Rev. Shirley Lynn	1987–1993
Rev. Jim Mulroy	1989–
Rev. Rick Kirchoff	1991–
Rev. Linda Gabriel	1992–
Rev. Bradley W. Gabriel	1993–
Rev. Matt Hook	1993–
Rev. Don Burford	1993–
Rev. Win Green	1993–

Diaconal Ministers

Mr. Donald L. Sanford	1970–1982
Mrs. Shirley G. Lynn	1972–1987
Mr. Marvin H. Budd	1981–1991
Mr. Charles Bagley	1987–1990
Mr. Pat Whaley	1990–
Miss Elaine Friedrich	1993–
Mrs. Dorree Jane Smith	1993–

Pastoral Ministers

Rev. Gene Barnes	1988–

THE ADMINISTRATIVE BOARD

THE ADMINISTRATIVE BOARD RESPONSIBILITIES AND CREATION OF THE EXECUTIVE COMMITTEE

This document outlines the responsibilities of the Administrative Board and documents the establishment of the Executive Committee in February 1992, and a modification in 1994.

As the executive agency of the local church, the Administrative Board is to oversee the ministry and administration of the congregation. The responsibilities of the Administrative Board include:

A. Serve as the executive agency, overseeing the program and administration of the church, providing advice and consent to the various groups and committees.

B. Create and annually review a Mission Statement for the church.

C. Upon recommendation of the program council, the Administrative Board will review and approve goals and objectives to carry out the mission of Christ Church.

D. Provide for an annual evaluation of the overall administration and ministry in light of the mission of the church.

E. Upon recommendation of the proper committees, the Board will determine and compile policies and authorize actions to carry out the program for the congregation.

F. Upon recommendation of the Finance Committee, establish the annual budget.

G. Upon recommendation of the Nominations Committee, fill vacancies between meetings of the Charge Conference.

Executive Committee. There will be an Executive Committee of the board (made up of 15 persons, officials and staff) which would meet monthly and would be empowered to make policy decisions between regular meetings of the board. Decisions of the Executive Committee must be reported to the Administrative Board for its action at the board's next regular meeting.

The Executive Committee would include: the senior minister, board chairperson, COM (program council) chair, lay leader, the chairpersons of finance, staff-parish, UMW and trustees, the business manager, the senior associate pastor, and five other laypersons, to be nominated by the Nominating Committee and elected by the Charge Conference. The original resolution was amended in the following manner: (changes are in italics)

There will be an Executive Committee of the board (made up of 16 persons, *lay* officials and staff) which would *meet monthly to make decisions within current church policy as established by the Administrative Board and/or Charge Conference. All decisions or actions* of the Executive Committee *will be* reported to the Administrative Board *for its response* and action at the board's next regular meeting. *The Executive Committee will also receive reports about the progress of the church in implementing the church's mission, key result areas and goals and will forward any conclusion and/or recommendations to the Administrative Board for information and/or action.*

The Executive *Committee* would include: the senior minister; board chairperson; program council chairperson; lay leader; the chairpersons of finance, staff parish, UMW, *Joel* and trustees; the business manager; the senior associate pastor; and five *additional* laypersons, to be nominated by the Nominating Committee and elected by the Charge Conference.

✤ ✤ ✤

Annual Net Membership and Budget

Year	Members	Budget
1956	876	$193,422
1957	1,119	$165,635
1958	1,316	$555,505
1959	1,413	$235,181
1960	1,489	$414,613
1961	1,579	$358,848
1962	1,684	$358,806
1963	1,893	$463,027
1964	1,941	$408,082
1965	2,091	$421,410
1966	2,275	$366,701
1967	2,501	$400,265
1968	2,615	$441,800
1969	2,592	$554,144
1970	2,610	$450,335

The Administrative Board

Year	Membership	Budget
1971	2,677	$209,708
1972	2,728	$403,988
1973	2,745	$459,376
1974	2,800	$689,270
1975	2,871	$524,747
1976	2,916	$556,956
1977	3,067	$684,375
1978	3,165	$753,148
1979	3,260	$864,648
1980	3,316	$944,935
1981	3,396	$916,365
1982	3,495	$1,066,172
1983	3,571	$1,100,468
1984	3,703	$1,809,968
1985	3,754	$1,575,092
1986	3,827	$1,899,026
1987	3,755	$2,155,428
1988	3,977	$2,205,677
1989	4,421	$2,360,864
1990	4,632	$2,445,453
1991	4,972	$2,652,033
1992	5,311	$3,541,918
1993	5,796	$4,246,088

* Membership and budget totals are from the *Memphis Annual Conference Journals*

HISTORY OF COUNSELING AND FAMILY LIFE CENTER 1984–1994

Rev. Fred Morton

The counseling center was born of the vision of senior minister Maxie Dunnam and the generosity of several laymen. Rev. Edward Horton, a minister in the Memphis Annual Conference, was appointed as counselor. The center was housed in the refurbished former parsonage on Poplar Avenue, and Reverend Horton remained as primary counselor for about a year. George Atkinson, a graduate student in clinical psychology, served as a temporary counselor. Mrs. Jerry Johnston was recruited to serve as secretary and business manager during a time of transition.

In January 1986, a new permanent director was secured when Rev. Fred Morton, a minister in the Memphis Conference, was appointed to the staff of Christ United Methodist Church with pastoral duties as well as responsibility for directing the counseling center. Reverend Morton, who held a graduate degree in clinical psychology, had served as a university chaplain at Murray State University and had served churches in the Memphis Conference since his ordination in 1967. The counseling center operated under a strong advisory committee chaired by Ms. Martha Vandervoort with able committee members Mr. Ted Medlin, Dr. Tom Shipmon, Mrs. Julia Atkinson, Mrs. Doris Smith, Mr. Erie Henrich, and Mr. Orin Johnson.

Over the next eight years under Dr. Dunnam's ministry, the counseling center's programs would expand to include a number of permanent services and a wide variety of counseling personnel. Among the various programs initiated by the counseling center were Christian Parenting, Marriage Enrichment, Preparation for Marriage Workshops, a Lay Chaplains' Ministry to the Homebound, and the provision for a wide variety of support and recovery groups, such as Alcoholics Anonymous (AA) and Al-Anon. Because the counseling center was the only center approved by the University of Memphis for graduate training in church-based counseling, over a score of counseling interns would serve on the counseling staff. Ms. Lou Martin and Ms. Ann Marston Orr served as interns and both continued as permanent counseling staff, working primarily with children. Also Mr. Don Howdeshell was added as a financial counselor along with career counselor Mr. Warren Morrison. A close working relationship for referrals was developed with local psychiatrists, clinical psychologists, and treatment centers.

Among the more significant and enduring programs during this era was the emergence of the Career Support Ministry. In 1988, in response to an initiative from several individuals in the Lamplighters Sunday school class seeking to bring support to several of their number who had lost jobs, a coordinated response was devised to provide spiritual support and practical assistance to the increasing number of persons affected by downsizing in the corporate world. An Advisory Committee was formed under the leadership of John Allen, Burns Landess, Mike Sheahan, Horace Branch, and Roger Watson. An ongoing program was developed to provide regular workshops and resources for those in job transition in the counseling center. A dedicated and effective career counselor, Mr. Jack Quinlan, served as career counselor for monthly sessions that reached nearly one thousand persons those first four years of the ministry. A corps of volunteer persons lent ongoing support at Tuesday morning breakfasts. Currently there are two career counselors and a permanent resource center for the Career Support Ministry, which comprise a regular part of the counseling ministry services. Those counselors, who were initiated to the ministry as they were serving graduate internships at the center, are Deborah Schadt, Ph.D., and Pat Stanley, M.S. Their services continue to be available at no charge to the unemployed in the entire community. The Tuesday breakfasts first held at a local restaurant are now held in Seabrook Hall. Of all the career support services that have emerged in both church and secular settings locally and nationally, Christ Church has the reputation of being one of the first and consistently best.

Christians in Recovery was an intentional response to the growing awareness of the problems of drug addiction as it affected our church families. Specific programs, even a Sunday school class for recovering persons, was developed as encouraged by senior minister Maxie Dunnam. Christ United Methodist Church had historically supported recovery work. In the Seabrook addition (1988) a room was dedicated for use by recovery groups (AA and Al-Anon). By the end of Dr. Dunnam's tenure, an alcohol and drug counselor, Mr. Steve Watts, was added to the counseling center staff.

Other programs initiated in this time were Divorce Care Workshop, developed cooperatively with singles' ministry courses in dealing with anxiety and depression, and a ministry for women recovering from abuse. An additional clergy counselor was added when Rev. Linda Gabriel was appointed in 1992 as counselor and director of Stephen Ministries to strengthen our volunteer lay ministry to sick and hurting persons.

With the use of new facilities in the Seabrook Building, the center was located on ground level with three offices. By the conclusion of Dr. Dunnam's tenure, the counseling staff had grown to over a dozen part-time counselors, which included Dr. Larry Semrau, a marriage and family counselor; Mr. Burns Landess, an additional financial counselor; and a part-time ministry assistant in career support.

Under Reverend Morton's leadership as counselor and director, the center had grown from its early beginnings to that of a major ministry, serving a wide constituency in the entire faith community through a variety of programs and with a diverse and highly capable professional staff of Christian counselors.

✢ ✢ ✢

STEPHEN MINISTRY (LAY MINISTERS)
by Rev. Linda Gabriel

I love the church. I am in love with the liveliness, the courage, the joy and deeply caring love I see in the people who are the church. God is placing before us ever growing opportunities to equip and empower God's people to reach the world with Christ's desperately needed love.

What is God calling you to do and to be? How is God calling you to share the impact of the Gospel with the world? If your love for the church calls you to service—please read what D. Elton Trueblood writes of ministry . . .

> If you are a Christian, you are a minister. This proposition is absolutely basic to any contemporary understanding of the Christian movement. A non-ministering Christian is a contradiction in terms. The Christian faith is not made up of spectators listening to professionals and is not for individuals who are seeking, primarily, to save their own souls. It is necessarily made up of persons who are called to serve as representatives of Christ in the world, and to serve means to minister. Ministry is intrinsic to the Christian life. Ministry is not something added or a means to an end; it is central and ineradicable.

The notion that a Christian must minister arose, in the beginning, from the example of Christ, Himself. Early Christians realized that they were called to minister because Christ ministered and they were called to follow Him. "For I have given you an example," He said "that you also should do as I have done to you" (John 13:15 RSV). Though this conception of what a Christian is was well understood in the beginning, it was lost, or at least neglected, for many years, and is now being rediscovered in a powerful way. The degree to which the idea of the universal ministry is being rediscovered and seriously intended in our generation is the most hopeful single factor in contemporary Christianity. If it could be really understood and practiced, it would produce a new Reformation.

It is important for Christians to realize how revolutionary the idea of the ministry is. Christ really turned existing ethical values upside down when He put on the garb of a servant and washed the feet of His followers. He knew that words were not really effective and that, consequently, He needed to engage in an acted parable. He had told His followers, earlier, that the struggle for prestige and personal eminence was wholly alien to His movement, but apparently they did not understand. It was after much powerful teaching that "an argument arose among them as to which of them was the greatest" (Luke 9:46 RSV). His rebuke to them for even raising the question was the blunt statement that "He who is least among you all is the one who is great" (Luke 9:48 RSV).

As long as we have the ideal of the ministry, there is real hope for the Christian movement. Whenever we return to this ideal, we have a potent challenge to our practices of selfishness and personal ease or comfort. As long as we know that we are called to be servants, we can realize that religion is meant to be a stimulus to service rather than a means of self-gratification.

If you know truly that you are a minister, you will still have problems and the tasks are barely begun, but you are at least embarked on the most fruitful road which man knows. You will not be at your destination, but you will be on the way. It is Christ's way! If you want to become more equipped for ministry, think and pray about becoming a Stephen Minister.

ONE MONTH IN DR. DUNNAM'S FIRST YEAR AT CHRIST CHURCH

This record shows Maxie's willingness to share his beliefs and to make this short period of time become the springboard from which a very successful twelve years at Christ Church were launched.

The reader can gain a great deal of insight into the Methodist Church and Maxie Dunnam's participation in the changes that have taken place in recent years.

Maxie approached the questions in the minds of many members of all ages and experience with a great deal of openness. All were workers and leaders in the life of Christ Church. He didn't hold back on stating his beliefs and action, and the people in the three meetings did the same in a quiet and understanding way.

The results of the meetings are stated in the last few lines in bold print.

The entire exchange lasted for only three consecutive Sunday afternoons, and every participant put their shoulder to the wheel and Christ Church experienced tremendous growth in its missions and ministries, in its membership, and in the facilities needed to support them. Not one of the participants left Christ Church.

Budget and building pledges were paid and all obligations of the church were retired.

In early February 1983 Harry A. Johnson Jr. received a call from Emmett Marston (legal counsel for CUMC) and his wife Betty. They stated that they were concerned, and several other people were equally concerned, about the course the senior minister, Maxie Dunnam, was taking and setting for the church. They asked Harry if he would be willing to chair a meeting the next Sunday of these people. They said they thought he would conduct a fair and impartial meeting. Harry agreed to do this and the following people, all leaders in the church, met the next Sunday. Harry asked D. A. Noel, chairman of the Pastor-Parish Committee, to come and listen to the discussion.

In addition to D. A. and Harry, others included Betty and Emmett Marston, Beth and Meade Moore, Ella McVean, Ruth and Kurt Meierhofer, Clarence Hampton, Eloise and Sam Mays, Dorris and Carlos Smith, Nancy Moore, J. J. Doughtie, Melinda Rauscher, Ann and Harry Orr, Anne and Jackie Miller, Lillie and Ben Carpenter, Jean and J. P. Tucker, Jack Moore, Sewell Dunkin, Mary Condra, Bettye and Gordon Slappey, Faye and Skip Daniel, Sara Jane and Dan Scott, Vikki and Bob Roberts, Julie and Dan Sutch, Liza Ozier, Ann and Jonathan Page, Charlotte Snow, Virginia Hollon, Virginia and Howard Boone, Elizabeth Poole, Martha Anne Johnston, Lee McCormick, Jack Renshaw, Margaret and Clarence Colby, and Agnes Thomas.

Harry opened the meetings with a statement that went like this:

I think I speak for all of us when I say that we believe in intercessory prayer and in divine healing but we also believe what Paul said, "If eating meat offends then quit eating the meat." The healing service held last Sunday night was the beginning of the healing ministry. We know that CUMC is big enough to embrace all areas of Methodist beliefs, but an individual does not need to embrace all areas of a movement to be a committed part of it.

Prophecy, speaking in tongues, and snake handling are all based on the Bible. So when you remind us that healing and the laying on of hands is Bible-based, it offers little comfort. All denominations and all sects of Christianity are Bible-based. But all are not Methodist.

The elitism of the Emmaus Walk, the fact that this is becoming a major program within the church, yet it is not a part of the church's program through the Council on Ministries, the Official Board, etc. Our senior minister is using his time, the time of his secretary, and much of his thought and energy promoting a program that we are not paying him to do.

One leader asked Maxie, before he was appointed as senior minister, if he would change the Sunday school literature when he came to the church. The leader was saying that something was wrong with the literature or he would not have asked the question. Why do we need a Curriculum Committee that is not answerable to the Work Area on Education? We have withstood the jolt and the violence of Harold Beaty's death, but there have been too many changes, too fast.

The *I* ministry is too much; how great is a deed of mercy if the individual has to put it in the bulletin? There are many unsung heroes in the church who don't ask for, nor get, any recognition. Wouldn't our senior pastor do better to seek out the anonymous heroes of the church and put their stories in the bulletin, instead of his own praises.

There are a large number of unhappy members and the only difference has been the appearance of a new senior minister. In the twenty-eight-year history of this church, there has been only one year of dissent to this degree. The church has embraced extremists over the years. Some of these individuals could not embrace the church and left us to go to Central Church or First Evangelical Church.

There was a full and long discussion of all of the foregoing and D. A. Noel said he would report to the P&P Committee and then talk with Maxie Dunnam.

D. A. did this and, after talking to Maxie, met with the Pastor-Parish Committee the next Sunday.

When the group met the next Sunday, Harry made the following statement:

We want each of you on the Pastor-Parish Committee to know that you, Dr. Dunnam, and the church have been in our prayers constantly since our meeting last Sunday and especially on Wednesday afternoon when D. A. met with Dr. Dunnam. We thank you again for listening to us with love, respect, and restraint last Sunday.

To the group of concerned members: we have agreed to listen to the committee today using the same rules as last Sunday, but with a reversal of roles.

After the meeting with the committee, we will meet in this room for the purpose of deciding whether to end what we have started or what the next step will be.

The P&P Committee gave us the answers that Maxie had given them in general but did not specifically answer our questions.

The group asked Harry to meet with Maxie to see if the situation could be resolved.

Harry met with Maxie in his office for more than an hour. Their discussion is contained in the remarks on the following pages.

Harry made the following statement to open the discussion with Maxie:

The Christian Church is made up of millions of individuals who are divided into denominations from the Roman Catholic Church to the most basic denominations. We are the Methodist Church, more specifically, Christ United Methodist Church. Within our congregation for twenty-eight years we have supported individuals from one extreme to the other. Once in a while an individual or family decides that their specific needs are not being met by CUMC and moves their membership to one of the other denominations. If the congregation of this church had wanted it to be more fundamentalist than it is, that would have been established long ago. When you, in word and deed, indicate that your future course for the church is to have healing services to include the laying on of hands by both clergy and lay members and using a proxy for this ceremony, then you conjure up in the minds of many people that you also embrace the other areas of the charismatic movement to include prophecy, speaking in tongues, snake handling and such. All of these practices by fundamentalist churches are based in Scripture so the answer given us last Sunday by the P&P Committee was not sufficient.

In the conversation that week, Harry expressed his opinion that Maxie made a very grave error in putting his healing ministry into practice in the way he did; without notifying the congregation so that only those who wanted to participate could attend and those who did not want to participate would not. Would Maxie agree that services that are desired by a group within the church which services are out of the ordinary worship services normally held in this church should be advertised as such? Maxie's answer was that he would agree to this method.

Emmaus. The next thing discussed, which was also a major tactical error, was the Emmaus movement. This movement was brought to CUMC by Maxie, and he was head of it in this church, starting what is perceived by many to be an elitist group of Christians within the church membership, but not approved by, or a part of, the program of the church.

Maxie's answer as understood by Harry was that he agreed that it was an error not to have cleared it as a program of the church. He would do this with a full explanation to the proper committees and a statement would be placed in the paper mailed to all members within the next week.

Maxie stated that he would not initiate a new program in the church without clearing it through the proper committees and/or boards of the church.

Empire Building. Some of the members think Maxie came to CUMC to build his empire.

Maxie's answer to Harry was, "I came from a job as editor of *The Upper Room* that provided far more discretionary money, more contacts throughout the world, more honor, and easy access to the leaders of the Methodist Church in addition to probably the most widely read publication within the church. Empire building could better and more easily be done in that position than this one." Maxie had no intention of empire building and the purpose for coming to CUMC was and is to return to the ministry of the local church and a closer contact with fellow Christians on a continuing basis.

Maxie gave Harry copies of the statements that he had given to D. A. Noel. They are as follows:

Memo
To: Mr. D. A. Noel, Chairman, Pastor-Parish Committee
Pastor-Parish Committee

From: Maxie D. Dunnam

The following is a dictated word from the notes and my recall of our meeting Wednesday afternoon.

1. Whether Maxie Dunnam is in the mainline of the United Methodist church. The question has been raised as to whether I am in the mainline of the United Methodist church. There are some obvious signs and involvement on the part of myself which are clear indications of my being at the very center of the United Methodist church. Some of those are: (a) one could not be the editor of *The Upper Room* for six years and not be a mainline Methodist. There is nothing in United Methodism more at the center than *The Upper Room*. I doubt if there is anything more at the center of the Christian faith than *The Upper Room*. (b) I am a member of the Executive Committee of the World Methodist Council and serving now as the chairperson of the Program Committee to prepare for the world gathering of the United Methodist council in 1986. That's rather mainstream! (c) I have been invited for the fourth straight year to write the study for Lent. This little booklet is published yearly by the Methodist publishing house, and is one of the most popular publications the publishing house prints. Between 400,000 and 500,000 copies of these are sold each year. It is very doubtful that they would be inviting either a wide-eyed leftist or rightist or closet charismatic or fundamentalist to do the writing of this nature. (d) I have been invited to speak in the Annual Conferences of three different bishops this year; Bishop [Ellis] Finger, of the Holston Conference; Bishop [Frederick] Wertz, of the Washington D.C. area; and Bishop Armstrong of the Indiana area. This says something about whether I am in the mainline of the Church or not.

2. *The issue of our Sunday school literature.* I'm told that probably the largest number of people at the meeting were concerned about that issue. This really is not an issue for the pastor-parish relations committee, but for the curriculum committee, the work area on education, and the council on ministries. It needs to be noted, however, that this is not related to my leadership in Christ Methodist church. This literature issue had been under debate for at least two years before my coming to Christ Church. It was not my prerogative to contest the decision of a duly-established committee, when I had been pastor here only a few months. Both Jerry Corlew and Marvin Budd felt that this was the case, and also felt that the decision of the committee should be carried out in light of how the committee had been established, and the many months of research and work they had done.

It has been my position since I came here for the issue of literature to be an ongoing one, and for that reason the Curriculum Committee was appointed by the Quarterly Conference in December and will work with the work area on education and the council on ministries. It is certainly my wish that Methodist literature be used where possible within the life of Christ United Methodist Church. I am totally committed to the United Methodist church and am delighted that a new literature has been provided for children as a result of the concern of churches all across the nation during the 10 or 12 years. It is my hope that this new children's literature will be adequate for use in our Church School.

3. *The question of the charismatic movement.* Some people have thought that I was a member of an organized charismatic movement, and was seeking to carry the church in that direction. There is a charismatic organization in the United Methodist church, called the United Methodists Renewal Services Fellowship, but I have never been a member of that organization. The person who presented this notion to the PPR Committee produced some paper which referred to my speaking to the first national gathering of this group. I did. I see no more significance in that fact than in the fact that I also keynoted the national gathering of the contact teleministries in Huntington, West Virginia a few months ago. I also was one of the keynote speakers at the national convocation of the United Methodist men. Because one addresses a group does not make one a member of that group. I'm quite certain that I said nothing at that gathering, or any of the other gatherings to which I speak that I would not say at Christ Church.

It does need to be noted that, prior to the general conference of 1976, I was a member of a staff committee for the Board of Discipleship, when I was serving with *The Upper Room*, to design some guidelines for the board to present to the General Conference as guidelines for the United Methodist Church and the charismatic movement. These guidelines, along with some explanation for the charismatic movement in its historic base and Wesleyan framework, is available through Discipleship Resources of the United Methodist Church. The members of the committee who prepared these guidelines are listed in the introductory statement. It would be well for any United Methodist to read these guidelines which the church has approved by action of the 1976 General Conference.

Some clarity about the whole matter may be needed. This is my perspective. The so-called charismatic movement has played for the past 15 years, and continues to play a significant role in the life of the whole church. I doubt if anything, other than Vatican II, and the base church movement in Latin America, has played a more significant role in the Catholic Church of the 20th Century. So significant is it that the present pope has assigned Cardinal Suenens of Belgium to give oversight to the movement within the Catholic Church, and in many dioceses, Roman Catholic bishops appoint priests to this concern. The Methodist Renewal Services Fellowship was organized to meet that sort of need among Methodists. And this organization has its staff at the board of discipleship of the United Methodist church in Nashville.

Though I am not a member of the so-called charismatic movement, I do feel that we need to understand what, at the heart of it, this movement is all about. In order to do that, we need to understand terminology. Most of us understood what was meant when Winston Churchill was referred to as a charismatic leader, or someone talked about the charisma of John Kennedy or Winfield Dunn.

But there's been given little attention to the meaning of the word in the New Testament. In various forms it comes out *charis*, *charisms*, and *charismata*, all of which may be translated *grace* or *gifts*. The big idea in the New Testament is that Christians are those who received God's grace, or are grace-gifted by the Holy Spirit, and are given gifts (charisms) for ministry that the whole body of Christ, the Church, might be a fellowship of the Holy Spirit. This is what I talked about in a Sermon a few weeks ago, using the term *koinonia*, the Greek word Paul used for fellowship in Christ, which is a gift of God.

So when we see the word in this fashion, not in the stereotype we realize that it refers to that which should be normative for the Christian. But now, there is so-called charismatic movement, and unfortunately it is seen as an extreme (for some even bizarre) expression, with an exaggerated emphasis on dramatic gifts of the spirit, such as speaking in tongues, healing, prophecy. And that's the reason for such nervousness about the label charismatic. In this latter sense of using that word, I would certainly deny being called a charismatic.

Having said all that, we need to recognize that the Christian church has always taught that the Holy Spirit gives gifts to all Christians—and those gifts are given to equip us for ministry. Also the Holy Spirit produces fruit in our lives as indicated in Galatians 5:22–25. In my volume, *The Communicator's Commentary on Galatians* (published by Word Books) one can find a reflection upon my understanding of this scripture. Also, on pages 202–204 there is more commentary on the meaning of the Spirit in the life of the church. My book entitled *Alive in Christ*, the basis from which came a number of sermons I preached in a series by that title here at Christ Church, expresses my understanding of the Holy Spirit. Pages 47–50 have particular application to the question.

4. *The question of healing.* One of the things that excited me about this congregation, and listening to Harold Beaty's tapes when I first arrived, was the tremendous emphasis on intercession. Over and over again that note has been sounded. And as I have become familiar with the life of the church I have noted that most adult Sunday School classes have an emphasis on intercessory prayer for healing, and the administrative board closes every meeting with a time of intercession for healing. I've never known of such an emphasis on healing prayer. How anyone can think I have introduced anything new in the area of prayer for healing surprises me, for this church is permeated with that idea. And that I should continue that emphasis should surprise no one. I wrote a workbook on intercessory prayer three years ago which is being used through the United Methodist Church as well as in other denominations.

We did have a healing service for Sandra Brady, and in that service we prayed for the healing of others. This service came about as the concern expressed by countless persons that we do something special in the way of prayer for Sandra. I did what I think is the finest tradition of the United Methodist Church, the Episcopal Church, the Roman Catholic Church, and many other denominations. While I understand that there was some negative response to that service, the personal response that I received was overwhelmingly positive—in fact, there's nothing I have done since coming to Christ Church that people spoke to me more positively about.

It seems as though some questions center around the act of laying on of hands and specific prayer healing. I understand that it was suggested that this was an extreme expression such as that that we have seen in the past with persons like Oral Roberts. I suppose the one church in Memphis that would be the farthest removed from the style of Oral Roberts is Calvary Episcopal, downtown. I am told that it is the Episcopal Church to which to belong—a place where the socially elite, much wealth and culture are centered. Yet, every Thursday at noon at Calvary Episcopal Church, Father Doug Bailey and his associate rector conduct a healing service, not only practicing the laying on of hands, but anointing with oil.

I have no idea whether other United Methodist churches in our city have healing services. I know that United Methodist churches across the nation do—also, Presbyterian, Lutheran, Episcopalian, other Protestants and Roman Catholic Churches. I was in Murray, Kentucky, last week, and learned they have healing services during seasons of the year when they are having special services.

As is true with many areas of Christian experience and practice, when the church fails to give attention to and provide adequate teaching, extreme expressions grow up outside the church. Most of us cringe as I do at the stereotypical tent meeting faith healers. That makes it even more important that we keep perspective, that we root ourselves in scripture, and that the fellowship of the church be a healing community.

How this expresses itself in the church may certainly vary—as indeed it does. I don't have any design for what is to be done at Christ church in that area, though I am committed to continue the significant emphasis on intercessory prayer that has been a part of this church's life. I do believe it is proper and in the tradition of the church from the first century on that the church as a body, as a part of its corporate life, pray for the healing of persons. If we ignore that, we will disregard a huge part of the New Testament.

Just a word about the laying on of hands—because that may have been the upsetting issue. That practice of laying on of hands is not only scriptural, it is at the heart of the tradition of the whole church. The minister—and this is certainly true of me—makes no claim of special power when he lays on hands; in fact, I disclaimed any special gift of healing at the service we had. But in ordination, in baptism, in confirmation, and sometimes even in marriage, and certainly in prayer for healing, the laying on of hands has become the representative act of the ordained clergy on behalf of the whole church, as a symbolic conferring of the power of the indwelling spirit of Christ. Those who have problems with that will question the whole tradition from Jesus' day until now.

I happen to believe that it is very meaningful to connect our prayers for healing with the celebration of Holy Communion. That keeps the perspective clear. It is Christ present with us in the power of his spirit, who is the great physician.

✤ ✤ ✤

Additional Comments by Dr. Maxie D. Dunnam (in writing)
February 25, 1983

Charismatic Movement. I am not, nor have I ever been a member of the so-called charismatic movement. I would not consider myself a charismatic in the stereotype fashion that word is commonly used. I do not, nor have I ever spoken in tongues, nor have I experienced some of the so-called extraordinary gifts, such as healing and prophesy, which come to some peoples' minds when they hear the word *charismatic*.

My involvement:

1. I served with staff committee of the board of discipleship to prepare guidelines for the United Methodist Church and the charismatic movement, which were approved by the General Conference of 1976—a copy, which is readily available.

2. I spoke at the national meeting of this group some years ago—in the same fashion I am requested to speak at many national gatherings.

3. Have recently been invited by the United Methodist Renewal Services Fellowship to serve as a member of a rather large advisory council. Accepted this because of my belief, as the General Conference indicated, that this should not be a splinter group in the church or a cause for divisiveness.

4. I have written a lot about my understanding and experience of the Holy Spirit and certainly this is present in my preaching. *Alive in Christ* actually addresses this matter in my *Communicator's*

Commentary, pages 202–204, and pages 114–120 in my Commentary on specific scripture related to the Holy Spirit may be found.

5. I hope the deepest commitment of my life is to the indwelling Christ who is one with the Holy Spirit and my desire is to be responsive to Christ's leading. That is the reason I preached for 11 weeks about cultivating an awareness of and responding, to the indwelling Christ in my sermon series *Alive in Christ.*

I believe the church is a healing community. I believe that Christ United Methodist Church has marvelously demonstrated this in its tremendous emphasis on intercessory prayer which is focused in the Sunday school, in worship, and even in the administrative board.

The service we had, especially for Sandra Brady, has absolutely no connection with the meetings and faith healing of that sort, but is clearly rooted in scripture and the tradition of the church. Rather than being compared to Oral Roberts, the best example of an ongoing nature of what we did in that service is at Calvary Episcopal Church, downtown Memphis, where a healing service is held each Thursday at noon.

I do not claim any gift of healing but believe the whole church is to be a dynamic fellowship of healing of mind, body, emotions, and spirit.

The laying on of hands is in the tradition of the scripture and the practice of the church from Jesus' time until now. We lay on hands in ordination in baptism, in confirmation and when we pray for persons. We claim no special power in that act.

Like so much of what we do in the church, laying on of hands is symbolic—but meaningful still. It is, primarily, an act of a person representing the church as a channel of God's grace and power even when I pray for persons in the hospital I usually touch them—hold their hand, place my hand on their head or shoulder simply as an act of contact. It is not totally unlike what many of us do in our own families when we hold hands around the dinner table to offer prayers of gratitude.

My commitment is that the worship services and everything else we do in the church will always be grounded in scripture and in our Wesleyan United Methodist Christian tradition.

At the risk of overstatement, I think you would be hard-put to find anyone who knows the United Methodist Church nationally and as a world communion, who would indicate that I am anywhere but at the center and in the mainstream of United Methodism.

Walk to Emmaus. One of the most effective models of the renewal and growth for individuals and the church is the Walk to Emmaus. This model has been developed by the Board of Discipleship of the United Methodist Church, through *The Upper Room.* Bob Wood of *The Upper*

Room staff is primarily responsible for making this experience available to Methodist annual conferences throughout the nation, and other Protestant denominations as well. For many months persons from Christ Church have been attending Emmaus Walks in Birmingham, Nashville, and Myrtle Beach. Ninety-eight people from our church and ministers and members of other Methodist churches in the city as well as other denominations have gone. We have sought to deliberately seek persons representing all ages and groups in our church to attend so that interpretive sharing can take place.

We have had enough people attend in other places that we can now make the experience available in Memphis. Our first weekend for men is April 28–May 1; for women, May 19–22 at the Country Place in Moscow. It will not be a Christ Church Event but, interdenominational.

The Emmaus walk centers in the theology of grace, God's unmerited love offered to all. The goal is inspiration, renewal, and challenge for persons to live out the Christian faith through their church in their community. There is a sense in which it is a call and preparation for the ministry of all Christians. A seventy-two-hour conference-retreat type experience, beginning on Thursday evening and closing Sunday evening, is the pivotal experience. In the weekend persons listen to talks by clergy and laity on central themes of the Christian life, share together in small table groups in response to the talks in order to clarify and appropriate meaning, pray together, worship together, celebrate Holy Communion and in essence experience the love of Christ in a small group of people committed to making that love real. The gospel story of the Emmaus walk is the motif. Jesus walked with the disciples on the road to Emmaus, opened the scripture to them, rehearsed God's action, and was then known to them in the breaking of bread.

There is small group sharing and efforts on the part of those who continue "The Walk" to grow in their faith and become more effective servants of Christ, to undergird the church and assist the church in being all that God calls us to be.

✣ ✣ ✣

Harry took all of Maxie's answers and agreements to the group of concerned leaders and they all agreed to discontinue the meetings, and if Maxie followed his agreements never to meet again.

Harry gave Maxie the answer, and he honored all of his promises and the church set a course with Maxie as its leader which caused it to grow by leaps and bounds.

Everyone gained by this process and made the church processes more open to all its members.

THE JOEL COMMITTEE

THE FIRST JOEL COMMITTEE
1992–1993

Jim Eoff	Chuck Gadd
Robert Rogers	Robin Taylor
Mat Lipscomb	Dick Ross
Robbie McQuiston	Suzanne Schaeffer
Randy Noel	Miller Delgadillo
Rick Kirchoff	Maxie Dunnam

Boyd Rhodes, Chairman

The first report of the Joel Committee to the Administrative Board outlines the planning porcess to set up this committee which was appointed to set up short- and long-range overall planning for Christ United Methodist Church.

Report of the Joel Committee.
INTRODUCTION: As Christ United Methodist Church approaches its fortieth anniversary, it is one of a relative small number of United Methodist churches showing continued growth in members, programs, missions, and resources. Because of our senior minister's worldwide reputation as a preacher, author, and leader in church evangelism, and our historic emphasis on mission, Christ Church is recognized locally, nationally, and internationally as a leader in both its denomination and all Christendom.

Jesus said, "To whom much is given, much is expected!" Recognizing the many ways God has blessed this congregation, Christ Church has responded with the development of a bold mission statement and more than 250 programs to carry out the great commandment of love and service of neighbor and the Great Commission of taking the gospel throughout the world.

During 1992, the formation of the Joel Committee was authorized by the Administrative Board to serve as the Planning Committee of the church, identifying those steps that will need to be taken to ensure continuous attention to, and execution of our mission. For more than a year, the Joel Committee has assessed where we are from the standpoint of facilities, staff, and programs designed to nurture, make disciples, and evangelize. Numerous books on church trends and evangelism were read and shared to provide insight and instruction on the best ways to share God's grace and meet human needs. A sample is included.

The committee visited and studied other dynamic, growing churches, both denominational and non-denominational, seeking benchmark ministries that might be used at Christ Church. We sought to brainstorm that which we had learned to fit within our own Christ Church mission statement.

A demographic study of our parish and outlying areas was commissioned to provide insight into their makeup now, and in the years ahead.

A questionnaire was mailed to a representative sample of our congregation to obtain both demographic data as well as information related to church participation, personal beliefs, social and political attitudes, spiritual life, and life's satisfaction and concerns.

With all of these sources to draw from, the planning process was initiated. Our mission statement served to remind us of who we are and the vision outlined for Christ Church. Values that would serve as guidelines and parameters for future plans were established.

Brainstorming sessions yielded a list of strengths of Christ Church as well as perceived weaknesses. Critical opportunities as well as critical threats to church growth and effectiveness were examined.

We then addressed key areas from which specific goals and objectives would be selected. They are:

1. Space
2. Staff
3. Worship
4. Caregiving
5. Assimilation and Discipleship
6. Stewardship
7. Evangelism and Outreach
8. Transformation of Our City

Finally, the specific goals and recommendations relative to achieving them were determined.

Mission.

As the Body of Christ, we will celebrate Christ in Worship;
Honor Christ in all we do;
Reveal Christ in our witness and fellowship;
Instruct persons for discipleship and ministry;
Serve persons in Christ's name;
Transform the world by "spreading scriptural holiness."

Values.

Christ is central.
People are primary.

The Joel Committee

Discipleship is demanded.
Mission is intentional.

Concerns.
- Achieve adequate space and facilities.
- Effective staffing for flexibility and responsiveness.
- Offer dynamic worship experiences that respond to diverse needs.
- Create a climate of Christian love and concern.
- Develop committment, teach the basics, and establish significant relational groups.
- Increase average yearly contributions to six percent of personal income.
- Make Christ's last commandment our first concern by encouraging people outside the church to make a life changing connection with Jesus Christ.
- Transform our city by responding to the needs of a demographically diverse community.

The location of Christ Church has been one of the more important reasons for its growth and ministries. Its visibility and easy access are appealing to those seeking a new church home. We are committed to remaining and growing at this location.

Our congregation is growing by an addition of 500–600 members each year. This rate of growth is expected to continue for at least five years and perhaps longer. The successful development of new Methodist churches in both downtown and east Shelby County may slow the rate of growth but it seems certain that Christ Church will have a membership of 10,000 by the year 2000—if there is space for them. Our worship attendance at 9:45 and 11:00 A.M., Sunday services, consistently utilizes 95–100 percent of seating space in both Seabrook Hall and the sanctuary. The recent improvement in our nursery facilities is a stopgap measure at best. Office space for our increased church staff is exhausted and offices are scattered across our church campus. It is necessary that we address our space needs now. Accordingly, the Joel Committee has established the following goals related to space.

Goal: Provide adequate space and facilities.

Short-Term Objectives:
1. By December 1993, clearly communicate to the congregation and community our commitment to stay in the heart of the city. Responsibility: Maxie and the director of communications.

2. To attain a professionally designed master plan for maximum effective use of property and facilities by March 1994. Responsibility: Board of Trustees.

3. Develop and implement a short-term plan to accommodate increasing attendance at the 9:45 worship service and holiday worship services by March 1, 1994. Responsibility: Board of Trustees/Worship Committee and staff.

4. By March 1, 1994, develop a plan for the quiet and systematic acquisition of property adjacent and nearby to the church. Responsibility: task force of Board of Trustees.

5. Implement the accessibility plan developed by the task force on ministry to persons with disabilities by March 1, 1994. Responsibility: task force of Board of Trustees/Property Committee.

6. Formalize a long-term parking agreement with adjacent shopping centers by June 1994. Responsibility: trustees and business manager.

7. By March 1, 1994, develop an interim plan to provide for wedding reception space that is needed since Seabrook Hall is in use for the Saturday worship service. Responsibility: trustees.

Long-Range Objectives:
1. Consistent with master plan, have a sanctuary designed "in the round" suitable for various types of worship services, seating 2,500 to 3,000 people by January 1997. Responsibility: input from Board of Trustees.

2. Consistent with master plan, increase the fellowship space of Seabrook Hall by approximately 100 percent by January 1997. Responsibility: Administrative Board, input from Board of Trustees.

3. Consistent with master plan, double the size of nursery suite, add classrooms and expand the administrative office complex by January 1997. Responsibility: input from Board of Trustees.

4. Consistent with master plan, provide adequate on-site parking for a 10,000-member congregation by January 1, 1997. Responsibility: input from Board of Trustees.

STAFF

The growth in membership, programs and mission has demanded constant reassessment and ultimately additions to both our clergy and non-clergy staff. A projected membership of 10,000 by the year 2000 indicates that this trend will continue. We must staff the church to provide the most efficient execution of its programs and outreach and maximize the effectiveness of our clergy. This is particularly important as it relates to our senior minister, Dr. Dunnam, whose preaching, writing, and witness ministries are important not only to Christ Church but to Memphis, the United Methodist Church, and to all of Christendom. Planning must take into consideration his eventual departure.

Accordingly, the Joel Committee makes the following recommendation for execution by our Staff-Parish Committee.

Goal: Effective staffing to offer flexibility and responsiveness to diverse membership and constituency.

Objectives:
1. By June 1994, staff-parish will conduct a thorough analysis of current and future staffing design and needs, emphasizing involvement of lay ministry. Responsibility: Staff-Parish Committee.

2. By July 1, 1994, develop a staffing plan that will maximize the strengths, tenure, and impact of Maxie Dunnam's ministry, while minimizing the church's dependence on Maxie. Responsibility: Staff-Parish Committee.

3. Develop a plan for staff involvement in biracial civic and community life of the city by July 1, 1994. Responsibility: Staff and Staff-Parish Committee.

4. By January 1, 1995, develop an ongoing process to evaluate all requests for new staff in light of our commitment to volunteer ministry. Responsibility: Staff-Parish Committee.

WORSHIP

Our demographic studies as well as our congregational questionnaire have confirmed that persons are drawn to Christ Church to a large extent because of its preaching ministry. These same studies also pointed out that an increasing diversity of style of worship is needed to attract a broad cross section of our population. We have already responded to this need in the differentiation of our 8:30, 9:45, and 11:00 Sunday services. The assurance of dynamic worship must continue to be a key area for future planning. A strong music ministry must be an integral part of worship. Herb Miller, in his book *The Vital Congregation*, states that most churchgoers want music to be at least 40 percent of the worship service. We must be receptive to different styles of music and worship as long as they reflect the glory and adoration of God, the Father, Jesus, the Christ, and the Holy Spirit.

The Joel Committee recommends the following goals related to dynamic worship.

Goal: Offer dynamic worship experiences that respond to diverse needs of congregation and community.

Objectives:
1. Develop by November 6, 1993, a Saturday evening worship service similar to the 9:45 service. Responsibility: clergy.

2. To increase overall participation in the music program by the following standards:

   A. By March 1994, develop an additional worship band to provide music leadership for the Saturday evening service.
   B. By January 1995, develop an 11:00 choir of 100 voices.
   C. By January 1995, develop a 75-member youth choir.
   D. By January 1996, develop a 15-20 piece volunteer orchestra.
   E. By January 1997, develop an 8:30 choir of 50 voices.

   Responsibility: special music task force, designated by the Executive Committee, director of music, and Matt Hook.

3. By July 1, 1994, develop and implement a plan to make our facilities, parking areas, and our Saturday night and Sunday morning worship times visitor friendly. Responsibility: task force assigned by Program Council.

CAREGIVING

From its inception, one of the great concepts of the church has been that it be an instrument of active concern and nurture for its members. An important dynamic of early Methodism was the spirit of responsibility and accountability of its members, one for another. This sense of caring needs to be strengthened and expanded within Christ Church. We must become more sensitive and responsive to members who are sick or recovering from sickness; who are homebound and lonely; who need assistance or encouragement. We need the structure and determination to assure that all calls for help are answered—that no person is ignored. In this spirit, the Joel Committee recommends the following:

Goals: Create a climate of Christian love, care, and acceptance. Establish a task force to develop a comprehensive congregational caregiving plan by August 1994. This plan would include but not be limited to:

Objectives:
1. An organized system by which our members who are shut-in or have long-term illness are visited regularly and remembered in special ways.

2. An organized program which ensures that our members feel loved and supported by the clergy and other laypersons during times of stress such as hospitalization and bereavement.

3. An organized system to bring each member into a relational group.

4. A plan to assure that all telephone calls are responded to with friendliness and caring concern.

5. A well understood feedback system that will enable members to share problems and ideas.

6. Training for all classes and groups in caregiving.

7. A comprehensive intercessory prayer program.

Responsibility: Staff-Parish and Program Council.

Assimilation and Discipleship

The assimilation of new members into the life of the church is important to their becoming good disciples and good stewards.

Christ Church offers many opportunities for spiritual growth and service, but we must be more intentional in bringing these opportunities to our members. Our studies, contact with other churches as well as our own experience at Christ Church have pointed to the importance of church school and other smaller groups and ministries in activating members and making them true disciples of Jesus. To develop a witnessing community who joyfully share the Christian faith and to assure a church environment that welcomes new members and assists all members to find their role in the Body of Christ, the Joel Committee recommends the following:

Goals: Teach the Basics; Develop Significant Relational Groups; and Increase Commitment.

Teach the Basics:
1. Develop comprehensive program for teaching the basics by September 1995, which includes: new member orientation, the basic Christianity course, the course in Methodist beliefs, volunteer ministry orientation, and basic Bible study skills. Responsibility: Assimilation.

2. By January 1996, it will be expected that each new member will attend orientation and during their first two years of membership will attend the basics courses. Responsibility: senior minister, Group Life, and Assimilation.

3. Offer orientation and assimilation classes at alternate times by January 1996. Responsibility: Assimilation.

4. Develop ways of sharing and/or teaching what we've successfully implemented in areas of assimilation with other churches by January, 1997. Responsibility: Assimilation, Volunteer Ministry, Group Life, and Program Council.

5. Appoint a task force made up of persons who are committed to Christian education. The mission of the task force will be to study the trends that will impact the future of Christian education, develop a master plan for Christian education in the twenty-first century and report by January 1995. Responsibility: laypersons, diaconal ministers, and clergy appointed by the Executive Committee.

Develop Significant Relational Groups:
1. By the end of 1998, we will increase to 60 percent the number of members in relational groups. Responsibility: Assimilation.

2. By August 1994, develop a plan to begin unlimited numbers of home fellowship groups across the metro area. Responsibility: Group Life.

3. Implement a plan to provide group leadership and trained teachers by January 1994. Responsibility: Group Life.

4. Develop and implement a plan to bring all new members and church leadership into a significant relational group by June 1995. Responsibility: Assimilation and Group Life.

5. Beginning in 1994, provide the resources necessary to fully implement the adult group life pan. Responsibility: Program Council, Staff-Parish, and Finance.

6. Develop and implement a plan so that by the end of 1995, Christ Church has five complete Sunday school programs; three on Sunday mornings, one on Wednesday evening and another on Saturday night. Responsibility: Program Council.

Commitment:
1. That by June of 1995 we will have developed a plan to communicate the meaning of church membership to all church members and to all who choose to become members of Christ Church. Responsibility: Assimilation.

2. All who choose to accept the nomination as an elected leader for 1995 will be expected to: make a commitment to tithe or grow toward a tithe; be an active member of a Sunday school class or other small, ongoing group; attend worship at least three times a month; pray regularly; agree to sponsor new members; be a volunteer for ministry in an area of lay ministry sponsored by Christ Church. Responsibility: senior staff, Nominations, Administrative Board.

The Joel Committee

3. Beginning in January 1995, all new members will be expected to make a commitment to tithe or grow toward a tithe; be active in a Sunday school class or other ongoing group; attend worship at least three times a month; pray regularly; agree to sponsor new members; be a volunteer in an area of lay ministry sponsored by Christ Church. Responsibility: Evangelism and Assimilation.

4. By January 1995 all church members will have been given the opportunity to renew their membership vows and make the same commitment that our leaders are making and that will be asking of new members. Responsibility: Assimilation.

5. Develop computer methods for tracking each member's involvement in presence, giving, and service by December 1994. Responsibility: Larry Pennington and Brad Gabriel.

STEWARDSHIP

The support of the church by our gifts is a promise of membership and an expectation of God. Giving should be looked at as an opportunity and a joy.

Our congregation as a whole falls far short of the tithe, that amount most commonly set by Christians as the expected level of giving. Based upon the responses to our congregational questionnaire, our level of giving is approximately four percent. The recommended expansion of our outreach ministries, as well as the programs and facilities that are recommended for Christ Church will require a higher commitment of congregational giving. To achieve this from a congregation that has always risen to the challenge before them, the Joel Committee recommends the following.

Goal: Increase average yearly contribution of personal income from active members to an average six percent by December 31, 1998.

Objectives:
1. Develop procedures to provide the congregation more complete financial information beginning February 1994. Responsibility: Stewardship, Finance Committee and Communications.

2. Develop a plan to share more frequently with the congregation how their giving makes a difference, both in Memphis and across the world by June 1994. Responsibility: Stewardship, Finance, Communications.

3. Obtain or create an appropriate data processing program that will provide information related to congregational giving and giving patterns by December 31, 1994. Responsibility: business manager.

4. Design and implement a planned giving program by September 1994. Responsibility: task force assigned by Stewardship and Finance.

5. Beginning January 1994, seek to have at least one CUMC member actively involved in each ministry and mission we support. This is for the purpose of accountability as well as hands-on involvement. Responsibility: Missions.

6. Beginning with 1994, have at least two special giving opportunities for our congregation. Responsibility: Stewardship, Finance.

7. By 1995, develop a comprehensive stewardship education plan that encourages all members to tithe or grow toward a tithe. Responsibility: Stewardship, Finance.

EVANGELISM AND OUTREACH

Evangelism and outreach sum up, to a large extent, what the church is about. Christ Church must continue its commitment to offering Jesus to the world and caring for our neighbor both locally and abroad. We are now the largest denominational congregation within the city limits of Memphis and as such, have the best opportunity (and obligation) to make a difference in our city. Perceptions and programs such as our Mediation and Restitution/Reconciliation Services that is just beginning, have initiated a feeling that Christ Church cares. However, our studies have indicated that we need to develop better strategies to reach certain groups of people such as single males, blue collar families, single parents, youth and college age persons, members of ethnic minorities, and persons in mid-life.

At the same time, we must not miss the opportunity to ignite the fires of the church in those areas of the world that have recently been opened to evangelism. We are called to help our brothers and sisters wherever they are. In addition to the current evangelism programs of Christ Church, the Joel Committee recommends adoption of the following goals.

Goal: To make Christ's last command our first concern by encouraging people outside the church to experience a life-changing connection with Jesus Christ.

1. Beginning in 1995, increase the broadcast of *Perceptions* by 10 percent each year for the next five years. Responsibility: Maxie and Work Areas on Evangelism and Communications.

2. Implement a quarterly *Bring a Friend* emphasis to encourage our members to invite their friends and acquaintances to visit our worship services beginning June 1994. Responsibility: Work Area on Evangelism.

The Joel Committee

3. By January 1, 1995 develop and implement a plan to train our people in faith sharing that seeks to make this a value among our people. Responsibility: Evangelism Work Area, in cooperation with Adult, Youth, and Children's Ministries.

4. By 1995, develop, prioritize, and implement a plan to become a place of hospitality that seeks to reach out to the following: single males, blue collar families, single parents, youth and college age persons, members of ethnic minorities, and persons in mid-life. Responsibility: Evangelism and Adult Group Ministries.

5. Develop by June 1994, a work area on ministries with the Disabled. Responsibility: Program Council and Nominations Committee.

6. To employ an additional full-time director of evangelism by January 1995. Responsibility: Staff-Parish.

Additional suggestions: Continue to emphasize our support for the world evangelism initiatives.

Transformation of Our City

Racial and ethnic conflict in Memphis and Shelby County impact significantly on the problems of our city. A large number of leaders in all aspects of community affairs believe that this conflict can be resolved only by the Body of Christ, the church of Jesus Christ. The size, resources, and influence of Christ United Methodist Church demand that it play an increasing role in the transformation of our city. Our clergy, because of their active participation in citywide Christian projects such as Life Focus and in other interfaith activities, are well known in both the white and African-American communities. Within our congregation are persons in leadership positions in most aspects of community life. Once again, because Christ Church is so blessed, it is also so challenged. Accordingly, the Joel Committee recommends the following.

Goal: Transform our city by responding to needs of a demographically diverse community.

Objectives:
1. To create a multicongregational parish (Central Church, Mt. Vernon Baptist Church, Mississippi Boulevard Christian, and Christ Church) to develop joint, interracial ministries in our city by June 1994. Responsibility: Maxie and Program Council.

2. Add part-time African-American staff to the CUMC staff to enable the development of house church congregations in economically depressed areas

of Memphis by October 1994. Responsibility: missions and staff-parish.

3. Continue to develop volunteer mission ministries in partnership with existing inner-city ministries and develop new opportunities for CUMC members to engage in hands-on ministry in the inner city. Responsibility: missions.

4. By July 1994 encourage Maxie to exercise Christian influence by building relationships with religious leaders, with emphasis on partnership in inner-city areas. Responsibility: staff-parish.

5. As part of our witness and as a way of enabling our ministry to African-Americans, add at least one African-American to our full-time program or clergy staff and two African-American persons to our support staff, by June 1995. Responsibility: staff parish and senior staff.

6. Create a strong work area on church and society by January 1994. Responsibility: Nominations Committee.

7. Develop plans for outpost ministries including a new congregational downtown Christian community and house churches among the poor and marginalized by January 1995. Responsibility: staff parish, evangelism, and missions.

   A. Develop a plan by April 15, 1994, to enable CUMC to sponsor development of a congregation in Cordova. The plan that is developed should be one that minimizes any adverse effect on the plans and programs of Christ Church. Responsibility: senior minister and appointed task force.

ARCHIVES HISTORY

Before 1987, the history of the church was kept in closets at the church and much of it at times in people's homes.

All of this changed when the Dunnam Building was finished and a small, cramped space was walled off behind the library. This space was a great leap forward in keeping the records safe and more accessible.

When volunteers came to help organize the records, they had to use the only table and chairs available, which were in the library. This, of course, infringed on the usable space in the library.

The following pages record some of the work that it took to get the archival room usable as such.

Jane Isbell Haynes will agree that she gave D. A. Noel, chair of the Building Committee, a few restless days and nights.

She didn't get everything she wanted, but it was tremendous improvement on the past.

PREFACE

> The thing that hath been, it is that which shall be;
> and that which is done is that which shall be done. Ecclesiastes 1:9 (KJV)

> That which hath been is now; and that which is to be hath already been;
> and God requireth that which is past. Ecclesiastes 3:15 (KJV)

> ... what's past is prologue ...
> —*The Tempest* II, I

The bound volumes, Volume I–Volume XXXVI, constitute a uniform format of copies of the extant original minutes, reports, and letters of Christ United Methodist Church, Memphis, Tennessee for the years 1955–1987. All available pages of the original records have been kept intact and are housed in the church archives. In spite of their sometimes fragile, frayed, brittle or discolored condition, no original pages or parts of pages have been discarded or deleted. If a significant church record sometimes is missing in these copies, the cause is that its location in the original records is undiscovered; additionally, a few pages of the original records are not included in these volumes because their condition prevented a clear or legible copy. The original pages that were not dated posed a problem when they were originally filed under a subject heading. Sometimes the page contents provided a clue regarding the date; on other occasions when no clue was found, we hoped we guessed correctly in assigning an approximate date to the undated pages.

In seeking whatever permanence is possible all the while keeping in mind Matthew 6:19 (KJV), ". . . where moth and rust doth corrupt, and where thieves break through . . ." we have copied the records onto archival bond acid-free paper with a sheet life of 300 years; the binding is library cloth. This conservation of records was deemed important even if, and especially if, laser discs or other computerized methods of preservation, storage and retrieval are adopted later. In 1987, the life of film is yet undetermined, so perhaps these bound volumes will outlive that method of storage that we did not choose.

Especial gratitude is due to Avis Davidson Allen and Trudy Manning (Mrs. Warren L.) Simpson, members of the Records and History Committee, who helped to reassemble into chronological order the original records after their disarray that was caused unavoidably by the copying process. They also helped collate the copies to be bound. A debt is owed to Dr. Susan Ruby Breland (Mrs. Wayne A.) Lamb, our committee consultant; and to Ben M. Carpenter for photographic assistance for materials for the archive photographic file. Thanks are due to the following church volunteers, who helped reassemble, sort and file:

> Ruth Green (Mrs. C. Lasseter) Woodard
> C. Lasseter Woodard
> Lorraine Brown Bradford
> Mary Clyde McKnight
> Mary Ward Morrison

The church office staff were helpful and genial when we invaded their offices looking for non-current records. We thank Gynette O. (Mrs. J. Milton) Bennett and Mary Knapp (Mrs. Michael A.) Marino, whom we bothered the most; J. Milton Bennett patiently unlocked and locked consecutively doors, cabinets, closets, and basements during our quest. We cordially thank Dr. Maxie D. Dunnam, senior minister, and Reverend Earl A. Johnston, executive minister, who were unfailingly supportive of this preservation idea from its beginning; their support was indispensable.

Our largest debt is to God, and so we offer a prayer of thanksgiving to Him who gave us sustenance during this two-year project that is dedicated to the glory of God, in whose cause we worked and to whom we look for the unrestrained grace, peace, and joy that He can provide to fortify and enrich all of our lives.

> Respectfully Submitted,
> Jane Isbell Haynes, Chair
> Committee on Records and History

Archives History 49

✣ ✣ ✣

Detailed Description of the Church Archive
Christ United Methodist Church, Memphis, Tennessee
Requested by Records and History Committee
Jane Isbell Haynes, Chair

Definition. As distinguished from a library, an archive serves a different function and does not house primarily books; it houses documentary materials such as non-current records, minutes, journals, reports, business materials, church bulletins and pamphlets, church letters, papers, directories, manuscripts, church photographic file, old architectural drawings, the first communion service not now in use, the gold shovel used for groundbreaking for the buildings, along with other historical artifacts. An archive is a depository for the permanent retention of local church records of fiscal, historical, legal and administrative value to the local church.

Use. To house the above listed materials and to be used as a Hall of History similar to the one at Second Presbyterian Church (but different shape and size) and to be used for periodic historical exhibits at key occasions in the church program.

Location. Near the church offices for their convenience in the housing and the retrieval of records.

Size. Approximately, or at least 25' x 30' with an adjoining walk-in workroom approximately, or at least 8' x 9' for accessioning and processing of materials and for storing supplies. This workroom needs countertops with cabinets above and below. We need a card catalogue in this area.

Special Climatic Control. Museum temperature and humidity with separate thermostat. A necessity to prevent either mold, mildew or brittleness and drying of papers and other materials.

Safety Control. Fireproof room with fire doors and smoke alarm. Entrance door to have different key from any other key. Locks on all cabinet doors with one key for all doors.

Furnishings:
1. Wooden built-in bookshelves with wooden cabinet doors with locks, with locked wooden cabinets underneath them (no countertops).

2. Wooden built-in bookshelves with glass cabinet doors with locks, with locked wooden cabinets underneath them (no countertops). We need twice as many

wooden cabinet doors as glass cabinet doors. Is there a choice of kinds of glass, e.g., reinforced? Inside the cabinets, the height of the bookshelves should vary to accommodate large minute books or smaller size books and materials.

3. Glass display cases to display historical artifacts: one upright case against wall and three table-type cases in center of room (museum-type cases).

4. Three (or more) built-in filing cabinets (four-drawer, 25 or 26 inches deep) with locks and wooden fronts if possible.

5. One library table (wooden) for research; four wooden (not metal) chairs at table.

6. A built-in manuscript file with shallow drawers to house large architectural drawings and maps.

Lighting. Commensurate with other parts of the building.

Problem and Question. Can a small unobtrusive number be put somewhere on each of the cabinet doors and drawers to serve as a means for locating materials that are listed in the card catalog? We wish to avoid the type of labels that are ordinarily on file cabinets; however, we wish to work out some plan to number the doors and drawers.

Respectfully submitted,
Jane Isbell Haynes, Chair
Records and History
17 January 1987

✤ ✤ ✤

Addendum I to Specifications for Archive Room in New Building

Notation to: Mr. D. A. Noel, Chairman
Building Committee

From: Jane Isbell Haynes, Chair Records and History Committee

Lighting. Archive lighting should be incandescent instead of commensurate with other parts of the new building as previously specified. Particularly, the lighting should not be fluorescent; sunlight should be avoided, so we request as few windows as possible, with none on the south or west or east. From the architect's drawing it seems that there are no windows, which is very acceptable for an archive.

✥ ✥ ✥

Addendum II to Specifications for Archive Room in New Building

22 March 1987
Notation to: Mr. D. A. Noel, Chairman
Building Committee

From: Jane Isbell Haynes, Chair Records and History Committee

Shelving. Archive shelving inside the cabinets should be metal shelving instead of wooden as previously specified. (I have visited the University of South Carolina and the University of Virginia to gather data, even though we do not wish to duplicate a university facility.) We want the archive room to have a wooden cabinet look instead of an office look. At the appropriate time in the future, may I talk to the person furnishing the room?

THE HISTORY OF THE CHRIST UNITED METHODIST CHURCH LIBRARY

May 1985–December 1993

The first library was established in 1961 as evidenced by the newspaper article in the *Memphis Press Scimitar*:

Beginning in 1961, the church library was located in the homes of members. It was shifted from place to place, eventually residing in a small room in Fellowship Hall (now the Rash Building).

THE HISTORY OF CHRIST UNITED METHODIST CHURCH LIBRARY FROM MAY 1985 TO DECEMBER 1993
by Karen (Mrs. Ernest) Jetton

As early as 1973, the church library was located in a small room off the second floor entrance to the present Rash Building. A restroom is located in the area now. It was moved at some point to the day school library in room 106 of the Rash Building. The children's books were circulated through the day school and the adult books occupied shelf space.

Mrs. S. K. McKenzie, chairman of the Library Committee, and Clay Shelton, chairman of the Commission on Education, in the new Christ Methodist Church library, February 4, 1961. Memphis Press-Scimitar photo.

In May of 1985 Sallie Simmons (Mrs. David) Grant and Karen Henrich (Mrs. Ernest A.) Jetton began revitalization of the church library. Over the summer months of 1985, Mrs. Grant and Mrs. Jetton sorted through the books and started adding new resources to the collection of approximately two thousand books with five hundred dollars from the work area on education.

In the fall of 1985, a Library Committee was formed consisting of Mrs. Jetton, chairman, Mrs. Grant, Margaret (Mrs. Erie S.) Henrich, Sara Kane, and Virginia (Mrs. James III) Eoff. In December of 1985 the work area on education gave the Library Committee (an extension of the work area on education) one thousand dollars to spend on library resources and supplies.

Between September 1985 and May 1986, the library was open on Sunday mornings from 9:30 A.M.–10:30 A.M. On February 23, 1986, the first library open house was held in room 106 of the Rash Building. Hundreds of people came between 9:15 A.M. and 10:45 A.M. During the summer months of 1986, a preschool story time was planned for children between the ages of three and five.

Approximately twenty-five to thirty children enjoyed Bible stories, songs, and crafts. The inventory as of June 1986 was 1,659 books.

In June of 1986, the library was moved to room 134 of the Beaty Building. The move allowed the library to be opened Monday, Wednesday, and Friday from 10:00 A.M.–12:00 noon. Because the room was used by a Sunday school class, it was not open on Sunday mornings.

In September of 1987, the inventory grew to 2,645 books. At that time plans were submitted to the Building Planning Committee of the church for a new library. By June of 1988 the library had 3,501 books and 287 audiovisual materials.

In December of 1988 the library was closed because of the building program.

In September of 1989 the library resources were moved to the present location in the Dunnam Building. The library was renamed the Lamppost Library. It adopted a logo and began distributing brochures and bookmarks.

Because of the generosity of Mr. and Mrs. Erie S. Henrich the library space and furnishings were realized.

The Library Committee in 1989 included Karen Jetton, chairman, Sallie Grant, Irma Roberts, Helen Purinton, Kartha Stires, Elva Lyles, Ruthie Samaha, and Wilma Hawkins. The budget for 1990 was five hundred dollaras. On April 22, 1990, the library held its second open house between 9:30 A.M.–11:00 A.M.

Circulation was handled through a computer. The budget for 1991 was $1,735. Karen Jetton was placed on staff at the church in January 1992. The budget for 1992 was $1,735. In the summer of that year the Keys to Summer Reading program was established for first through third graders. A preschool story time was held during the summer in conjunction with the reading program. A puppeteer program was established with performances for the preschool story time. Library Week was October 18–23 with open house on October 18 at 9:00 A.M.–12:00 noon.

The budget for 1993 was $6,420. God's Little Lambs & Ewe preschool story time was scheduled Wednesdays 5:00 P.M.–5:20 P.M. Keys to Summer Reading continued during the summer. The library open house was September 19 from 8:30 A.M.–12:00 noon with special events during the week including an oral book review.

The name of the library was changed to the Lamppost Library & Resource Center. A new logo was incorporated at the same time. The Library Committee included Lynda Smith, chairman, Sallie Grant, Irma Roberts, Helen Purinton, Elva Lyles, Ruthie Samaha, Wilma Hawkins, and Karen Jetton, library director. Leslie Morgan was added to the committee for 1994.

Respectfully submitted,
Karen Jetton
Library Director
1993

LAY DELEGATES
TO ANNUAL CONFERENCE

1982
Avis Allen
Larry Hawkins
Anne Howdeshell
Don Howdeshell
Kate Joyner
Dr. Susan Ruby Lamb
Henry Weber
Martha Weber
John Williams

1983
Avis Allen
Clarence Hampton
Larry Hawkins
Don Howdeshell
Kate Joyner
Dr. Susan Ruby Lamb
Shirley Lynn
Henry Weber
Martha Weber
John Williams

1984
Avis Allen
Marvin Budd
Mary Louise Caldwell
Clarence Hampton
Larry Hawkins
Don Howdeshell
Kate Joyner
Dr. Susan Ruby Lamb
Shirley Lynn
Henry Weber
Martha Weber

1985
Clarence Hampton
Martha Anne Johnston
Henry Weber
Alternates:
Mrs. J. J. Doughtie
Byron Fisher
Don Howdeshell
Shirley Lynn
Jack Morris
Dr. Dick Ross
Mary Elizabeth Thomas

1986
Mary Louise Caldwell
Martha Anne Johnston
Alternates:
Mrs. J. J. Doughtie
Bert Ferguson
Byron Fisher
Don Howdeshell
Shirley Lynn
Jack Morris
Dr. Dick Ross
H. Clay Shelton Jr.
Henry C. Shelton III
Mary Elizabeth Thomas
John Whitsitt

1987
Margaret Colby
Tom Dyer
Harry A. Johnson Jr.
Dr. Richard Ross
Henry C. Shelton III
Alternates:
Kate Davenport
J. J. Doughtie
Jane Isbell Haynes
Dr. Susan Ruby Lamb
Ann Orr
H. Clay Shelton Jr.
Gordon Slappey

Lay Delegates to Annual Conference 55

1988
Margaret Colby
Tom Dyer
E. C. Handorf
Harry A. Johnson Jr.
Dr. Richard Ross
Henry C. Shelton III
Alternates:
Kate Davenport
J. J. Doughtie
Jane Isbell Haynes
Dr. Susan Ruby Lamb
Ann Orr
H. Clay Shelton Jr.
Gordon Slappey

1989
Margaret Colby
Harry A. Johnson Jr.
Alternates:
Kate Davenport
Thomas R. Dyer
Becky Ford
John S. Ford
Jane Isbell Haynes
Penny Johnson
Charles H. Johnston
Martha Ann Johnston
Randall D. Noel
Ann Ross
Dr. Richard T. Ross
Gordon Slappey Jr.

1990
Kate Davenport
Thomas R. Dyer
John S. Ford
Jane Isbell Haynes
Harry A. Johnson Jr.
Randall D. Noel
Dr. Richard T. Ross
Phoebe Smith
Alternates:
Mary Condra
Becky Ford
Penny Johnson
Charles H. Johnston
Martha Ann Johnston
Ann Ross

1991
John S. Ford
Jane Isbell Haynes
Preston McDaniel
Philip Mischke
Jack Morris
Randall D. Noel
Lou Payne
Phoebe Smith
Don Wood
Alternates:
Mary Condra
Becky Ford
Penny Johnson
Charles H. Johnston
Martha Anne Johnston
Ann Ross

1992
Becky Ford
John S. Ford
Harry A. Johnson Jr.
Penny Johnson
Charles H. Johnston
Martha Ann Johnston
Preston McDaniel
Philip Mischke
Jack Morris
Lou Payne
Wayne Pyeatt
Ann Ross
Flo Seward
Henry C. Shelton III
Phoebe Smith
Don Wood

1993
Mary Condra
Tom Dyer
Harry A. Johnson Jr.
Philip Mischke
Jack Morris
Lou Payne
Suzanne Schaeffer
Flo Seward
Henry C. Shelton III
Wally Simpson
Alternates:
Becky Ford
Charles H. Johnston
Martha Anne Johnston
Wayne Pyeatt
Ann Ross

1994
Tom Dyer
Harry A. Johnson Jr.
Jack Morris
Suzanne Schaeffer
Flo Seward
Henry C. Shelton III
Trudy Simpson
Wally Simpson
Phoebe Smith

Alternates:
Mary Condra
Becky Ford
Charles H. Johnston
Martha Anne Johnston
Ann Ross

ANNUAL CONFERENCE
1986

CHRIST CHURCH HOSTS ANNUAL CONFERENCE 1986

The 1986 session of the Memphis Annual Conference will convene on Sunday, June 1, at 4:30 P.M. in our church and will continue through Wednesday afternoon, June 4, when the ministerial appointments for a new year will be read by our presiding bishop, Ernest W. Newman. This will be only the second time in Christ Church's history that we have hosted the meeting of the Annual Conference, the last one being in 1965.

The conference begins with a memorial service Sunday afternoon, memorializing the clergy and wives of clergy who have died since last June 1. The Reverend George Comes, pastor of Wesleyan Hills Church, has been selected to preach that service. It will be followed by a Communion service led by our own senior and executive ministers.

Sunday evening at 7:30 P.M. there is a service of worship designed as a rally of Methodists from the Memphis area. All our membership are invited to the entire proceedings of the week and especially urged to attend the Sunday evening service. Dr. William P. Bailey Jr., our district superintendent, will preach at that service and our Christ Church Chancel Choir will be singing two anthems.

Bishop Newman will call to order the first business session at 10:20 A.M. on Monday, following an executive session at 8:30 A.M. to examine clergy and candidates for ministry. The welcome will be extended by the mayors of Memphis and Shelby County, Dr. Dunnam, and Harry A. Johnson Jr., chairman of the Host Committee.

On Monday at 11:30 A.M., Dr. Norman E. Dewire, general secretary of the General Council on Ministries of the United Methodist Church, will preach. On Tuesday and Wednesday at 11:00 A.M. Bishop Joel McDavid, retired bishop from Atlanta, will be the preacher as well as on Tuesday evening at the 7:30 P.M. ordination service, which is one of the highest and holiest times of the week.

Cokesbury will set up a bookstore in the gym and various organizations in the conference will have displays surrounding the bookstore.

Conference continues through Wednesday afternoon when our bishop is scheduled to read the ministerial appointments of all clergy about 3:00 P.M.

A committee has been working diligently for the better part of the past year, preparing for the more than nine hundred lay and clergy delegates who will attend. Serving with the chairman, Harry A. Johnson Jr., has been Dr. William P. Bailey Jr., Gary Barta, Reverend Robert Crump, Brad Conder, Jerry Dunnam,

Annual Conference: 1986 57

Reverend Earl Johnston, Jean Martin, Jackie Miller, Frances Parsons, Ed P. Segner Jr., Hank Shelton, Steve Shular, and Julie Sutch.

Many improvements have been made in our property, too, as the maintenance crew, working with Milton Bennett, have planted hundreds of shrubs, polished floors, painted, and improved many areas. We are grateful to them. In addition, many of our people are volunteering to serve in various areas. Food will be served; the courtyard will be alive with food, fun, and fellowship.

Again, let us urge you to attend one or more sessions of the conference. It is a unique experience every United Methodist should know about firsthand.

In an official way the following are delegates representing Christ United Methodist Church: Mary Louise Caldwell, J. J. Doughtie, Bert Ferguson, Don Howdeshell, Martha Anne Johnston, Jack Morris, Ann Orr, Hank Shelton, Henry Weber, plus the ordained ministers and diaconals of our staff.

ANNUAL CONFERENCE
1991

Host Committee Meeting Minutes
Memphis Annual Conference
January 13, 1991

Present: Harry A. Johnson Jr.   Al Ingram   Maggie Hollabaugh
          Gary Barta   Earl Johnston   Leann Leathers
          Miller Delgadillo   Art Massey   Jeanette Watkins
          Bob Crump   Francie Brunt

The correct dates for the conference are June 2–6. We expect 900–1200 participants at the conference. The participants come and go, rarely will they all be present at once. Harry Johnson has requested that no weddings or special meetings be scheduled at the church from May 29 through the end of the conference.

Harry Johnson has a copy of the budget approved by the Annual Conference Committee. It is unclear how bills are to be paid and where various financial responsibilities lie. Earl Johnston told Harry to contact Joe Pevahouse (Corner Drugstore, Henderson, Tennessee) to learn how that is handled.

Food (Jeanette Watkins):
1. Methodist Hospital will give a reception in Seabrook Hall on June 2.

2. The Wesleyan Fellowship will expect a luncheon. Earl Johnston will give Jeanette the name of the appropriate person in that organization who will help her understand their needs as well as choose a date.

3. The Board of Pensions will have a luncheon, probably on Monday, June 3. Dr. John Clarke in Fulton, Kentucky, will help Jeanette with details. This luncheon will feed around two hundred retired ministers and spouses as well as the bishop and his cabinet. It will probably take place in Seabrook Hall.

4. The bishop and his cabinet will have working lunches daily, except for Monday. We expect that they will be served in the parlor. Jeanette must ask the bishop how many people to count on each day.

Various theological schools usually host reunion lunches. As the alumni groups begin asking where these lunches might be held, this committee has

Annual Conference: 1991   59

decided not to have these events at CUMC. Other Methodist churches in the area would probably enjoy providing facilities.

Jeanette has written both mayors. Mayor [William] Morris has promised to make an appearance at the conference. Mayor [Richard] Hackett is checking his schedule.

Our youth program will be selling food (donuts, coffee, soft drinks, sandwiches, snacks) in order to meet the needs of conference participants who are not included in luncheon groups. Braxton Brady will coordinate this project.

Buildings, Grounds, Umbrella Tables, In-Church Displays (Maggie Hollabaugh):
Do we have a theme? Reverend Crump says the Conference Committee will come up with a theme. He will encourage them to hurry.

Will we receive a banner? Leann and Reverend Crump think we will and that it should be hung in the sanctuary. Reverend Crump will ask the committee about a banner.

Maggie asked Miller Delgadillo to accept responsibility for hostess badges as well as badges for conference participants. Miller said yes.

Maggie suggests having a hospitality room equipped with necessary items for ladies as well as some fun things.

Jerry Dunnam can tell Maggie who to call regarding umbrella tables. These tables will be set up in the courtyard, weather permitting. Part of the Fellowship Hall will be reserved for this purpose in case of rain.

Maggie requests a master plan so that she will know where each group will be meeting and exactly which rooms will be in use.

Conference Secretary (Reverend Crump):
Reverend Crump thanked CUMC on behalf of the Conference Committee for agreeing to host this Annual Conference.

Reverend Crump requests two small rooms or one large room for tellers to count ballots. The room should be close to the sanctuary and be equipped electrically to handle two computer systems. It should be a secure room to protect this expensive equipment. David Lewis is in charge of ballot counting.

Registration (Miller Delgadillo):
Miller's main responsibility is the packet that conference goers receive on arrival at the church as well as badges. Much of what goes inside the packet will come from conference headquarters in Jackson, Tennessee (Reverened Crump will help get this material); however, Miller will include city maps (call Phil Mischke), CUMC maps, schedules, etc. Harry Johnson is asking Methodist Hospital to provide attractive folders.

Miller will also send out a preregistration letter that will provide information and will contain an actual registration form. This form will include questions regarding nursery needs.

CONFERENCE 1991

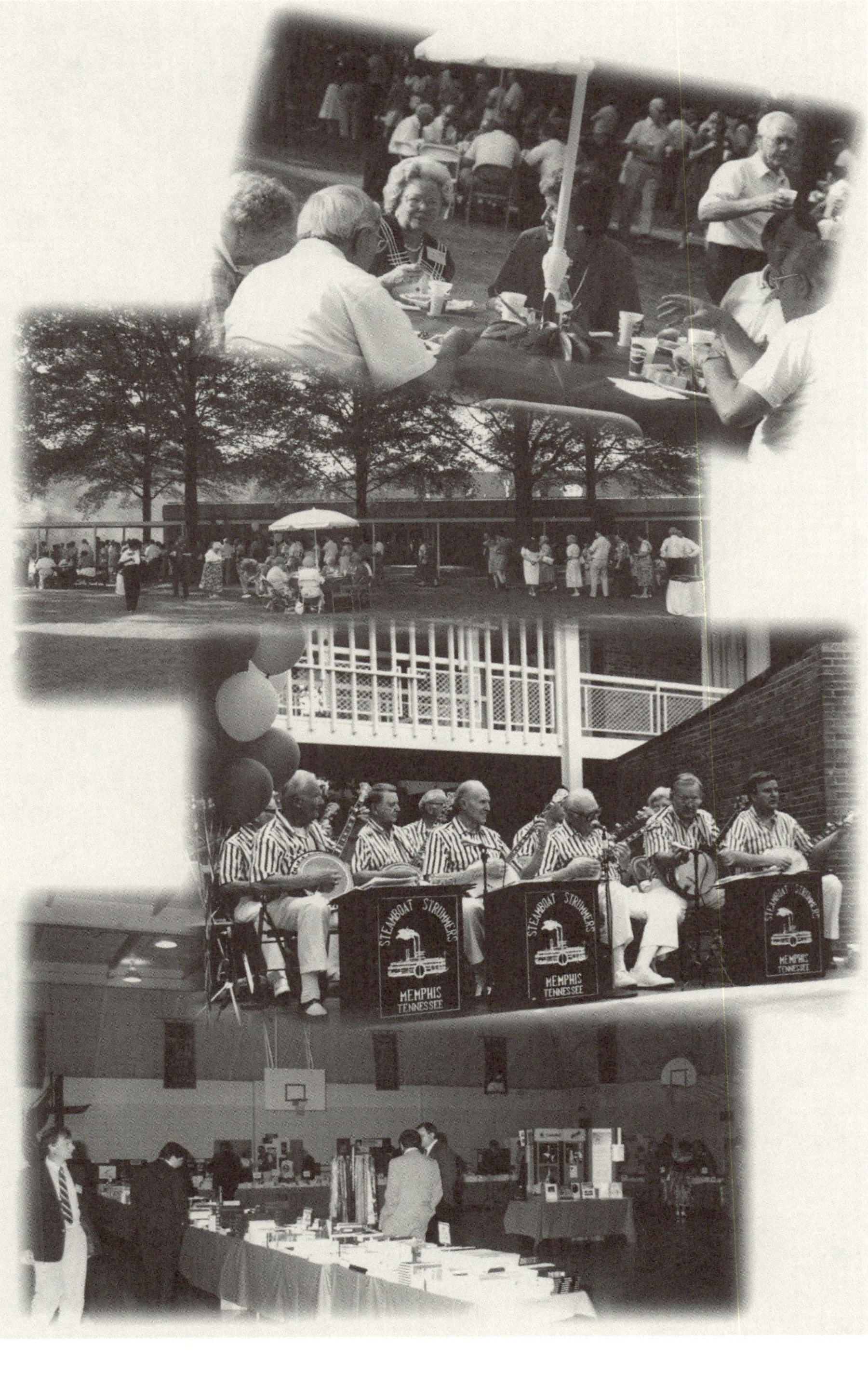
STEAMBOAT STRUMMERS
MEMPHIS
TENNESSEE

Miller will be in charge of setting up a registration area at the church and will secure volunteers to man the tables. She will also secure hosts and hostesses. Maggie gave Miller a list of hostesses from the conference held at CUMC four years ago.

Signs, Church Sketch (Gary Barta):
Gary needs a list of groups that will require signs. He needs a list of vendors in the gym. (Francie Brunt will give him that list when she learns who is coming.) Gary needs the names of those requiring reserved parking. He plans to make place cards and make signs for information tables, press tables, etc. Gary expects an architect's sketch of our entire facility. He will see that it is reproduced and placed in necessary areas.

Parking, Security (Art Massey):
Art will get volunteers to help with parking. He will see that at least one security person is on guard at night. The courtyard will need attention because of umbrella tables and rented equipment from Coca-Cola.

Tours for Spouses, Special Events, Information Center (Al Ingram):
Al expects information and help from the Visitors and Conventions Bureau. He will set up an information center that will include a message board and telephone access.

Nursery, Agency Displays, First Aid (Francie Brunt):
Registration forms will tell us what our nursery needs are. Pat Whaley will then be contacted so that he can arrange for sitters.

First Aid Needs:
A quiet room for someone to stretch out, possibly the Bride's Room.

Near this room, an area for personnel from Methodist Hospital to provide usual services for participants (blood pressures, general first aid). David Compton at Methodist Hospital is the contact person. Is this service free?

The display area will probably be in the old gym. CCOM [Conference Council on Ministries] office manager Martha Manuel will provide Francie with a list of possible exhibitors. Francie must write these people to determine their needs.

Any committee chairman who has specific needs, such as umbrella tables, or volunteer needs, such as hostesses, should give a list to Harry Johnson. Harry will get an article in the *Courier* in March making these requests.

✣ ✣ ✣

HOST COMMITTEE MEETING MINUTES
Memphis Annual Conference
April 28, 1991

Annual Conference: 1991

Present: Harry A. Johnson Jr.   Miller Delgadillo   Tom Marino
             Gary Barta   Francie Brunt   Byron Fisher
             Leann Leathers   Art Massey   Bob Crump

Harry began by telling Tom Marino that he needs to submit a menu with prices to Harry by May 15. An average of 1200 people per day may be buying food at the church. Tom said he would try to get that together by the fifteenth.

Young people from CUMC will be needed in the sanctuary to hand out bundles of papers. The kids will also operate the message center.

Harry told Francie to distribute a letter he has written to church neighbors informing them of the conference. Art offered to distribute the letters to shops in the Oak Court Mall.

Maggie Hollabaugh: Maggie has carried on an elaborate cleanup campaign. Her plans are set for the courtyard seating and decor. Interior decorations are planned as well. She is on schedule.

Jeanette Watkins: Jeanette has gotten 50 tables and 500 chairs donated for the Bar-B-Q. All of this will be taken away Monday morning. She has gotten all table linens for luncheons donated. Well done, Jeanette!

Art Massey: What are the hours that we will require security guards? Answer: Friday night, May 31 through June 6.

Art wants badges for his parking attendants. He also wants maps of church property that include the parking areas.

Francie Brunt: A concrete marker arrives in mid-May. She needs to alert Mr. Boda that it is coming and tell him it will be displayed on Tuesday, June 4.

She will call Pat Whaley regarding the nursery.

Gary Barta will get the display table signs to her before May 31. We have had late requests for display space. We will see if we can find more space and tables.

Gary Barta: Gary has found host tags. He will order the tags, which will be ready in two weeks. We must be sure to collect the tags so they can be used again.

Gary will make two signs for each district, one for clergy and one for laymen. Harry has reserved parking signs that will be placed by Mr. [Richard] Boda.

Miller Delgadillo: Miller has volunteers to man the registration tables from noon on Sunday till noon on Monday. Rev. Crump suggests she have at least one person there throughout the rest of the conference to take care of latecomers.

Al Ingram: No treasury problems. Al will have a table near registration to hand out tourist info. A tour of Neighborhood Centers will be arranged by Betty Evans.

Byron Fisher: Reverend Crump helped Byron with table and seating arrangements for the front of the sanctuary. We should have an extra chair handy for any visiting bishops. Byron would like to rent furniture from Aaron Rents. He thinks the cost will be around $200. Bob recommends a cloth to hide the bishop's legs. Byron may use plants instead. (Harry said to ask Maggie if that is ok; we don't want to mess up her plans.)

Bob reminded us of his need for a microphone. He will talk to Jim Holmes about all of the microphones needed in that room.

Byron has the equipment for the message center. He will set it up and test it and teach the youth to use it.

Problem: How to get nonvoters to sit in a designated visitors' area?

Leann Leathers: Leann has tickets for the Bar-B-Q Committee members and spouses are expected to attend this affair. It starts at 3:30 P.M.

Submitted by:
Francie Brunt

✣ ✣ ✣

August 6, 1991

Dr. Maxie Dunnam
Christ United Methodist Church

Dear Maxie:

This is the final report of the Annual Conference 1991 Host Committee.

I asked the Budget Committee for $5,000 to be used by the Annual Conference Host Committee. They granted the request but we never asked for the money and have no need for it. I therefore ask that it be returned to the general fund for other uses.

The youth working with Tom Marino distributed literature to the Conference when needed, operated the overhead projector message center and cooked and sold food for snacks and lunch each day of the Conference. They cleared about $2,000, which was distributed to those who worked, to be used for their Colorado trip. They made a considerable contribution to the needs of the Conference.

We recovered the following from the Conference for expenses incurred by the church directly attributable to the Conference.

Taping of all sessions $209.57
Maintenance Crew Expense $595.00
Office Expense $689.00
Total $1,493.57

Food services provided by the church and paid for by the group holding the function, by individuals, and/or the Conference.

June 2	Methodist Health Systems	600 people	$1,200.00
June 3	Pension Lunch	190 people	$1,034.00
June 3	Diaconals Lunch	50 people	$250.00
June 4	Emory Lunch	38 people	$190.00

Annual Conference: 1991

June 4	Minister's wives lunch	155 people	$775.00
June 5	Ordinand's Reception	200 people	$400.00
June 5	Credit Union Cont. Bkft.	40 people	$70.00
June 4	Bishop's Lunch	30 people	$120.00
June 5	Bishop's Lunch	30 people	$120.00
June 6	Bishop's Lunch	30 people	$120.00
	Total Food Services		$4,279.00

The Bar-B-Q on Sunday, June 2, was a tremendous success. The food, decorations, entertainment, and general atmosphere accomplished the purpose for it. The Bar-B-Q cost $4,900 and was paid for by the sale of tickets at $7 each. We actually fed 707 people.

Expenses incurred by CUMC $1,493.57
Food services $4,279.00
Balance to the church $4,050.85
Total check to CUMC $9,823.42
Total income from all Conference activities $17,120.93
The total expense $13,070.08
....$4,050.85

The balance turned over to the church $4,050.85 is there because the members of the Host Committee were able to get many contributions from without and within the church and gave so much of themselves, their time, and talent.

The Conference was tremendously successful because of the magnificent way in which the committee and the many volunteers, as well as many staff members, gave of themselves.

It has been a wonderful experience in what people can accomplish when they want to do so.

Sincerely
Harry A. Johnson Jr.

P. S. I would like to propose that the $4,050.85 surplus coming to the church be used in the following way: $2,000 to be used for the top priority decorations or furniture on the list as made up by Maggie Hollabaugh, and those who helped her during the Conference.

And, in keeping with the commitment of the church to give 50 percent to others, that the balance of slightly over $2,000 be given to the group in the church who will use it for materials only to improve the living conditions of one or more families. We would prefer that it be used to buy materials for those who are willing to help themselves by using own labor, and the help of those willing church members, or those who cannot help themselves.

It is further requested that both these funds be given in honor of the 1991 Host Committee members who created this surplus.

THE CHURCH SCHOOL

In 1981, Marvin Budd, a diaconal minister, joined the staff at Christ Church as the director of Christian education.

Marvin was a quiet man who performed his duties in a very organized way and was truly dedicated to the education of all church members.

In 1990, Patrick Whaley, also a diaconal minister, joined the staff as the director of children's ministries, where he did an excellent job and later switched to director of adult ministries where he has contributed greatly to the expansion and quality of the ministry to all adults.

1990

Earl Johnston, who is teaching the Bible class during April, called Harry and said that he wanted to serve Communion during Sunday school on Easter Sunday. He wanted Harry to get the Communion trays with the little glasses that have been used for many, many years. The church now uses a large cup to hold the juice and the wafer is dipped in. The little glasses become a real problem when one serves as many people as now attend.

It was hard to find them, but Thomas Mungen, the maintenance superintendent knew exactly where they were. Harry went with him up to "Ernest Stubblefield's apartment." Ernest Stubblefield is the man who kidnapped the [Leslie] Gattas girl many years ago and after several months was found living in the storage area below the balcony in the church. When he was found he had keys to many churches in Memphis, not just Christ Church. They survived by using the facilities of the church and getting food out of the church kitchen.

Carolyn Grizzard gave Harry several cans of grape juice and a bag of Communion wafers.

CHRIST METHODIST DAY SCHOOL

The Christ Church day school acquired a new director, David Fox, who was employed following the resignation of Sam Drash. The day school continued to enjoy a fine reputation for excellent training and quality education. From kindergarten through the sixth grade, the enrollment at present is 410 pupils, with 150 children enrolled in the Parents' Day Out program, under the auspices of the day school.

MISSIONS
1982–1993

The following recollections give an overall view of the scope and commitment to missions.

- Reverend James Loftin comes to Christ United Methodist Church

- "Recollections of Fourteen Years at Christ United Methodist Church" by Rev. James L. Loftin

- Volunteers in mission trip to Atlixco, Mexico

- Mission Volunteers to San Salvador, El Salvador

- Trip to Russia (from Don Green's diary)

- "Service Over Self (SOS) in Memphis" by Dick Klenz

- "I Didn't Drive a Single Nail" by Dr. Maxie D. Dunnam

- Mediation and Restitution/Reconcilation Services (MARRS)

- Neighborhood Centers and MIFA (Metropolitan Inter-Faith Association) supported

- Eight local and foreign missionaries supported

- Nash Vickers (CUMC member) commissioned by the General Board of Missions to serve in Zaire

The Missions Ministry of Christ Church
Stages of Development
by Rev. James L. Loftin

Stage I. Charity. From its birth in 1955 Christ Church has always had a heart for missions. This has been voiced by members over the decades with words like, "Let's do as much for others as we do for ourselves." The early emphasis of the missions outreach was on the donation of resources to support the work of missionaries and agencies. Though some of this work was in evangelism, most projects targeted the physical needs of people (food, clothing, housing, etc.). Much of the work was relief in nature—meeting immediate, short-term, crisis needs. The long-term conditions of the persons were not specifically addressed. In this phase of our church's outreach, the dominant strategy was the provision of financial support so that others could do outreach for us.

Stage II. Partnership. In the early nineties Christ Church began to develop a new strategy of outreach. Though the church continued to donate financial resources to many Christian ministries in Memphis and around the world, a new emphasis surfaced. The desire was to do ministry *with* others. The key word became *partnership*. Support from Christ Church included volunteers as well as dollars. The church sought to be a viable part of the ministry, including decision-making and hands-on involvement. In this phase there was a growing emphasis on the long-term conditions of persons, with the understanding that evangelism and discipleship are meeting the long-term needs of people—their eternal needs. MARRS [Mediation and Restitution/Reconciliation Services] and SOS [Service Over Self] developed as partnerships during this stage. Charity and relief work must always be a part of the church's response to suffering and poverty. However, by itself, charity does not change lives. Another key word for this phase was *development*.

Stage III. Empowerment. In 1996 the missions ministry of Christ Church seemed to move into a new stage. More and more attention is being given to the sending of Christ Church members into full-time missionary service and the equipping of indigenous leaders. God has opened many doors for the members of Christ Church to minister in the inner city and in foreign lands such as El Salvador, Russia, and Morocco. Though numerous, these ministry efforts generally involve a few hours or days of a person's time. There is an awareness that God is calling Christ Church to continue this mobilization of volunteers but to also participate in the sending of people into full-time missionary service. The key word is *send*.

Another part of this new focus is the empowering of men and women to minister to their own peoples. Who can more effectively minister in Binghampton than an African-American Christian who lives there and has been discipled and trained for ministry? Berbers to the Berber residents of North Africa. Russians to Russians. The key word here is *empowerment*. There is still a need for westerners to minister in the Far East and for European-Americans to minister in African-American neighborhoods. Nevertheless, the training and deployment of indigenous Christian leaders is a crucial strategy in effectively transforming the world.

During 1996 the missions leadership of Christ Church adopted a new plan to reach the world for Christ. The key word is *neighborhood*. This strategy involves redeeming the world one community or neighborhood at a time. Therefore the Missions Committee has decided to focus our local ministry in the Binghampton neighborhood and our international ministry in what is called the 10/40 window. This refers to the section of our globe that includes North Africa, the Middle East, India, Pakistan, China, and Indonesia. Ninety-seven percent of the people in the world who have not had opportunity to hear the gospel of Christ live here.

Missionary Personnel Overseas
Mr. & Mrs. Loreto Crisologo
Fiji Islands

Rev. & Mrs. Joe Stroud
Japan

Mr. & Mrs. Donald E. Rugh
India

Mr. & Mrs. Dean Louis Schowengerdt
Korea

Rev. & Mrs. Richard Cabbage
Africa

Missionaries
1956—Dr. & Mrs. Harold Brewster	Sarawak, Borneo
1958—Dr. Loreto & Mrs. Dorothy Crisologo	Sarawak, Borneo
1958—Edward & Jane Heyer	Southern Rhodesia and Sierra Leone
1963—Jim & Ila Gravely	Brazil
1965—Louise Morris	Japan
1965—John O. Studstill	Congo
1965—Stanley & Joanne Maughlin	Congo (Zaire)
1981–82—Marvin Pouco	Trips to Jamaica/Haiti

✣ ✣ ✣

JAMES LOFTIN MISSIONS RECOLLECTIONS
1983–1993

Rev. James Loftin came to Christ Church from Meridian, Mississippi, to become the youth director, but in 1991 became the director of missions where he has made his most lasting contribution.

1984. A training class for workers interested in the Prison Fellowship was set up for the second Tuesday of every month in the activities building. A program called Willing Workers was set up by Mike Sheahan so twenty-five to thirty men can do yard work to try and rehabilitate themselves. PCS [Positive Christian Singles] contributed fifty dollars and the Men's Bible Class one hundred dollars to buy equipment for this program.

Dud Curry announced the completion of the first Habitat for Humanity house with more planned in Rossville. Beck Beckwith made a work trip to Brazil with others to build a community center. Funds and books were donated to Methodist churches being organized in Czechoslovakia. Donations were made to the Bethany Home for unwed mothers and to the ethnic minority local church.

A team of Christ Church volunteers went to Brazil to help Gordon and Teca Greathouse set up a day care center for the large number of orphaned and homeless children. Beck Beckwith, Mary Louise Caldwell, Pam Harsh, Virginia and Sherman Parry, Nash Vickers, and Marvin Budd made up this mission team.

1985. The Prison Fellowship will send six prison inmates to help during June and July to rehabilitate several selected houses under the leadership of Fred Mills. Three truckloads of used clothing were distributed to Neighborhood Centers and MIFA [Metropolitan Inter-Faith Association]. This project was headed by Julia Atkinson.

A van was purchased by the church and presented to the United Methodist Neighborhood Centers.

A total of $61,595 was allocated for the support of the following ministries:

Mr. & Mrs. Douglas Crowder—Zaire, Africa
Mr. & Mrs. Gordon Greathouse—Brazil
Mr. Franklin Perry—Memphis inner city
Mr. & Mrs. Richard A. Mott—Zaire, Africa
Mr. & Mrs. Dean Schowengardt—Korea
Mr. & Mrs. Joe Stroud II—Japan
Rev. Billy Joe Jackson—Memphis
Mr. Jeff Walker—Memphis

Nash Vickers was commissioned as a United Methodist missionary on October 24, 1985, by the General Board of Missions and left on November 9 for his assignment to the North Shaba Conference in Lubumbashi, Zaire.

VOLUNTEERS IN MISSION TRIP TO ATLIXCO, MEXICO
Atlixco United Methodist Church, Summer 1982
(Author Unknown)

My first mission trip was filled with as much excitement and wonder as most any first time experience, including the awkwardness of misplaced expectations. For me, this trip and experience opened my eyes to a new view of Christian service and commitment. I honestly do not think I was alone in this assessment as less than half of the team of eight had ever been on a mission trip before.

The Team. Ann and Tommy Tanner of Jackson, Tennessee, led our team. Their experience and learning from previous trips was invaluable to all of us who may have been having some doubts about what we were really getting involved in. Barbara Markum from around Ripley, Tennessee, and Ray Marcum from Lexington, Tennessee, seemed to be full of confidence and knowledge even though this was their initial trip. It was quite a challenge to introduce them and try to distinguish their last names in such a way that our local friends would know that they were not related to each other beyond the cross of Jesus!

There were four of us who were a bit younger (at the time) than the others. Tim Johnson from Emmanuel United Methodist here in Memphis and John Laverty from St. Johns United Methodist were either just out of college or still in at the time. Patty was a young mother who left her young family in the care of her husband to join us for two weeks. Ethyl joined the team as the second member from St. John's United Methodist. For Paul Mulroy and myself, we were both just beginning our working careers in our chosen fields.

The Project. Atlixco is a small town by Mexico standards of about forty thousand people and is located about one hundred miles southeast of Mexico City. It is nestled near the base of Popocatepetl, a 17,887-foot volcano cinder cone that is snow-capped throughout the year. Situated in a field of volcanic activity, Atlixco has several other small volcanic mountains in the surrounding area, which are just large enough at their summits to accommodate a small Catholic church.

A couple of years prior to our visit, Atlixco had been ravaged by an earthquake, which severely damaged the United Methodist church and adjacent parsonage. Rubble and debris were still surrounding the sanctuary and courtyard making it impossible to walk around the grounds without first carefully navigating the terrain. The building structures appeared to be in good condition despite some cracks. It was apparent that the congregation had worked on repairing the most essential facility structures.

Funding had also been a limited factor to the rehabilitation of the church property. In fact, the United Methodist church, which was located adjacent to the downtown square, stood in stark contrast to the beautifully ornate Catholic churches in the town. Our local hosts indicated that this was a difference in tithing and gift-giving philosophies of the two churches: the Catholic church encourages stewardship in support of the edifice even to the sacrifice of the family themselves while the Methodist church focused first on the welfare of the families and community of believers.

The Family of Christ. Our accommodations were in the homes of the church members which for Tim, John, Paul, and I was within walking distance of the church. This was essentially a two-room house with a living area which included a kitchen and eating area and second room which was the sleeping room for the family of four. This family gave up their bed and room for us! Their hospitality was truly remarkable.

I remember coming home to them each night after a long day laboring at the church. Our beautiful hosts wanted to talk and share culturally while we were tired, dirty, and exhausted! Their lack of knowledge in English was matched by our lack of knowledge in Spanish. A sentence of conversation took about five minutes of each side flipping through our respective language dictionaries. But oh, their smiles and Christian love said it all!

Initial Impressions. Amidst all the rubble and debris that greeted us as we arrived was a small baby whose cradle was much like a hammock suspended on two ropes across the parsonage. Such a different, yet so very effective way to do something! I know that we all came in with ideas that we could help make their work better but soon we were proven so wrong.

A good example of this was when we were reworking the roof of the parsonage. First of all, we weren't entirely sure we had translated the instructions correctly when they told us to start breaking up the flat roof, which was made of bricks and mortar. When it came time to replace the mortar with new concrete, we rigged up a pulley system that lasted all of about thirty seconds! Our local friends sure did get a good laugh at our attempt at bringing them our Yankee ingenuity! We needed to listen and learn from them!

Concluding Thoughts. Overall, I was amazed at the level of joy and happiness that our new friends at Atlixco United Methodist Church seem to exude. Even though their lives were so very simple and austere, their joy and love for the Lord was so deeply rooted even to the point of providing so sacrificially for us. If there was ever anyone with whom I had had contact that had, what I thought, was a reason to complain or be disgruntled, it was our Atlixco Christians. However, to my astonishment, their sense of joy, which had its source in the heart of their faith, was much more substantial than even my own!

I had set out on this mission trip feeling that I would be going out and ministering to the lives of a needy people. In the end, I discovered that I was really the needy person, and they had ministered to me through God's grace, love, and glory showing through their lives.

VOLUNTEERS IN MISSION
San Salvador, El Salvador
February 20–28, 1993
by Julie Ferrell

Our team consisted of twenty-seven people: eleven physicians (nine M.D.s, two dentists), nine nurse/assistants, an audiologist, and the rest non-medical support persons of various backgrounds. Our team leader was Dr. Tom Long.

Our objective was to boost the ongoing work of our host church, Iglesia Nazaret, within their community and in the rural poverty areas.

Iglesia Nazaret is a church that is alive with the love of Christ. The congregation has recognized many of the needs in the community and is acting in faith to show God's love to meet those needs. There are local dentists and physicians who are willing to give of their time to work in a clinic at the church to provide care for the poor people. Part of our team worked in this environment.

Another part of our team went to an inner-city poverty area called Bambelar. We set up our clinic in a shack and distributed medicines, love, and clothing to the patients there.

Another part of our team visited a local outreach ministry called LoveLink. This is a shelter for abandoned and/or sick children whose parents cannot or will not take care of them. These children live with missionaries Sam and Julie Hawkins until adoption is arranged.

Another part of the outreach of Iglesia Nazaret took us to a rural area called Tapaluacha. In this community, the families live in one-room mud brick houses. There is a one-room concrete building that is the church. In this building we set up our clinic for two doctors to examine patients while the pharmacy and the dentist set up under the trees outside. Members of the congregation and some of our non-medical team members entertained the children with skits and games while they waited, sharing the message of Jesus Christ's love in song, medicines, and hugs.

It is my understanding that members of the congregation of Iglesia Nazaret Church visit these areas regularly and minister to the needs there. It was awesome to witness our common bond, the love of Christ for all people.

February 20–28, 1993, CUMC Medical Mission Team to San Salvador. Dr. Bob Hollabaugh seeing patients in the clinic.

Team Members

Caryline Adkins	Physical Therapist
Virginia S. (Genie) Ashworth, R.N.	Registered Nurse
Marion Bailey, D.D.S.	General Denistry
Cheryl Farnsworth	Dental Assistant
Julie Ferrell, R.N.	Registered Nurse
Thad Ferrell, M.D.	Plastic Surgery
Norman Fournier	Physician's Assistant
Sarah Green, M.A.	Audiology
Billy G. Hall Jr., D.D.S.,	General Denistry
O. B. Harrington, M.D.	Thoracic/Cardiovascular Surgery
Barbara Harrington	Homemaker/Designer
Robert S. (Bob) Hollabaugh, M.D.	Pediatric Surgery
José Huerta-Mendez	Pilot, Federal Express
Peggy Huerta-Mendez	Management, Federal Express
John G. Knepper, M.D.	Pediatrics
James Loftin	Minister
Carolyn Loftin	Homemaker
Diane Long, M.D.	Obstetrics/Gynecology
Tom Long, M.D.	Otolaryngology
Suzanne Medford, R.N.	Registered Nurse, Surgery

February 5–13, 1994, CUMC Medical Missions Team to San Salvador. Dr. Tom Long (seated) talking with a patient while many are waiting. Rev. James Loftin, director of CUMC Missions Ministry, standing far right.

Doreen Neal, R.N. . . . . .Registered Nurse, Surgery/Pediatrics
Matthew Ochs, M.D. . . . . .Internal Medicine
Karen Raley, R.N. . . . . .Registered Nurse
Jim Robinson . . . . .Certified Surgical Assistant
Bart Turner . . . . .Farmer
Deborah L. Williams, M.D. . . . . .Radiology
Sid Wilroy, M.D. . . . . .Pediatrics/Genetics

✣ ✣ ✣

Trip to Russia
May 2, 1993–May 13, 1993
(source information courtesy of Don Green)

A missions team from Christ Church consisting of Sherry Saunders, Don Green, Nash Vickers, Jerry Dunnam, Carolyn Loftin, James Loftin, Amy Melton, Skip Burzumato, Lisa Hays, and Curt Parham left Memphis on Delta Airlines in the afternoon of May 2, 1993, and arrived in Moscow, Russia, in the afternoon of May 3, 1993.

The following is taken from a diary kept by Don Green. Don had to give the life history of his flute. The customs agent recorded the serial number, etc. They had to declare how many dollars they were taking into Russia and then keep up with customs declarations so they could leave the country. They were met by a tour guide named Olga, a pretty and sweet person who took good care of the group while they were in Russia. The sky was sunny and the temperature 68 degrees as they boarded a Globetrotters tour bus to the Minsk Hotel. Their dinner consisted of steak, French fries, cabbage, Pepsi, cucumber (Don says it was fantastic), bread, tongue (good), salami, and ice cream with currant sauce (very, very good). A band played while they ate, so their welcome to Russia was fit for a czar.

After dinner they walked to Red Square which was fascinatingly beautiful. St. Basil's Cathedral and the Kremlin were aglow under the full moon. The bus took them back to the Hotel Minsk where they encountered beggars and teenagers trying to sell Yeltsin dolls (the dolls were really "stacked" according to Don). He told one of the teenagers that his wife Sandi said she'd shoot him if he bought one. Olga (the guide) bought them an ice cream costing ten cents each.

Skip gave a neat devotional about seeing a need and fulfilling it versus our safety. The decision is for each individual to make.

Can you imagine Don, who is a big man, taking a shower in a 30" x 30" tub/shower? There was no soap in the bathroom and the toilet paper was like sandpaper.

Breakfast was eggs, cheese, salami, bread (white and dark), and tea on May 4, 1993. After breakfast, all went back to the fifth floor lobby where Jerry Dunnam gave the devotional about the blind person who could feel. They took a bus tour of Moscow, stopping at several kiosks and flea markets. Don bought five army hats. The early morning weather was partly cloudy and 50 degrees, a near perfect day for sightseeing. But they were bombarded by people selling Gorbie dolls.

The lunch at the Moscow Hotel included beef tips, cucumbers, ham, borscht (needed some basil), bread, and ice cream. They visited the Russian Orthodox Church, Moscow University, Tass News Agency, "The White House" (Czar Nicholas II's house), Gorbachev's house, Kruschev's cemetery, and a swimming pool that had been the site of a beautiful cathedral. Josef Stalin had the cathedral blown up and tried building another building on the spot but it sank. He kept trying to build at that location to no avail. He finally made a swimming pool out of it. They saw St. Basil's Cathedral in Red Square again. St. Basil's was built by Ivan the Terrible and when it was finished, he had the architects blinded to keep them from building anything else as beautiful.

They saw the convent where Peter the Great put his wife, and then had a very humbling experience when Chris Henna took them to her apartment. They stopped at a couple of other apartments to pick up New Testaments for the church in Pskov. The temperature on this sunny day rose to 77 degrees. Back to the hotel for dinner—chicken Kiev, potatoes, cucumbers, orange soda, mushroom soufflé, bread, butter, good coffee, and ice cream. They took the bus to Red Square to shop at Gumm's Department Store, but it was closed. They walked to Arbal Street looking for bottled water but none was to be found. Don bought two roses for Olga to show appreciation. There were women lined up against a wall selling perfume, candy, shoes, hosiery, etc. Not one of them smiled which gave you a very eerie feeling. To bed at 11:00 P.M. on May 4 after interesting day.

They woke up to a sixty-degree, partly cloudy day on May 5. Breakfast consisted of salami, cheese, bread, a mystery breaded meat patty, potatoes, and marmalade. They toured the Kremlin where they saw a lot of Russian history—relics of the czars, carriages, jewels, clothes, thrones, etc. United States Secretary of State Warren Christopher was meeting with Boris Yeltsin while the group was at the Kremlin. They watched the changing of the guard at Lenin's Tomb, saw four churches on the Kremlin grounds, and went to Gumm's, the world's largest department store. It's really a large collection of shops, more like a mall. On a side street Don found a religious kiosk and bought a nice crucifix for $2.50. They ate lunch at the Moscow City Council Canteen and had steak, borscht, potato salad, coffee, bread, slaw, cream of mushroom soup, tuna salad, and a relish tray with pickles, onions, tomatoes, etc. They had looked everywhere for bottled water but couldn't find any, but Olga brought some to lunch.

They went back to the hotel to pack up for train ride to Pskov overnight and had supper at the hotel before boarding the train—cucumbers, fish with onion sauce, scalloped potatoes, and ice cream. Saw thousands of people (mostly poor) on way to the train station to board for Pskov. Don and Nash Vickers shared a compartment that was small but nice, pleasant, and efficient. Talked a long time with Jerry Dunnam and Olga; then to bed at 11:30 P.M. Don gave Olga a Pavarotti tape and a compilation tape of classical music. She loves opera so this was a great and exciting gift for her.

May 6 started with 50 degrees and clear weather that stayed clear and got up to 80 degrees in the afternoon. Don was up at 5:00 A.M., excited in anticipation of their arrival in Pskov. The train arrived on time at 8:40 A.M. and the group was met by fifteen people as excited as they were. They went to the hotel and freshened up; then toured Pskov and its A.D. 903 Kremlin. After Don's devotion on humility, they divided into groups of three. Nash, Jerry, and Don went to Leana's apartment for lunch and the afternoon. They ate like kings: fresh raw cabbage, fresh bread, mineral water, and pancakes with fresh strawberry jam. Don says it was heavenly and Jerry demonstrated the same by mopping her plate clean. Don had six cups of Russian tea.

After lunch they shared pictures of their families. They told Don that his wife was beautiful, and then laughed and giggled when he told them that he and Sandi were newlyweds. When Jerry Dunnam asked them what they wanted to discuss, gears changed to overdrive, and they found themselves in the fourth quarter with two-minute warning. They had a real problem with prayer and could not comprehend how they could achieve peace in their hearts as long as their parents were sick, unemployed, and two hundred miles away. How do they feel good about themselves as long as they are broke, their kids need clothes, the electric bill needs to be paid, the rent and other bills are delinquent?

Don told them that we live like that too, but we take it one day at a time and trust God who gives us faith in ourselves. Don played the flute for them. They had two lovely daughters, Sasha and Julia.

The group went to a meeting at 7:00 P.M. and heard the Boys Choir (with men) sing "What a Friend We Have in Jesus" in Russian, and Don says it was so moving he couldn't hold the tears. They sang "Silent Night," "Alleluia," and "Ave Maria." James Loftin spoke about Jesus being our friend and over twelve people stayed to ask questions and to accept Jesus as their friend. Skip taught ten kids how to sing "Humble Yourself in the Sight of the Lord." They had supper at 9:30 P.M., sunset at 10:00 P.M., and it was still light at 11:00 P.M.

May 7 started out clear and 75 degrees. They went to visit the hospital which was very antiquated but with 235 doctors and had a visit with the mayor of Pskov. They went to a soup kitchen, then walked along the river and then to Nadia and Alexander's apartment for lunch. There was baked chicken, mashed potatoes, oranges, cucumbers, sour cream cake, and Don played the flute. Olga, Nash, and Don walked back to the hotel at 5:00 P.M. All went to a meeting at 7:30 P.M. but the door was locked so they went in through the stage door. Fourteen people were saved. Amy Melton sang a solo, Don played the flute, and Skip the guitar. After the meeting they went to Leana's apartment to eat pancakes and strawberries. Then walked one and a half miles back to the hotel at midnight.

It was 60 degrees and clear the morning of May 8, but Don had a queasy stomach (I wonder why.), so breakfast was not appealing. After breakfast, they boarded a bus that transported them to an old fort that was built in 900 A.D. and then to a monastery just three kilometers from the Estonia border. They stopped by a lake on the way back to Pskov and had a picnic (evidently the queasy stomach disappeared). Then to church at 6:00 P.M. May 9, Mother's Day in the U.S., had low temperature of 65 degrees and high 80 degrees. They went to a service in a big Orthodox church and then back for breakfast. They saw a very moving tribute and memorial to Russian Unknown Soldiers which included a parade with military bands, troops, and a lot of veterans covered with medals. A twenty-one-gun salute topped off a very nostalgic experience.

They went to the Estonian border for a picnic by the lake with the people of the Pskov church. This location is a retreat for railroad workers, a neat place amid whispering pines. Many of the pines were infested with beetles or acid rain. It was a great picnic after which the bus took us to the border checkpoint with Estonia. Some got off the bus and took pictures of the guards, who didn't think it was very amusing. The guards demanded the film from the cameras. James Loftin reloaded with new film. The guard took it and exposed it, then declared the camera clear.

Back to the hotel, Don changed clothes and went to Denis's apartment for dinner. His mother had prepared a six-course meal for six people. It was delicious, but his mother tried to get Don to eat all six meals. Denis never knew his father who was an alcoholic. Don and Denis walked to the church for a meeting that was very emotional. It was so emotional that Don lost his composure while playing "Amazing Grace" on the flute. Not many of the forty-eight people had dry eyes.

The people of Pskov touched Don's heart in a way he had not experienced before. Denis's mother is a seamstress and gave Don a bolt of material for Sandi. This was all that she had to give which reminded Don of the widow's mite. Don gave gifts to several people including his umbrella to Leana's grandmother. It hadn't rained a drop in a week but as soon as they left the meeting, it started raining. Don says he was glad the grandmother didn't get wet walking home—but he sure did. During a prayer service back at the hotel, Jerry Dunnam thanked God for Don, his heart, and his tears. Afterwards, Jerry and Don made a pact to lose twenty pounds each by Labor Day.

> May 10—Another beautiful day for our trip to St. Petersburg which is truly the Venice of Russia. Happy day! I talked to Sandi and she will meet me at the airport when we get home. I'm in my room by myself for a little quiet time, but my heart and thoughts are still with the people at the First United Methodist Church of Pskov.

> May 11—We ate breakfast after Lisa's devotional, then went to the Hermitage Museum. We saw some of the highlights of Peter the Great's collection. He built the Hermitage Museum for Elizabeth, but she died very young. Catherine the Great collected great art

from all over the world. There were two paintings by Leonardo da Vinci and several by Rembrandt, Van Gogh, Picasso, and Monet. The collection is unbelievable. We ate lunch at the St. Petersburg Astoria Hotel. This hotel is the one that Hitler chose for his victory banquet when he defeated Russia. He made all arrangements for this banquet, but the Russian people were never defeated so his arrangements were in vain. We toured the big and beautiful St. Isaac's Cathedral where they hid the artworks from the Hermitage during World War II. The story goes that they covered the roof of St. Isaacs with paintings of flowers during the summer and of snow in the winter to camouflage it from German bombers.

We went to Peter and Paul Island where Peter the Great first established the City of St. Petersburg. It was a beautiful sunny day and many people were out sunbathing. This was a strange and unexpected sight since St. Petersburg is on the same latitude as Anchorage, Alaska. All but two Russian czars are buried on Peter and Paul Island.

Nash Vickers and I are still roommates and what better way to get to know someone. After spending some time writing letters and postcards, we went to Floor B and had some chai in a little café.

The first thing Don did on May 12 was to go and check on Jerry Dunnam at 6:30 A.M. Jerry said that her experience in Russia related more to Nash and Don than anyone else. During this early morning visit, Jerry confided that she scaled the sea wall on their walk last night rather than walk back to the steps. This must have been quite a sight to see considering Jerry's lack of athletic ability.

We paid a visit to a Bible school teaching Russians to be preachers, then to Pushkin, the home of a famous Post and on to two summer places of Peter the Great; they were magnificent. The Germans did a great deal of damage during the nine-hundred-day siege of Leningrad (St. Petersburg), but the Russian people and the winters wouldn't give up. The restoration of these palaces has been going on for forty-eight years and still isn't finished. The palace in Pushkin had a bedroom sixty yards long. There was a man playing a flute on the front steps, and I gave him some money to play some Mozart and he did a great job of it. The other palace is on the Gulf of Finland, with beautiful gardens and the view is breathtaking.

Back in the hotel we had a wonderful view of St. Petersburg with two hot air balloons floating by. For our devotion at 10:00 P.M., we made a list of the people we had met in Russia and knelt around the bed and prayed for our new friends, and especially for Olga, our guide. Nash said that he saw a woman who was six foot six and the most beautiful and well-dressed that he had seen in Russia. He was told that she was a prostitute for the Russian Mafia.

Up at 4:00 A.M. on May 13 to finish packing and leave for the airport at 5:15 A.M. Olga gave me a lacquered chalice to take home to Sandi. I made it through customs okay, but James and Carolyn Loftin had to open their bags and the customs officials went through everything. Nash, Carolyn, Jerry, and Lisa had crosses and an icon confiscated. Olga took them and said she would get them out through customs in Moscow. There weren't many people on this first leg of the flight but we stopped in Warsaw, Poland. We had our third breakfast of the day on the flight from Warsaw to Frankfurt.

It was 60 degrees but a yucky fog and rain when the plane landed in Frankfurt, thirty minutes late. The flight to Atlanta was forty-five minutes late taking off. We had lamb with asparagus for lunch over the Helvides Islands, 3,682 miles from Atlanta.

Don says the trip made him realize how much he missed and loved Sandi and how thankful he is to have someone who can love him as he is—the same as Jesus does.

✣ ✣ ✣

Don Green's Observation of a Happening
On 6 May, 1993 8:30 A.M. at the Minsk Hotel in Moscow, Russia
Jerry Dunnam was having trouble opening her hotel room door after breakfast, and a nice Russian lady hotel employee came to her aid. Jerry was so excited by this woman's help that she wanted to show her gratitude by saying thank you in Russian (spa-cee'-ba) but could not think of the correct pronunciation. Frantically, Jerry looked around seeing me silently laughing. Her eyes pleaded for help but none was forthcoming. The Russian woman knew that Jerry had something very important to say; so she politely smiled, waiting for Jerry to speak.

At that moment and being totally frustrated, Jerry blurts out "Bethsheba!" I rolled on the floor laughing and Jerry started laughing. Then the Russian lady joined in, and we all three started laughing. Jerry began to apologize in English to this "Good Samaritan" Russian woman who nodded as if she understood every word. The more she nodded, the faster Jerry's rambling (English) apology became. When the incident was over, Jerry tried to throw me out of the fourth floor lobby window.

Don Green's Unexpected Gift from Tamara, Denis's Mother
Just when we least expect it, God humbles us. On my first visit to Pskov, Russia, in May 1993, I could hardly contain my excitement. Here I was in Russia! Having a lot of preconceived notions about Russia and her people, I was not quite prepared for what God had in mind for me. In Pskov I was befriended by a young man of eighteen named Denis (Deniece). He kept insisting that I come to his apartment and experience his mother's cooking. Finally I relented after making Denis take some money to buy food.

Like most Russians, Denis and his mother Tamara didn't have much. His father had been gone from the family most of Denis's life and Tamara had been laid off from the factory where she was a seamstress making elegant evening attire for women. Since the breakup of the USSR, there were no parties in which to go. Since there were no parties, who would buy an evening gown? So the factory shut its doors and fifty-five-year-old Tamara was out of a job. I felt that this was what God wanted me to do. It was, and I felt pretty smug. But God had other things in store for me. It was a feast, and I ate until I almost popped. As is the custom, after the meal I presented a small gift to Tamara. That's when it happened.

Russians are very proud, and Tamara began to cry, then ran out of the room. Thinking that I had offended her, I looked over at Denis. His face was as blank as mine. A few moments later, Tamara emerged carrying two extremely small bolts of inexpensive cloth. She reciprocated my gift with one of her own. Then it hit me, and I was speechless. That's when God hit me with a large dose of humility. Here was a woman . . . a stranger . . . a poor but reciprocating Russian presenting me with the only thing of value to her . . . the cloth. She told me to take it to Sandi so that she could make something nice.

At the time I felt so bad about taking some of her means of income—sewing for friends and neighbors—that I didn't have a clue as to what Sandi would make out of it, if anything. I am embarrassed to say that I can't even remember my meaningless gift to Tamara, but I'll never forget her gift to me—not what it was but what it represented. She sacrificed to give me that cloth, and I would have offended her if I refused it. I brought the cloth home with no idea of its use except that it had taken on a very special significance, so whatever was to be made of it must be special.

God opens the doors in front of us at just the precise moment and on His timetable. Six months after my return I found out that the Emmaus community didn't have Communion linens. Sandi went to work sewing. A set of yellow Communion linens was presented to the Memphis Emmaus community. A set of blue Communion linens was presented to the Altar Guild here at Christ United Methodist Church. Both sets have been used in Communion services since 1993. The nondescript cloth humbly given was transformed into a beautiful gift to God. For someone who doesn't know the story of Tamara and the cloth, it's not impressive. It would look very plain. But to me and those to whom this story touches, these Communion linens represent God's infinite grace and wisdom and that He is in control. Of a more personal note, this whole incident humbled me incredibly, and any thoughts of that experience humble me even now.

BLESSINGS RECEIVED BY DON GREEN ON HIS MISSION TO RUSSIA

Life-changing experiences are rare for me; traumatic can describe most of them before I decided to trust God more than myself. Since then, the biggest life-changing experience besides having Sandi put in my life has been my trips to Pskov, Russia, where there is now a living, breathing, Christ-centered band of believers: the Pskov United Methodist Church.

I recently completed my third visit with my Christian brothers and sisters in a city that is as old as Russia itself. I participated in a fifth anniversary celebration of the church there.

Every life experience on a personal level is made relative only by a comparison to other experiences; i.e., the more experiences, the more relevance. Deep friendships have emerged, and I am grateful to God that He allowed me to receive that rare gift, one which can never be bought at any price! To know that I have true Christian friends on the other side of the world who pray for me every day blesses me and humbles me at the same time. I thought that I was going to share my faith with these people of whom I was taught in my youth to distrust. I didn't take God to Russia—He was there over nine hundred years ago; I saw the onion-domed cathedrals!

To describe the blessings I received is easy; to describe the depth of my feelings is impossible. I would like to share some descriptions of blessings I received while sharing my faith story with people who hung on every word.

- Becoming overwhelmed with emotion while playing the flute as Amy Melton Harvill sang the song "Beautiful" in Russian.

- Feeling the warmth of genuine friendship while sharing a meal with a Russian family.

- To be touched by gut-wrenching emotion as our train slowly pulled away from the station, tearfully waving good-bye to Denis and Lara, who I thought I would never see again.

- To witness a real paradox on my first trip—being in an auditorium filled with people, looking at the stage, to the left of which was a likeness of Karl Marx, and to the right of the stage, Lenin. No big deal except that the Men and Boys Chorus of Pskov were singing "What a Friend We Have in Jesus."

- Sharing Victory Over Fascist Day (V-E Day) celebration with a former cold-war enemy.

- Sitting with new friends sharing a cup of tea and pictures of our children.

To receive God-sent blessings feels great; to be humbled by God gets one's attention. Again, describing the experience is one thing, relating the feeling is quite another. Here are a few moments:

- Sharing a crowded bus—no, a cram-packed bus—feeling very uncomfortable, and then realizing that for most Russians a bus ride is a luxury.

- Walking with Lara, whose family is struggling to survive and where paychecks arrive as much as six months apart; watching her reach into her purse, take out money, and give it to a beggar woman with an infant from Kazakhstan.

- Passing by a small street market and witnessing an old woman selling her family pictures for a few rubles in order to buy some food.

✣ ✣ ✣

WHAT IS SOS?
by Richard (Dick) Klenz

For ten years this ministry has provided an opportunity for high school students, ages fifteen to eighteen, to spend one week in the inner city making desperately needed repairs on homes belonging to economically disadvantaged families. Four Memphis churches have now come together to cosponser SOS: the resources and leadership of Mississippi Boulevard Christian Church, Central Church, Mt. Vernon Baptist Church, and Christ United Methodist Church have allowed SOS to be more effective in reaching our city.

Participating youth groups organize student volunteers and adult counselors into seven- or eight-person work teams. The work teams are housed, fed, showered, and provided a complete program at the SOS center.

Although each team needs at least one person with some carpentry skill, it is not necessary for anyone to be an expert.

Each work team is assigned a different family to work with for one week. The work performed is carried out with a loving and accepting attitude, seeing in the recipient families the common bond we all share as God's children.

What Is the Impact? Groups participating in SOS should be prepared to work, sweat, love, cry, share, learn, and . . . grow!

In many mission efforts, recipients of services are very thankful to God and the contributing church, but the church may be separated from further contact with the family due to geography or culture. With SOS, all homes receiving help are managed through local churches and agencies. We try to ensure that there are Christians right in the recipients' neighborhood who can follow up and welcome them into the church. Recipients already involved in a church discover that their church is truly alive, and that the volunteer work completed on their home is an act of love arranged by their own pastor and congregation.

Perhaps the greatest impact is on the lives of the volunteers. In the exciting closing session, comments flow about what has been learned about race, poverty, Christian servanthood, and life. Many assumptions about the poor and about life's real meaning are challenged. Most students feel they have received more from the families and from SOS than they have given.

How, When, and Where? SOS begins with the arrival of work teams on Sunday afternoon and ends with breakfast the following Saturday.

Two or more youth groups will be participating in each session. Breakfasts, lunches, and suppers are provided by SOS. Since work teams will more than likely be in different locations, it is necessary for each team to have its own set of tools and its own vehicle that can haul team members and supplies. Most jobs will be a twenty- to thirty-minute drive from the SOS center.

Each morning begins with a devotional. Supplies are then loaded and teams head out to the homes. The work done by each team varies and may include roofing, painting, replacing sheetrock, flooring, and fixing broken windows. The families are invited and encouraged to help with the work. Sack lunches that were prepared at the center are eaten at the work site. Each evening, a program is offered which relates the day's work to Christ's call to servanthood. There is group singing, small group interaction, and discussions on poverty, stewardship, servanthood, and love.

Family Day. On Thursday afternoon, all the work teams invite the families they are working with to a picnic for volleyball, hot dogs, singing, sharing, watermelon, and fun!

A Great Opportunity:

- to put your love for God and His children into action.
- to build relationships with some of His children in the Binghamption neighborhood.
- to make some homes a little drier, warmer, and safer.
- to develop a better perspective on our world.

✣ ✣ ✣

SERVICE OVER SELF (SOS)
Memphis, Tennessee 1993
by Dick Klenz, Job Site Supervisor

Out on the high seas, a ship in desperate need of help signals—dot-dot-dot-dash-dash-dash-dot-dot-dot—SOS (Save Our Ship). In the inner city of Memphis, Tennessee, homes in desperate need of repairs are being worked on by Christ United Methodist's own SOS (Service Over Self) program. On July 4, young people from across the Mid-South began to arrive in Memphis in efforts to repair homes where the owners were unable to maintain them. By the end of the month twenty-two homes were worked on and drastically improved.

Over the course of the summer, seven teams arrived the first week; followed by six teams on July 11; five on July 18; and nine on July 25, including seven teams from our own church. The teams came from Mississippi, Texas, Georgia, Alabama, and Tennessee. Each team receives guidance from one or more adult supervisors that come and stay with the youth throughout the week at the church. During the day they work on homes in the inner city and in the evening they gather for fellowship and special devotional programs.

The work during the day is hard, dirty, and challenging. The weather is typical Memphis in July—hot, hot, hot. As in past years, the young people tackle the work with almost unbelievable spirit and energy. Repairing roofs, shingling, replacing floors, walls and ceilings, removing and repairing porches, fixing plumbing, and painting are all in a day's (or many days') work. During the course of their week's stay, they develop a warm and loving relationship with the families with whom they work. Each Thursday they bring their new families to the church grounds for a picnic. It is not uncommon for more than a few tears to be shed as they bid farewell to the families on Friday.

In this day and age when we often criticize our young people for being self-absorbed and interested only in material things, the SOS program is a revelation! To watch several hundred Christian youth truly dedicating their time and money to help those less fortunate than themselves is amazing. They willingly take on tough demanding work under the worst of conditions. Their love of the families for which they are working demonstrates an approach to racial relations that all of us would do well to emulate. We all should be truly proud of these miracle workers. In addition to the 209 volunteers that worked on houses, the following Christ Church volunteers made this ministry possible:

SOS CHRIST CHURCH VOLUNTEERS
A list of Christ Church volunteers that it took for one summer to support the youth who came in from all over the country.

Job Site Supervisors
Dick Klenz
John Knepper
Bob Moore
George Ramsey

Team Leaders (on site)
Skip Burzamato
Walter Chambliss
George Cook
Lashlee Dorman
Steve Leuze
Margaret Libby
Frank & Mary Marino
Nash Neyland
Andy Rambo
Jeff Seabold

Food Service Coordinators
Richard & Ann Zambetti

Food Service Volunteers
Barry & Carol Adams
Rob & Lisa Ayerst
Gene Bailey

Lori Beckham
John Bobango
Don & Paula Bourland
Jean Branch
Larry & Christy Brooks
Jack & Terry Brown
Susan Burnett
Kim Carnes
Betty Cook
Jeff & Mary Lynn Davis
Russell & Sharon Day
Jane Dike
Debbie Dorman
Ken & Barbara Draffin
Steve & JoEllen Druelinger
Tommy & Kay Floyd
John Ford
Ben & Terry Foy
Lisa Gilliam
Mark & Laura Godbold
Bill Gossett
Chris & Leanne Gruenwald
Billy & Diane Hall
Mark & Mandy Hall
David & Sallie Harris

Stuart & Pam Hudsmith
John & Lynn Huggins
Randy & Patti Jelinek
Bob & Carol Johnson
Larry & Renee Karban
David & Elizabeth Kirby
Eva Lang
David & Donna Libby
Scott & Amy Linder
Carolyn & Ashley Loftin
Sanford Lyon
Mary Madden
Richard, Donna, & Dayle Marsh
Jerry & Elizabeth Marshall
Jane McMullen
Mark & Suzanne Medford
Mark & Barbara Melton
Lisa Mischke
Steve Mitchener
Meade & Beth Moore
Harry & Ann Orr
Jonathan Page
Keith Parsons
Nancy & Lauren Perrine
Steve Popernik
Carl & Paige Rackley
Anita Lotz Ramsey
Beth Ramsey
Boyd & Trudy Rhodes
Bob & Vikki Roberts
Todd Ross
Drew & Charlene Rucker
Julia Sayle
Whit Simmons
Brenda Sippel
Mark & Missy Sistrunk
Vince & Debbie Smith
Ned & Mary Spangler
Richard & Trish Spore
Clinton Stewart
Lisa Taylor
Gary & Melanie Thompson
Paul & Kathy Tuberville

Tom Twardzik
David & Paige Walker
Mike & Deborah White
Debbie Williams
Ben & Stephanie Witt
Denise Wyont
Terry & Katherine Young
Wade & Ellen Zambetti

Communications Volunteers
Shirley Bryant
Linda Echols
JoAnn Farras
Margie Ford
Helen Knepper
Mary Lou Liming
Sandy McNatt
Amy Stevens
Laura Stevens
Marsha Thompson
Debbie Williams

Locating & Evaluating Homes
Bill Crosby
Steve Druelinger
Ann Earle
Sonny Humphreys
Dick Klenz
Pat Madden
Suzanne Medford
Bob Moore
Ray Oldham
Keith Parsons
Jane Sullivan
Ron Whitney
Amy Wilson

Supply Delivery Volunteers
Bill Crosby
Steve Druelinger
Harry Murchison
Jim Ostner
Ralph & Helen Scherr

Missions: 1982–1993

Roy Thurmond
John Weeden
Jim Wittenberg

Young Barnabas Builders
C. J. Averwater
Michael Cook
Thomas Hickey
Emily McDonald
Amy Ray
Amy Wadsworth
Chris Wiseman

Program Resource Persons
Skip Burzamato
Ellen Eubank
Jay Harvill
Andy Rambo
Scott Walker
Terry Whitsitt

Program Assistants
Melissa Beck
Michael Cook
Rich Cook
Margie Ford
Drew Hays
Harris MacGruder
Lisa McGee
Andy Pierce
Amy Ray
Todd Ross

Elizabeth Ryan
Jeff Seabold
Sarah Allison Shafley
Jill Van Hoose
Adam Webster
David Zachery

Special Thanks to:
Bill Crosby, Chairman of the SOS Committee

Special Thanks to:
Church Staff
Melissa Beck
Richard Boda
Skip Burzamato
Janet Everett
Debby Favazza
Eddins Hopps
James Loftin
Tom Marino
Larry Pennington
Don Thompson

Donations
Jennifer Daniel (supplies)
Scott Edwards (lumber)
Gwatney Chevrolet (2 trucks)
Carolyn & Ashley Loftin
Melissa Neyland (supplies)
Tom Ryan, Delta Realty Investment Company (lumber & nails)

✣ ✣ ✣

"I Didn't Drive a Single Nail"
by Dr. Maxie D. Dunnam

I went to work one afternoon on an SOS project and didn't drive a single nail. The temperature was over 100 degrees, but that's not the reason I didn't drive a nail. We had more than enough workers on each of the projects. Young people and adults from our congregation have given themselves in a tremendous way to this ministry of sharing with others. Instead of working, I visited five of the work sites and saw the tremendous job that was being done.

I saw young people in scorching heat, their clothing drenched with sweat, doing physical labor in the name of Jesus.

I saw adults who had taken vacation time in order to make this contribution to needy folks in the name of Jesus. I met the recipients of this labor of love—and greeted in them the love of Jesus that inspires our church to be a part of this kind of ministry.

SOS (Service Over Self) makes desperately needed repairs to homes belonging to economically disadvantaged families in Shelby County. This summer, we will have worked on twenty-two different homes. Twenty-eight work crews with over two hundred workers have labored to make life better for persons in need.

Not only do our young people and adults do the actual labor; we have been the hosts for work crews who have come from Texas, Mississippi, Georgia, Alabama, Arkansas, and other towns and cities in Tennessee.

One home had a hole in the roof for over two years. The roofing job would have cost over two thousand dollars, but someone donated the shingles. Another home had not had hot water for three years because the woman could not afford a hot water heater.

This congregation is doing all sorts of things to meet human need, and, unfortunately, most of the story is never told. That's the reason I wanted to make this witness to what Jesus called us to do—that is to minister to the least of these.

It is exciting to know that we have hundreds of young people involved in our youth ministry, and that a part of that ministry is serving others in such a caring, unselfish sort of way. My hunch is that these young people and adults will never be the same again as a result of this exposure and their willingness to respond to human need. May their tribe increase!

✢ ✢ ✢

MEDIATION AND RESTITUTION/RECONCILIATION SERVICES
A New Urban Ministry by Christ Church
A proposal by Maxie Dunnam, Rick Kirchoff, and James Loftin
The Lord seems to be weaving three streams together: a vision, a need, and an opportunity.

Stream I: A Vision. Two months ago James Loftin felt called to ask the work area on missions to take a serious look at the missions work Christ Church is doing in the city. One big question is being asked: How many of these ministries are relief and how many are development? How many are giving fish away and how many are teaching people to fish? The work area is approaching the 1994 budget with a clean sheet of paper. They are prepared to make radical changes in the missions budget in order to do something big, addressing some needs unmet by existing community services, that will make a lasting impact on lives and on our community. A vision!

Stream II: A Need. Any survey of Memphians shows it. Shelby County Interfaith studies and Life Focus '93 findings confirm it. Crime is a major problem in Memphis. One difficult question is, "What do you do with persons once they are arrested?" Jails and prisons are overcrowded. Courtrooms are overloaded. All over the nation judges are forced to dismiss first- and second-time offenders due to the backlog of cases. Discussions are being held this month in several metropolitan areas about the possibility of not even processing misdemeanor cases due to the judicatory overload.

The problem is perhaps most acute in the youth culture. One sad truth is that once a youthful offender enters the legal and prison systems, they almost always get into more trouble with the law. Though some work is being done with juvenile delinquents in Memphis, relatively few youth are involved. Most of the work is relief in nature, and little is being done in the name of Christ. A need!

Stream III: An Opportunity. Christ Church is deepening its relationship with a local ministry named Memphis Leadership Foundation. The executive director, Dr. Larry Lloyd, is a nationally recognized expert in urban missiology. Totally unaware that *Stream I: A Vision* was already in place, Larry approached Maxie on April 13 with a bold proposal. Enclosed is a copy of that proposal. Don Burford is trained in and is successful in ministries to troubled teenagers. He has the ability and heart to create such a program in Memphis. This ministry would intimately involve scores of Christ Church members. It is clearly development ministry that is not being done in Memphis. An opportunity!

PLAN

Stage I. Offer a staff position to Don Burford to begin September 1, 1993, for the formulation of a new ministry possibly called Mediation and Reconciliation Ministry (MARM). The offer would be contingent upon Stage II and the identification of funding for the remainder of 1993 (in place).

Stage II. Meet with Juvenile Court Judge [Kenneth] Turner to secure his endorsement of the ministry and his willingness to refer youth to the ministry (done).

Stage III. Don would serve as executive director of the ministry. A Board of Directors would be composed of representatives from Memphis Leadership Foundation, the community and Christ Church (majority). A 501(C3) status would be obtained. This would facilitate relationships with the courts and potential donors. Attorneys of Christ United Methodist Church would facilitate the drafting of the legal relationship between our church and this ministry.

Stage IV. Don would cultivate relationships in the juvenile court system and in urban churches. At the same time he would recruit and train volunteers to serve as mediators. One black mediator and one white mediator would be assigned to each case involving the juvenile offender and the victim(s).

Funding

1993—$18,000 is needed for the three months of 1993 for salary, benefits, and program expense. Of this $18,000, $9,000 has been committed by Memphis Leadership Foundation (MLF). Christ Church will need to provide $9,000 from the special requests line in the 1993 missions budget and/or the missions fund. Benefits, office space, and secretarial support will be provided by Christ Church.
1994—The 1994 Budget of MARM would be $72,000. Of this amount Christ Church would provide $36,000 out of the missions budget. Benefits, office space, and secretarial support would be provided by Christ Church. The balance would be paid by MLF and donations to the new ministry.
1995—Christ Church's financial commitment would continue at the 1994 level. Ever broadening community support would fund expansions of the ministry.

We realize that this is a totally new approach to staffing and ministry. We believe it is where Christ Church must move to have the community impact that our congregation wants. We feel that other similar ministries will begin as this one proves to be successful.

The Program

Mediation and restitution (reconciliation) programs are growing in number across the country, particularly with adults. They have had good records of success. There are an increasing number of these programs being tested with juveniles, again with good success. There is no such program in Memphis. We want to begin one as soon as September/October 1993.

The mediation and restitution ministry is a partnership between Christ United Methodist Church, Mississippi Boulevard Christian Church, Mt. Vernon Westwood Baptist Church, and the Memphis Leadership Foundation. The program design is simple. It is mainly a volunteer ministry directed by one staff person who must be experienced in mediation and restitution, and who holds educational degrees that would be esteemed by the Department of Human Services and Juvenile Court. A master's level degree in counseling or social work is a minimum. This person would then recruit volunteers from local churches. We desire to model the unity we find in Christ as well as effectively minister to the juveniles we serve. Therefore, we are committed to recruiting and training black/white mediation teams for this program. Each mediator would receive thirty to forty hours of training for the program.

Initially twenty-four to thirty mediators would be trained. This would make up between twelve and fifteen mediation teams. The first year they would be assigned two cases so that we would do twenty-four to thirty mediations in 1993–1994. This would give us opportunity to track the program, refine the training, and test the results.

A mediation consists of bringing the offender and the victim together in a neutral setting along with the mediators. This is done by court order as an alternative sentencing arrangement. If the victim is the state/city/county, then an appropriate representative would be present. Basically, the victim relates to the offender what the crime committed has done to him/her financially, emotionally, etc. The offender is given a chance to hear, firsthand, what his/her crime has done to a real person. This personalizes the behavior. The offender has an opportunity to state why he/she committed the crime. The victim is then asked to state terms of restitution and the juvenile is asked to respond. Basically, the dialogue continues until an acceptable restitution is agreed upon by both parties. An agreement is signed and the appropriate J. C. authority endorses it as acceptable. If the agreement is carried out then the juvenile's record is wiped clean.

After the confrontation, the mediators are in contact with both parties to make sure the terms of the restitution are being carried out. There are subsequent meetings as well with both parties to further discuss the crime and the process of restitution. Of course, the mediators are counseling the juvenile on a regular basis. We hope to get each juvenile to the point of understanding his/her behavior and the pain it has caused others. We want to teach the principle that there are logical consequences to one's behavior. And, we hope that the juvenile will come to a place of genuine remorse and be able to say "I'm sorry" to the victim.

The key to this mediation ministry is accountability and real consequences. The accountability comes through the mediators and the consequence through the restitution arrangement. There is plenty of documentation that this concept gets results in terms of deterring further criminal activity at far greater rates than incarceration. And, as already mentioned, there is little going on right now for the kind of offender we want to target.

Based on the success records of other programs across the country there should be substantial growth in the program in year two. We believe that we will be able to recruit and train an ample volunteer force for a ministry like this. We believe that the results in deterred criminal activity will be a major selling point as we seek funding and expansion of the ministry. As a part of the whole process, we will ask the court to place the juvenile under certain orders to make the program even more effective.

For example, a young person on probation now is ordered to attend the church of his/her choice on a regular basis. While there is little evidence that the terms of this order are consistently carried out in Memphis, we would hold those in our program accountable to this. With the network of churches that is open to the MLF, there will be ample churches to recommend and follow up on in case the juveniles are unchurched (which is most likely). In addition, there will be ample opportunities to witness to God's love and regenerative power made evident in Jesus Christ. Our mediators will be solid Christians, our director will be a solid Christian, and our board will be composed of solid Christians. Evangelism and discipleship will be part and parcel to everything we do. While we will not require kids to be Christians, nor will we require them to attend religious services, the relational aspect of ministry will be truly powerful.

THE BOARD OF TRUSTEES

THE CLOSING OF CHERRY ROAD
Board of Trustees Report to Administrative Board
Primarily the Closing of Cherry Road

Harry Johnson reported on damage to the carpet in the sanctuary that happened when the church was being painted last year. Eddins Hopps repaired it very satisfactorily. A sum of $13,000 has been received as an insurance settlement. Further attention will be given to the carpet if needed. He reported that the planned giving program is off to a good start. About ninety-five responses have been received to the last letter sent out by Barry Brindley, the new director. Mr. Johnson further reported on the status of the Cherry Road property. A meeting was held with the Police and Fire Departments, and it was decided that a rolled curb with shrubs and a closed barricade would be installed to close off the property access from Poplar. Fire and police vehicles can go across if required for emergency entrance but there will be a deterrent to general traffic.

Approximately eighty-five hundred children used the soccer field last year. Protection for them is greatly needed. This is the main reason for closing the street. The neighbors and residents of Cherry Road are very pleased and are raising the needed $14,000 through individual or family pledges. The full amount will be secured within two weeks. The Cherry Road entrance will be ours with easements and access for our own people.

✣ ✣ ✣

HISTORY OF THE PROPERTY DISPOSITION COMMITTEE
Over the years since Christ United Methodist Church was organized, generous members and nonmembers have given tangible items to the church. For years the giver would come to the church, offer some item of value, and any staff member would sign a document for the giver testifying to the value of the item and agreeing to its placement in a specific place on the church property. By 1984 the practice had gotten out of hand so the responsible body (the trustees), after much consultation with accountants, lawyers, etc., drew up a procedure by which the church would accept property.

No one can now sign for any property with a value placed on it.

No one can promise that it will be placed or used exactly as the giver specifies.

A well-qualified Property Disposition Committee with Ray Cummins as chairman was appointed in 1985 by the trustees. The committee had an accountant, a lawyer, an artist, and two antique experts as members. Their recommendations are now made to the trustees who make the final decision whether to place it on the property, sell it, or return it to the giver. There is a form covering all of this to be filled out and signed by the giver.

Original Committee:
Ray Cummins, Retired Chairman of the Board, Goldsmith's Department Store
J. W. McAllister, Certified Public Accountant
Charles Patton, Attorney
Jerry Dunnam, Artist
Randy Jones, Artist
Mary Glen Massey (Mrs. Art), Owner of Antique Shop
Ben Madden, Senior Vice President of Union Planters Bank

✤ ✤ ✤

HISTORY OF THE SPECIAL FUNDS AND PROJECTS POLICY COMMITTEE

The church provides very appealing ways for church members and others to give in honor of or in memory of those whom they admire or those who are near and dear to them.

Over the years when people decided to give to honor or to memorialize without a list of the needed projects in the church, they gave to projects that never existed or projects that had been completed. Funds accumulated in the bank and couldn't honestly be used; therefore, the need for a more effective handling of the various needs of the work areas, commissions, committees, and projects existed. The Board of Trustees attacked this problem in 1985 and after about a year of getting ideas from many areas of the church and rewriting the policy many, many times, they formulated a policy that was approved by the Official Board in December 1985. Copy of policy is attached.

Purpose: To establish a system for the most effective handling of the financial needs of the various work areas, committees, commissions, projects, etc. The specific need is to improve the budgeting process thereby supporting the entire program of the church.

1. Beginning January 1, 1986, the following funds are approved and A–G will be listed on the memorial gift envelopes.

    A. General Fund (a permanent fund to support the approved budget)
    B. The Capital Property Maintenance Endowment Trust (a permanent fund admin-istered by the Board or Trustees)

    C. Building Fund
    D. Mission Fund
    E. Music Fund
    F. Youth Fund
    G. Single Purpose Project Fund (as listed in the bulletin)
    H. Minister's Discretionary Fund
    I. Communion Fund
    J. Pension Fund

2. Should a work area, committee, commission, etc. find a special need subsequent to the establishment of the final budget for any fiscal year, such need shall be defined as a single purpose project. Such projects must be approved through normal channels by the Administrative Board. A special goal (amount) shall be established. The project will expire with the earlier, i.e., of achieving the stated goal, or on action of the Administrative Board.

3. The pension fund shall remain an entirely separate fund and shall be under the control of a three-member trust. The trustees of the pension fund shall be nominated by the Nominating Committee and elected by the Charge Conference. Each member shall be selected for a three-year term with one person's term expiring each year. The benefits provided shall be approved by the Administrative Board upon recommendation received from the trustees.

4. Each adult Sunday school class may adopt special charitable projects. Any project established for more than $1,500 must be approved by the Board of Trustees.

5. All funds will be subject to the annual audit at the end of each year. The committee responsible for those areas of ministry will meet with the Budget Committee and share in deciding on the use of excess funds consistent with the intent of the giver.

6. The operating budget should be developed with a provision for an addendum to be added to show special projects properly approved.

7. Neither the Budget Committee nor the Finance Committee has the power to eliminate programs. Only the Administrative Board has such power.

8. It is further suggested that the Budget Committee become a year-round functioning committee which could possibly do a far better job, as we grow into a multimillion dollar program, if they can stay abreast of requests, incomes and expenditures on a year-round basis.

The Board of Trustees

The purpose of this policy is to guide the giving processes of the church to help accomplish the overall mission of the church and in no case used to impede nor to alter that mission.

Approved projects will be listed at regular intervals in the *Courier*. A list of these projects should be maintained and updated on each appropriate desk hi the church office and designated gifts channeled to them. A mailing to the entire congregation, at least once each year, should be made listing those projects currently in effect and asking that special gifts be made to them so that the needs of the church may be met.

When this program has been approved, it should be disseminated to organized bodies, work areas, committees, commissions, etc. This policy should be given to all organizations at the beginning of each year henceforth and in conjunction with the annual budgeting process.

In no way does this program approve or promote aggressive solicitation of funds for any project except the budget and approved building funds of the church.

✣ ✣ ✣

October 10, 1985

Mr. Harry A. Johnson Jr.
Mr. Donald A. Thomas

Dear Harry and Don:

The tremendous debate that took place at the board meeting Monday night about the proposed policy concerning special funds and projects is a strong indication that there is great confusion about the issue. The fact that this has been presented to the board twice and did not pass, and the fact that it took so long to get it through the Finance Committee also underscores the fact that we are dealing with something that really needs very careful attention.

I feel that two issues are involved. One: the issue which I think brought about the definition of a policy in the first place, having to do with who is responsible for funds and how those funds are to be dealt with at the end of each calendar year. That is a very legitimate cause with which to deal. However, there is a second issue that I think is equally important—maybe even more important. That issue is the giving of memorial monies. The tradition for that is very strong in the life of this congregation; and, I feel, is a very worthy one. I am enclosing, for both of you, an envelope that I found when I came to this church, and I understand it's been used for many, many years. It was altered when I came only in putting my name on it to replace Dr. Beaty's. This means that memorial giving has been encouraged.

I believe in that. I believe it's far more meaningful, and productive, and Christian, for people to give money to the church as a memorial to persons who have died, or in honor of someone they want to remember, than it is to give flowers or something else, and I for one would certainly rather that money come to the church to be used in ministry than be given to secular organizations—though I am not opposed to that. I also feel that people making gifts of this sort are not affected in their pledging to the church. This is extra money that the church has to use for ministry, and we should be grateful for it. Not only should we be grateful, I don't think we should do anything to discourage it; in fact, I think we should do everything we can to encourage it.

I do feel strongly that the paper that has been written is an excellent one, and sets out the parameters for a big part of how people give, yet again, the confusion suggests for me that something needs to be added, and I would like to make a proposal for those who meet to refine this concept to consider.

My proposal is that the paper that describes the special funds and projects position of the church be amended in this fashion: Under recommendations, put a #1., which is not presently there. That #1. would say something like this: "There will be four ongoing funds to which people will be encouraged to give memorial and honorary gifts: missions, youth, building, and music. These funds will be used by the groups responsible for ministry in these different areas either to supplement or support the ongoing ministry of the church."

Now if you want to define more fully what might happen in those areas, you could put that in the paper, or have an understanding about it. That understanding may involve the fact that at the end of each calendar year, the persons responsible for these areas of ministry would meet with the Budget Committee and share in deciding about monies in the funds not used—what part of those monies, if any, would be carried over, and what would become a part of the general fund.

I think with this kind of addition, you could go on with the paper, and a distinction would be made between special funds and special projects. It seems to me that where we get into trouble is the definition of special projects, and that really is what the paper addresses. In this fashion, we could provide envelopes for people and advertise the fact that we have these four ongoing funds—then, when a special project has been approved in the fashion that is set forth by the paper, that also could be advertised; and people would always have opportunities to give as freely as they wanted to give for memorials and in honor of loved ones.

I hope this doesn't confuse the issue, but hope that it contributes to the spirit of people giving generously to the ministry of the church, but also giving above and beyond their pledges and regular gifts in memorial and honorary contributions.

Grace and Peace,
Maxie D. Dunnam

✤ ✤ ✤

THE "BECAUSE WE CARE" PROGRAM

As chairman of the Board of Trustees of Christ United Methodist Church, I always consulted the senior minister and the executive minister as well as the chairman of affected work areas before introducing property changes to the trustees and/or the Official Board.

Following this procedure, I invited Dr. Maxie Dunnam and Rev. Earl Johnston to lunch at the Summit Club on April 15, 1985.

We discussed the needs of the church, relating program to physical facilities, and I suggested that now was the time to build all the needed facilities to support the mission of the church and all the supporting facilities to reach the full potential of the sanctuary.

Dr. Dunnam asked how much I thought it would cost. My estimate (without any substantiation) was four to six million dollars. He asked if I thought we could raise that amount. My answer—if the church could ever do it, it could now. Christ United Methodist Church was/is growing with young successful people and most of the charter members are still around, so, you can't beat the timing. The sanctuary was built to support a membership of six thousand. The nursery only has twelve beds and this many babies are born each quarter. We don't have enough classroom space for the young adults we have now, much less for the needed new classes. If we don't take care of the young people and their children, then the church can only go downhill.

Every organization should always exploit success and Christ United Methodist Church is success in the Methodist Church. Our mission and programs are exploding in every direction and unless we support physically the growth of the church, then all our programs and missions will suffer.

It was agreed that I would ask the Council on Ministries to give us a picture of their needs. We received that and expanded the projection through the extensive efforts of Earl Johnston and Marvin Budd.

The Board of Trustees gathered a list of 132 architects and wrote to each, asking for their qualifications and interest in the project. We boiled this down to 10, then had in-depth interviews with their principals. The 10 narrowed to 3 and after additional interviews with them, we determined their ability, the interest of their principals, and the availability of their staff to concentrate on this project. The best qualified was McGehee, Nickolson, and Burke.

In November 1985, I asked for a special board meeting and requested $25,000 for 1985 so the architects could do the preliminary planning necessary to begin the project, and another $25,000 for 1986 if needed. Both sums were approved. The architects began the preliminary plans immediately.

On January 1, 1986, D. A. Noel was nominated and elected chairman of the Building Committee. That committee working with the architects has developed the building plan.

✣ ✣ ✣

History of the Planned Giving Committee

After the formation of the Capital Property Maintenance Endowment Trust fund in 1980, and after people began to contribute to it, the need for a vehicle to handle the other giving needs of individuals came to light. People wanted to give property, insurance, place the church in their wills, etc., while not always desiring to place these bequests in the endowment fund.

The trustees in 1985 decided to form a Planned Giving Committee and enlisted Lee B. McCormick to be its chairman. Lee and Harry Johnson, chairman of the trustees, in turn enlisted the help of Robert Sharpe, who is a recognized expert in the field of planned giving. He has written books and holds seminars nationwide to teach universities, etc., how best to do this job. He has developed a program and literature for mailings to support this program and contributed his knowledge and expertise to this committee. The church purchased the literature and has made consistent mailings since that time. He also has given free tuition to Reverend Earl Johnston to attend several of these seminars. The tuition has amounted to several thousand dollars, and so the church only had to pay for transportation, lodging, and meals.

Planned Gifts Program Guidelines

Statement of Purpose. These guidelines have been established by the Planned Gifts Advisory Committee of Christ United Methodist Church for the following reasons:

1. To define and set forth the working rules of the program.
2. To provide a consistent framework for the promotion of good public relations with members of the congregation, donors, prospective donors, and professional advisors.
3. The protection of the church and those individuals directly involved in the conduct of the program (ministers, staff, volunteers).

Guidelines:
1. Charitable intent. No gift will be accepted from any individual from whom there is not obvious charitable interest.

The Board of Trustees

2. Confidentiality. All information provided by a donor, prospective donor, or other advisors will be treated with utmost discretion and confidentiality.

3. Use of legal counsel. All donors need and should be urged to seek competent legal counsel. Staff members shall seek the advice of the church's legal counsel in all matters pertaining to the planned gifts program and shall execute no planned giving agreement without the advice of such counsel.

4. Gifts of real or personal property. Any written acceptance of such gifts should be simply a receipt of the item(s) and should not express or confirm an opinion of the value thereof.

5. Gifts requiring expenditure of funds. The trustees of the church must approve all gifts that will or may require expenditure of funds either at the time of the gifts or at some future date. Examples of the types of gifts that would need approval are all assets going into any form of charitable trust, charitable gift annuities, bargain sales, or outright gifts such as real estate that may place present or future obligations on the church.

6. Use of funds. The planned gifts program primarily seeks funds for capital improvements, replacement and expansion, and for the outreach mission of the church. Gifts designated for other purposes will be accepted upon the approval of the Advisory Committee and the trustees.

✢ ✢ ✢

THE CAPITAL PROPERTY MAINTENENCE ENDOWMENT TRUST
Proposed Resolution of the Charge Conference
Christ United Methodist Church of Memphis, Tennessee

WHEREAS, on the 23rd day of November 1988, the Board of Trustees of Christ United Methodist Church of Memphis, Tennessee (the "Church") created and established "the Property Maintenance Endowment Fund of Christ United Methodist Church of Memphis, Tennessee" (the "Fund") for the purpose of accumulating moneys and properties so that the income therefrom may be used for the maintenance of the buildings and the improvements of the Church and that no interest or income earned on the principal of the fund shall be used for any purpose until the Fund has reached the amount of One Million Dollars ($1,000,000.00), principal and interest, and, thereafter, only the income from said Fund shall used for the purpose of property maintenance of the Church;

WHEREAS, it is the opinion of the Board of Trustees of the Church that the establishment of a separate trust fund and Board of Trustees for the administration of such Fund would encourage future gifts to said trust fund and would otherwise be in the best interests of the Fund and the Church;

WHEREAS, the Charge Conference has received the recommendation of the Board of Trustees of the Church, as evidenced by its resolution of November 23, 1987, attached hereto, approving and recommending to the Charge Conference the creation of a trust for the charitable purposes as set forth in the Trust Agreement which is attached hereto (the "Trust Agreement"); and

WHEREAS, after review and discussion, the Charge Conference believes that the establishment of a separate trust fund and Board of Trustees for the administration of such Fund would encourage future gifts to said trust fund and would otherwise be in the best interests of the Fund and the Church.

NOW, THEREFORE, BE IT RESOLVED, that the Charge Conference does hereby approve the Trust Agreement and the creation of the trust fund and separate Board of Trustees as set forth in the Trust Agreement, all for the purposes as set forth in detail in the Trust Agreement.

FURTHER RESOLVED, that the Charge Conference does hereby point as trustees of said Trust the nominees recommended by the Committee on Nominations, which list of trustees is attached hereto.

FURTHER RESOLVED, that when in the opinion of both the Board Trustees of the Church and the trustees of the Trust it is established that the Trust is exempt from taxation pursuant to section 501(c)(3) of the Internal Revenue Code of 1986, and the laws of the State of Tennessee, the Board of Trustees of the Church, to the extent permitted by law, is hereby authorized and directed to transfer to said Trust all property which has been received or may be received, and the income thereon, as a part of the Fund which is currently being administered under the authority of the Board of Trustees of the Church. Further, if at such time as all property held by the Board of Trustees in the Fund has been transferred to the Trust, the Fund shall be terminated and wholly supplanted by the Trust.

FURTHER RESOLVED, that the Board of Trustees of the Church and other officials of the Church or its agents be, and hereby agree, authorized and directed to take all action necessary or appropriate to accomplish the intent of the foregoing solutions.

✤ ✤ ✤

Capital Property Maintenance Endowment Trust
Minutes of Meeting 3:00 P.M. January 23, 1989

Held in the Office of the Senior Minister

Members Present: Others Present:
Gene Williams   Dr. Maxie Dunnam
Don Thomas
Harry A. Johnson Jr.

The Board of Trustees

This meeting was called to consider the need for a broad foundation to be formed so that the church will be able to accept living trusts etc., in the future. The foundation is to be set up to accept funds for many purposes, as a ministry for the individual or family giving the money to execute the ministries for which the money was given, and to include the Capital Property Maintenance Endowment Trust.

Don Thomas agreed to see this project through to its conclusion.

All present at the meeting in the senior minister's office agreed to pursue the formation of the foundation. The meeting adjourned at 4:10 P.M.

Robert Sharpe, a nationally recognized authority in this area, met with Don Thomas and Harry Johnson for lunch on February 13, 1989. The foundation was discussed. Bob Sharpe quoted many sources of help and followed this with a letter.

Harry A. Johnson Jr.
Chairman

cc: Maxie Dunnam   Don Thomas
    Earl Johnston   Gene Williams
    Charles Bagley   Lee McCormick

✜ ✜ ✜

THE CHRIST UNITED METHODIST CHURCH FOUNDATION

A. The need for this ministry:

1. Many people have come to the ministers asking that the church perform the services the foundation can perform.

2. Many have wanted the church to care for their long-term wishes other than those provided for by the Capital Property Maintenance Endowment Trust.

    a. Lifetime assets to be invested and managed by the church to carry out the wishes of the donor.

3. Money or property set up in a trust—the income to go to one or more ministries of the church.

4. Assets in trust to care for family members or the donor until they die—then the income or the principal to be used to further a ministry or ministries of CUMC.

5. To assist widows, widowers and others who need help get social security benefits, etc.

B. How the foundation will function:

1. It will set up a long-term education and information program for the congregation.

2. Set up the mechanics for advising donors.

3. Set up a system for the receiving of assets and for their investment.

4. See that the donors' wishes are carried out for designated funds.

5. Carry out the wishes of the proper boards, committees, etc. of CUMC in the dispensing of undesignated funds.

C. Other churches all over the country have successful, functioning foundations. This one is patterned after these successful foundations.

D. For thirty-five years, this ministry has not been available to members of CUMC, with a resulting loss of funds to the varied ministries of the church. It is reasonable to assume that it won't be available for the next thirty-five years without this or a similar foundation to focus on the need which exists.

Harry A. Johnson Jr., 1990, to Maxie Dunnam

✜ ✜ ✜

To: The 1991 Capital Property Maintenance Endowment Trustees

From: Harry A. Johnson Jr.
Date: January 23, 1991

Attached is an accounting of the assets in the Trust as of December 31, 1990.
This Trust was established in 1980 to Christ United Methodist Church in the assurance that major maintenance needs, which would affect the ministry of the church in a negative way, would be taken care of outside of the operating budget. The people who have contributed to this Trust did so with the following understanding:

1. The Fund would be perpetual.
2. The principal assets of the Fund could not be used for any reason.

3. The interest income would not be used until the Fund has one million dollars in it.
4. The assets are not to be used to take care of the normal maintenance items normally covered by the annual budget.
5. That the interest become a part of the principal body of the Trust unless used for one or more major maintenance needs.
6. The principal body of the Trust be built up to and maintained in the minimum of one million dollars in 1987 dollars.

I'm sure you are aware of the fact that unless our property is kept in first-class condition, the membership and attendance will decline. As a consequence the effective ministries of the church for others will decline even faster.

It is hoped that a more aggressive approach can be taken to raising the principal amount now that the New Building Program is fully pledged. This will take a long-term, churchwide educational program.

I want to thank each of you for accepting this responsibility and to pledge my continued support of the program.

Sincerely,
Harry A. Johnson Jr.

cc: David Rogers   Maxie Dunnam
    Gene Williams   Earl Johnston
    Ed Richmond   Jamie Smith

P.S. Please see that the current document remains in force and that this Trust not become part of any future foundation or trust except as a separate entity within it.

✥ ✥ ✥

The History of the Property Committee

In 1991, P. D. Miller, chairman of the Board of Trustees, asked Harry Johnson to make a study of the property management and maintenance programs and to recommend any changes needed.

After many months of study, consultations with P. D. Miller and the Board of Trustees, the following was approved:

A Property Committee consisting of the chairpersons of eight subcommittees, architects, grounds, maintenance, property use, fine arts, decorating, property disposition, security, and Harry Johnson as chairman.

The first accomplishment of the Property Committee was the conversion of the cloakroom in Seabrook Hall lobby into the property and information office and hiring Sharon Cruser as property director.

The Property Committee interviewed the qualified architects for the next building phase. The architectural firm chosen included an outstanding church planner from Dallas, Texas.

Burgess Ledbetter, a preliminary master planner, had been gathering information for a year. When the total master plan was presented to the trustees, then to the Executive Committee and the Administrative Board, it was overwhelmingly approved.

A Study Committee was formed that made a thorough assessment of the feasibility of raising the money and doing the construction, as well as justifying the need. The committee also recommended a Building Committee to oversee the planning, construction, and the capital funds campaign.

The total program for construction was to take at least six years and cost in excess of $26 million. As this building program was being planned there were over eight hundred children under school age, several babies being baptized every Sunday, and it seemed that every young woman in the church was expecting.

✤ ✤ ✤

LAND AND BUILDINGS
The Dr. Maxie D. Dunnam Years
March 1982–April 1994
by D. A. Noel

- 1983 Beaty Building Expansion/Maintenance Building
- 1989 Dunnam Building, Seabrook Hall
- Wilson Chapel and Rogers Youth Center
- Beaty Activities Building Expansion

In December 1982 construction was started on a project which was to include a major expansion of the Beaty Activities Building, a new maintenance building, paving of an additional parking lot, and improvements to the Fellowship Hall Building.

The additions to the activities building consisted mainly of a wraparound design to provide classrooms and meeting rooms surrounding the gym. The contractors' bid for this part of the project was $444,717.89.

The parking lot, plus the new maintenance building and changes in the Fellowship Hall added $230,060.87 which brought the total cost for all projects including furnishings and equipment to $674,778.76 according to a report to the Administrative Board made by Building Committee chairman Edward R. Richmond on October 20, 1983.

The improvements to the Fellowship Hall consisted primarily of closing the breezeway to provide additional offices.

The Board of Trustees 105

The Building Committee for the projects was composed of Edward R. Richmond, chairman, Don Bourland, Jack Renshaw, Charles Johnston, Ed Thorn, Sewell Dunkin, Ken Markwell, Mrs. Nancy Beasley, Mrs. Trudy Simpson, Mrs. Judy VanSteenbert (secretary), and Rev. Jerry Corlew.

Architects were Thorn, Howe, Stratton, and Strong.

After architectural plans were completed, eleven contractors were invited to submit bids. The successful bidder was Robert E. Brown Construction Company.

THE DUNNAM BUILDING, SEABROOK HALL, WILSON CHAPEL, AND ROGERS YOUTH CENTER

In May 1988 the Charge Conference approved the largest building project ever projected for Christ United Methodist Church up to this date. Total cost was estimated to be about $7,500,000.

The master plan included construction of four new buildings plus extensive remodeling of existing buildings.

The Dunnam Building—The largest new building was designed to include adult and children's church school departments, pastor's study and church offices, bridal room, counseling center, parlor, library, archives, and large restrooms on all floors. An elevator was provided to serve all three levels. This building would be connected to the sanctuary on the east and to the chapel and Seabrook Hall on the West.

Wilson Chapel—The new chapel would seat an approximated three hundred plus forty seats in the choir section. After construction was completed, the Kemmons Wilson family also gave a fine organ specifically designed for the chapel.

Rogers Youth Center—The Rogers Youth Center was designed to provide much needed additional space for an ever-expanding youth program. The location immediately adjacent to the expanded Beaty Activities Building allowed for better utilization of both facilities. The youth center contained large meeting rooms, lounge areas, a multipurpose gym/activities room, showers, and office space.

Seabrook Hall—Seabrook Hall was also designed as a multipurpose building. The upper level served as a fellowship and worship service facility. A new and modern kitchen was included with four serving lines to provide rapid service for several hundred persons for Wednesday night fellowship dinners and other events. The new facility quickly was filled to capacity by the expanding contemporary service at 9:45 A.M. Sundays and 5:30 P.M. Saturdays.

The lower level of Seabrook Hall provided space for the counseling center and meeting rooms for other activities including part of the nursery department. Other areas were provided for the printing department, etc.

The Building Committee consisted of D. A. Noel, chairman, Kathryn S. Clark, William J. Crosby, C. Winston Hoover Jr., and Kenneth Markwell Jr.

UNITED METHODIST WOMEN
1982–1994

Very little is heard about the daily function of the United Methodist Women in the local church.

It is a good guess that a majority of the women who volunteer regularly have some connection with the UMW or women's Bible study groups.

These ladies are very supportive on a daily basis of many of the ministries of the church with which we come in contact. The Methodist Hospital Auxiliary and the Neighborhood Centers are just two of the vital programs in Memphis that have been supported both with money and personal labor by the United Methodist Women.

The first Tuesday of every month the many circles meet and socialize with lunch and participation in Bible studies.

The women in the UMW are always willing to serve special luncheons and dinners necessary to the ongoing ministries of the church.

They offer their homes for circle meetings and prepare and serve lunch to all who come. Some circles may have ten on a given Tuesday; others may have twenty to twenty-five in attendance.

The circles become the place where new friends are met, extending the closeness of the church family. It's a place where personal contacts are maintained with people they seldom see at other church activities.

These personal contacts keep the church community from feeling too big and too out of touch.

We need more gatherings where small groups can get to know each other as individuals and learn together what we must have to grow in the knowledge of God.

✧ ✧ ✧

Executive Committee
1982

President	Mrs. Erie Henrich
First Vice President	Mrs. Warren L. Simpson
Second Vice President	Mrs. Orin Johnson
Secretary	Mrs. Ernest A. Jetton

Corresponding
Secretary   Mrs. D. A. Noel
Treasurer   Mrs. Robert Condra

✤ ✤ ✤

EXECUTIVE COMMITTEE
1983

President   Mrs. Warren L. Simpson
First Vice President   Mrs. H. Clay Shelton Jr.
Second Vice President   Mrs. Jack C. Jayroe Jr.
Secretary   Mrs. Ernest A. Jetton
Corresponding
Secretary   Mrs. D. A. Noel
Treasurer   Mrs. Robert Edwards
Assistant Treasurer   Mrs. Conrad McCrary

✤ ✤ ✤

EXECUTIVE COMMITTEE
1984

President   Mrs. H. Clay Shelton Jr.
First Vice President   Mrs. Dwight Clark
Second Vice President   Mrs. Horace Branch
Secretary   Mrs. H. Allen Whitsitt III
Corresponding
Secretary   Mrs. Ben Carpenter
Treasurer   Mrs. Charles W. Newman
Assistant Treasurer   Mrs. Conrad McCrary

✤ ✤ ✤

EXECUTIVE COMMITTEE
1985

President   Mrs. Dwight Clark
First Vice President   Mrs. Conrad McCrary
Second Vice President   Mrs. David Grant
Secretary   Mrs. Ned French
Corresponding
Secretary   Mrs. W. H. Craig

Mrs. Erie Henrich
(Margaret)
Twenty-fourth President
United Methodist Women
1982

Mrs. Warren Simpson
(Trudy)
Twenty-fifth President
United Methodist Women
1983

Mrs. H. Clay Shelton Jr.
(Harriet)
Twenty-sixth President
United Methodist Women
1984

Treasurer	Mrs. William L. Hurdle
Assistant Treasurer	Mrs. William C. Smith
Parliamentarian	Dr. Susan Ruby Lamb

✣ ✣ ✣

EXECUTIVE COMMITTEE
1986

President	Mrs. Conrad McCrary
First Vice President	Mrs. Kenneth Markwell
Second Vice President	Mrs. David Grant
Secretary	Mrs. Ned French
Corresponding Secretary	Mrs. John Ford
Treasurer	Mrs. William L. Hurdle
Assistant Treasurer	Mrs. Alton G. Orr
Parliamentarian	Dr. Susan Ruby Lamb

✣ ✣ ✣

EXECUTIVE COMMITTEE
1987

President	Mrs. Kenneth Markwell
Vice President	Mrs. H. Edward Garrett
Secretary	Mrs. J. F. Bigger Jr.

United Methodist Women: 1982–1994   109

Mrs. Dwight A. Clark
(Kathy)
Twenty-seventh President
United Methodist Women
1985

Mrs. Conrad McCrary
(Yvonne)
Twenty-eighth President
United Methodist Women
1986

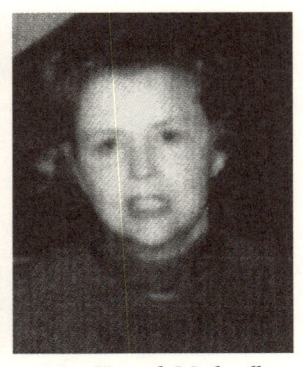

Mrs. Kenneth Markwell
(Helen)
Twenty-ninth President
United Methodist Women
1987

Treasurer   Mrs. Alton G. Orr
Assistant Treasurer   Mrs. Ned French
Secretary, Financial
Interpretation   Mrs. Warren Simpson
                                   Mrs. Robert Condra
Parliamentarian   Dr. Susan Ruby Lamb

✠ ✠ ✠

EXECUTIVE COMMITTEE
1988

President   Mrs. H. Edward Garrett
Vice President   Mrs. John S. Wilson
Secretary   Mrs. J. F. Bigger Jr.
Treasurer   Mrs. Alton Orr
Assistant Treasurer   Mrs. Conrad McCrary
Secretary, Financial
Interpretation   Mrs. Warren Simpson
Parliamentarian   Dr. Susan Ruby Lamb

✠ ✠ ✠

EXECUTIVE COMMITTEE
1989

President   Mrs. John S. Wilson
Vice President   Mrs. Ernest A. Jetton

Mrs. H. Edward Garrett
(Chris)
Thirtieth President
United Methodist Women
1988

Mrs. John S. Wilson
(Pat)
Thirty-first President
United Methodist Women
1989

Mrs. Ernest Jetton
(Karen)
Thirty-second President
United Methodist Women
1990

Secretary Mrs. J. F. Bigger Jr.
Treasurer Mrs. Harold W. Stewart
Assistant Treasurer Mrs. R. H. Roberts
Secretary, Financial
Interpretation Mrs. Warren Simpson
Parliamentarian Dr. Susan Ruby Lamb

✧ ✧ ✧

EXECUTIVE COMMITTEE
1990

President Karen Jetton
Vice President Lynn Holloway
Secretary Mrs. J. F. Bigger Jr.
Treasurer Alcidean Stewart
Assistant Treasurer Vikki Roberts
Secretary, Financial
Interpretation Trudy Simpson
Parliamentarian Harriet Shelton

✧ ✧ ✧

EXECUTIVE COMMITTEE
1991

President Lynn Holloway
Vice President Carole West

United Methodist Women: 1982–1994 111

Mrs. David Holloway
(Lynn)
Thirty-third President
United Methodist Women
1991

Mrs. William West
(Carole)
Thirty-fourth President
United Methodist Women
1992

Mrs. William Watkins
(Jeanette)
Thirty-fifth President
United Methodist Women
1993

Secretary   Nancy Thompson
Treasurer   Virginia McClain
Assistant Treasurer   Peggy Hampshire
Corresponding Secretary,
Secretary, Financial
Interpretation   Louise Clark
Parliamentarian   Harriett Shelton

✤ ✤ ✤

Executive Committee
1992

President   Carole West
Vice President   Jeanette Watkins
Secretary   Sharon Day
Treasurer   Linda Smith
Assistant Treasurer   Nancy Smith
Corresponding Secretary,
Secretary, Financial
Interpretation   Louise Clark
Parliamentarian   Harriett Shelton

EXECUTIVE COMMITTEE
1993

President	Jeanette Watkins
Vice President	Carolyn Rogers
Secretary	Ramona Seabold
Treasurer	Linda Smith
Assistant Treasurer	Virginia Darmody
Corresponding Secretary,	
Secretary, Financial	
Interpretation	Anne Curry
Parliamentarian	Harriett Shelton

✣ ✣ ✣

METHODIST HOSPITAL AUXILIARY

The Methodist Hospital Auxiliary was organized June 21, 1933, by Methodist Women. The membership has grown to over five thousand. The purpose of the auxiliary is to do the Lord's work by giving of your time, money, and interest to patients, nurses, and staff of our church-owned hospitals: Methodist Central, Methodist South, Methodist North.

We support this auxiliary by the appointment of our key woman, Mrs. Harry Johnson, who represents the UMW of Christ Church. She attends the monthly meetings which are held on the second Wednesday of each month at the Methodist School of Nursing located at 251 S[outh] Claybrook to bring to this unit information and needs of the auxiliary.

We further support this auxiliary by appointing a representative from each group to attend the monthly meetings so that she can be a contact person for the individual group.

We send supplies to The Love Ward such as:

- Clothes for the clothes closet.
- Personal items—powder, deodorant, toothbrushes and etc.
- Toys for the holding room, which is used by the children waiting to be taken in for surgery. The children are allowed to take the toy home.

Our unit also supports this ministry by each group attending at least one meeting a year. The auxiliary is fulfilling its purpose by:

- Providing tapes for Dial-A-Prayer.
- Furnishing *Upper Room* devotional guides for twenty-five areas of the Central Hospital and two satellite hospitals.

- Refurbishing prayer room at Central.
- Subscribing to newspapers and magazines for student nurses.
- Providing awards for graduating nurses having the highest scholastic achievement.
- Providing items such as rocking chairs for nursery—updating slides for Newborn Center and etc.
- Furnishing funds for grants and loans to needy student nurses.
- Sponsoring the Pink Lady Volunteers.

While the bazaar and the baby photos are fund-raising projects, the most important fund-raising remains the individual membership which is still one dollar per year, or honorary membership twenty-five dollars per year.

For just one dollar we can personally become a part of this outreach for one year. Let us make the UMW of Christ Church 100 percent participants for 1982.

Margaret Henrich,
President

✢ ✢ ✢

Report to the Official Board
United Methodist Women—November 14, 1983
United Methodist Women are responsive and caring about all aspects of life as they accept the call to grow and become whole persons through Jesus Christ.

And growing we are—just today I added our fiftieth new member to the rolls for 1983. With adjustments for deceased and transfers we total 447 to date. We have surpassed our goal for a ten-percent increase, which was 41 members for this year. Our young mothers group holds the record now with 55. This is exciting and it is truly thrilling to work with these dedicated and willing ladies. They are also very talented and participate in all the activities we are involved in and also serve on the Executive Committee.

Other goals that we have reached this year are: Five-and-one-fourth percent increase in our annual budget of seven thousand dollars, 100 percent participation in Methodist Hospital Auxiliary Memberships from Christ Church, for which we have received our first certificate. The Memphis Conference has awarded us two certificates of achievement for our Bible study of *Outside the Gate—Hebrews* and *People of the Silver Sea*—the Pacific Islands mission study.

We have sent approximately $400 to world missions for this study. This is in addition to the 80 percent of our annual budget already outlined for missions which includes undesignated, designated, local church, and community activities. To date we have received pledges for $8,005. We will be able to do a generous amount of giving when our Surplus Funds Committee meets in December. All funds over and above the budget will be used for special global missions, gifts to our church, and gifts to the community.

"Do you know—about 12 percent of the members of the United Methodist Church (those who choose to belong to UMW) are supplying 37 percent of the mission budget of the whole church through their undesignated giving?" This affects nine thousand programs and projects around the globe and touches the lives of millions of persons—persons already related to these programs and persons waiting to be touched by a Christian presence in mission.

Financial awareness was seen as an area of major import for women of the eighties. We have initiated a series of four seminars at Christ Church to help women solve their financial problems. Our second meeting is scheduled for November 29 at 7:00 P.M. The remaining two will be held early in 1984.

All district, conference, and spiritual retreats have been very well attended. It is a pleasure to represent Christ Church. We have members serving at the district and conference level this year and for the next two years.

We have a total of sixteen groups with the hope of adding another one next year. Currently eight study groups meet in the homes, with four service groups meeting at the chapel for study and then disbursing to function in their field. Our service group is busily engaged with the ceramic picture frames we give each new baby, helping with needs in the nursery, making book covers and stuffed toys, and the annual decorating for Advent, the altar, and the Chrismon tree. Our Neighborhood Centers group meets monthly at the center. Wesley Highland Manor group holds a meeting with music for those who can attend each month.

Our membership group is continually working on contacting all new members at Christ Church. Our two night groups meet one in homes and one in church. We hope to increase membership there next year.

We support the Reading Is Fundamental (RIF) program within our budget and ladies help distribute books three times a year at LaRose School.

Our members participate in mission service to Reelfoot Rural Ministry, the Sunshine Home, Memphis City Jail, Wesley Foundation, USO, Methodist Hospital Auxiliary, John Gaston Hospital Maternity Ward, and Church Women United.

Our local church chairman of the unit is assisted by the members in serving special church functions, banquets, dinners, luncheons, receptions, etc.

The unit sponsors Quiet Day—a call to prayer and self-denial, usually in February with our offering being divided between national and overseas missions. We also contribute to the World Thanks Offering in March.

Our collections are many—stamps, eyeglasses, Campbell's Soup labels for Reelfoot, and clothing, food and paper goods for Neighborhood Centers.

Our Purpose: The organized unit of United Methodist Women shall be a community of women whose purpose is to know God and to experience freedom as whole persons through Jesus Christ; to develop a creative supportive fellowship; and to expand concepts of mission through participation in the global ministries of the church.

We have had record attendance at both group and general meetings. We too are in the beginning of our Centennial Era Celebration 1983–1985. We are beginning 1984 with a special centennial program. We will continue to work to meet our challenges—growth and love for each other and willingness to serve Thee. All for the Glory of God.

We too have joined the world of computers! Our yearbook for 1984 is being compiled right now in a home computer—with a printer. Amazing—we are excited about this and very grateful to our member who so willingly agreed to do it for us.

Respectfully submitted,
Trudy Simpson, President

✜ ✜ ✜

Report to Charge Conference
Christ United Methodist Women
December 1, 1986

United Methodist Women are a community of women whose purpose is to know God and to experience freedom as whole persons through Jesus Christ; to develop a creative, supportive fellowship; and to expand concepts of mission through participating in the global ministries of the church.

We gained sixty new members this year, but due to death, transfers, and bringing our roll up-to-date we now have 485. We are very excited about two new circles that were formed this year. Circle 17 is a daytime circle for women forty to fifty-five and they are off to a great start. Circle 18 was formed last month for our young career women who will meet the second Tuesday night of each month.

A Study and Review Committee met and made recommendations that were adopted in June. There will be several changes for 1987. One will be a Bible study for our women taught by Maxie Dunnam in January. Other changes include more flexibility in the studies and fewer general meetings.

Our general meetings have been well attended this year with good programs and music. Mary Louise Caldwell has brought us a local mission each month. Some of these are MIFA, United Methodist Hospital, United Methodist Neighborhood Center, United Methodist Adoption Agency, and Wesley Foundation. We took the church vans and toured MIFA and Neighborhood Center. We also had Dr. Susan Ruby Lamb tell us about EWHA University in Korea and about her trip to Korea in May.

In addition to our $8,690 budget that we have met, we have given to St. John's soup kitchen, Wesley Highland Manor, MIFA, Church Women United for inner-city children, Neighborhood Center Arts Festival, EWHA University, tuition for cosmetology school for Charles Donalds of the Jubilee Ministry, and

Neighborhood Center for their Thanksgiving feast. We will disperse about $1,400 in surplus funds later this month.

We sent $317 from our Quiet Day Offering in February to conference. We had Evelyn McKee as our speaker from *The Upper Room* and our own Martha Vandervoort. The theme was *Toward Wholeness-Forgiveness*.

Our mission study this year, led by Mary Louise Caldwell, *Natives of North America,* was excellent. We had four sessions—two on Wednesday night after fellowship dinners and the third and fourth Tuesday in March. We received a certificate of excellence for this study at the School of Mission at Lambuth in July.

The second annual retreat was held at St. Columba Episcopal Conference Center with Abel and Freida Henricks as leaders. This was truly inspiring and rewarding.

All district and conference meetings have been attended. We are represented on the district and conference level with officers. October 1987 we will host Annual Conference.

We have three active service groups. Our Neighborhood Center group tutors, works in Neighborhood Center Thrift Store, and had a Bible school this past summer for the children.

Circle 12 makes ceramic picture frames for each new baby of the church and delivers them with a friendly visit. They have been working for a month repairing the ornaments for the Chrismon tree.

In addition to mission services already mentioned we support Reelfoot Rural Ministry, Sunshine Home, Memphis City Jail, Wesley Foundation, USO, Methodist Hospital Auxiliary, Wesley Highland Manor, Church Women United, and RIF at LaRose School.

We have participated in special church functions by decorating and serving tables such as conference in June, banquets, dinners, and luncheons.

We collect stamps, eyeglasses, Campbell's Soup labels for Reelfoot, clothing, and paper goods. We will again be 100 percent in membership to the Methodist Hospital Auxiliary. We gave $142 to the conference for their candle burning project for missions.

Many of our ladies participated in the reading program. We had three book reviews and luncheons during the year. We received a certificate of excellence for this. We will receive a certificate of excellence for the study of Daniel at next year's school of mission.

In April we entertained thirty-eight women from Winston-Salem on their way to California to assembly with a potluck and lots of fellowship. We had dinners for the USO and Wesley Foundation.

We have one more meeting December 16. At that time we will install the officers for 1987 and have a pledge service. During 1986 we have worked and shared together. The fellowship has been outstanding. Women of Christ United Methodist Church are truly dedicated to serving their Lord.

Respectfully submitted,
Yvonne McCrary, President

✧ ✧ ✧

REPORT TO CHARGE CONFERENCE
Christ United Methodist Women
November 2, 1987

United Methodist Women is a community of women whose purpose is to know God and to experience freedom as whole persons through Jesus Christ; to develop a creative supportive fellowship; and to expand concepts of mission through participation in the global ministries of the church.

Our membership as of October 15 was 512. We have gained 49 members so far this year but with a loss of 22 members—four deaths, seven transfers, seven moved out of the city, and four by request leaves a net gain of 27 members. We have about 60 prospective members who will be our guests at our Christmas general meeting and brunch in December.

In addition to our $9,355 budget which we have met, we have given $140 for carpets for the Neighborhood Center Church, $50 to UNICEF, and $305 to the Methodist Hospital Auxiliary to make us go 100 percent for our membership, and $410 to the conference for their candle burning project for missions. Any surplus funds will be used for local mission projects.

Our general meetings have been well attended. In January Dr. Dunnam's overview study of James got us off to a great start breaking all records with 179 in attendance. In fact, he was so popular he will teach again.

In February for Quiet Day we had Mary Ann Frazer as our guest speaker and our own Carolyn Loftin. Their theme was *Winning with Prayer*. It was a very inspiring day, well attended in spite of the inclement weather. We sent $274.71 from our Quiet Day offering to conference.

Our mission study this year on southeast Asia led by Millie Gedney was very interesting and informative. We now have a better understanding of problems in India and Nepal, Sri Lanka, and Pakistan.

Our third annual retreat with seventy present was again held at St. Columba Episcopal Conference Center in April with Dr. Dunnam as leader. His theme was *Adventures in Prayer*. This was truly an inspiring and rewarding experience in such a beautiful setting.

All district and conference meetings have been attended and we received a book for this award of excellence. We are represented on both the district and conference levels with officers. We were hosts for the Annual Conference on October 10 for the first time since 1967.

We have three active service groups.

1. Circle 12 (Church Service Group) makes ceramic picture frames for each new baby of the church and delivers them with a friendly visit. They are

now making articles to be sold at the Methodist Auxiliary Christmas Bazaar.

2. Circle 13 (Neighborhood Center Group) tutors, works in the Neighborhood Center Thrift Store, had a Vacation Bible School this past summer for the children, had about thirty-five for Neighborhood Seniors lunch, Monday–Friday, and Bread of Life Lunches for the young.

3. Circle 14 (Membership and Visitation Group) works very hard. Robbie McQuiston works almost full-time at this job.

In addition to mission services already mentioned, we help Reelfoot Rural Ministry, Sunshine Home, Memphis City Jail, Wesley Foundation, USO Methodist Hospital Auxiliary, Wesley Highland Manor, Church Women United, and RIF (Reading Is Fundamental) at LaRose School. Some members of the USO attended our church picnic in August. One circle has just started doing Meals on Wheels for MIFA.

We participated in one ecumenical project by serving Lenten lunches at Calvary Episcopal Church during March and April. Our younger daytime circles served the lunches and our treasury is $120 richer for this ecumenical service to a community tradition.

We have participated in special church functions by decorating and serving at the reception honoring Reverends Lynn and Lamb in June and at the Evangelism Training Day luncheon in September.

Our reading program has grown this year with more of our ladies participating. We had two book reviews and will have another one November 30. We received a certificate for our reading program.

We will have two more general meetings. Shirley Lynn will follow our national theme *Into the Future by Faith* when she speaks on November 17. On December 15, Dorothy Peel, our district president, will install our new officers before our Christmas musical program by Mimi Vestol which will be followed by a Christmas brunch.

During 1987 we have worked and shared together. One of our younger daytime circles (Circle 11, led by Ann Wilder) has won circle count at each of our general meetings for the first time ever. This indicates that our UMW has a bright future with our younger ladies becoming more active.

Respectfully submitted,
Helen Markwell, President

HISTORY OF WORSHIP
1982–1994

Mrs. William N. Crowson had been asked by Dr. Beaty to serve as the chairman of the work area on worship for 1982. One of her first concerns was to establish an altar guild. With the approval and encouragement of the new senior minister, Dr. Maxie Dunnam, an altar guild was established under the leadership of Mrs. Dwight Clark. Mrs. Crowson reported that the following activities and concerns were being addressed by the work area: the responsibility of the ushers during Communion; alternate ways of serving Communion; finding ways to involve more youth and young adults; better serving our handicapped; repair work on the hearing aids in the sanctuary; continuation of tape ministry; obtaining funds for replacing hymnals and Bibles; and rebrassing offering plates.

The duties of the newly established altar guild included working under the direction of the senior minister to provide a more beautiful and meaningful atmosphere for worship services by correctly preparing for all worship services and sacraments of the church. This involved the care and storage of the Communion vessels, altar linens, paraments, banners, vestments, and baptismal font in addition to the preparation of the elements of Holy Communion. The guild is responsible also for the interpretation to the congregation of the Christian symbolism, liturgical symbolism and seasons as they are used in the worship service. Another task is the appropriate preparation of the chancel for weddings, funerals, Christmas, Easter, and candlelight services.

Since 1982, many items have been given to the church to enhance worship in both Reeves Chapel and the sanctuary. These items were presented for dedication. In the chapel, the brass altar candlesticks were given in memory of Mr. Jesse Anderson by his family. The needlepoint wall hanging, in honor of Rev. Howard W. Rash, was designed, blocked, and mounted by Mr. Charles Roma, who also did the needlework with the help of Edith (Mrs. Carey) Middlecoff, Mary (Mrs. Keith) Kelley, Dorothy (Mrs. Noel) Stafford, and Frances (Mrs. George T. Jr.) Roberts. The brass altar cross was received from the Doddsville United Methodist Church, Doddsville, Mississippi, when it disbanded in 1982.

Two wooden processional crosses and their stands, used in the sanctuary worship services on Sunday, were made and donated by Mr. Clarence Colby. The silver bud vase which holds flowers for new babies each Sunday was a gift of Myra (Mrs. Jack C.) Barksdale. Three silver revere bowls are used for baptisms. One was given in memory of Marguerite Murphy Meador by the William J. Crosby family, and two were given by the Lowell G. Hays Jr. family. The purple, red, and white brocade paraments and the green linen one which cover the altar each Sunday, and are rotated to correspond with the colors of the liturgical calendar, were given in memory of Mr. Jesse Anderson by his family, as were the matching pulpit hangings and Bible markers.

In a report to the Charge Conference, December 6, 1982, Dr. Dunnam reported:

> There is nothing more vital to a congregation than Sunday morning worship. I celebrate the joy that I experience with you in worship on Sunday mornings, your gracious response to my preaching, the commitment of our choirs, and the changed lives that have come through worship. I celebrate our growing attendance. We must do whatever we can through music, congregational involvement, and preaching to enhance the quality, excitement, joy and meaning of this one time during the week when your congregation gathers as a family. I look forward to the day when at least 50 percent of our congregation will by present on any given Sunday.

In August 1985 a committee made the following recommendations regarding a new chapel: We need a chapel which will seat 250–350 people and have a church-like look, with traditional decor. Other specifications were suggested as well, but it was not until 1989 that this need became a reality.

A policy change in 1987 moved the annual memorial service from Memorial Day weekend to All Saints Sunday.

The October board minutes reported that the work area on worship included the altar guild, the music ministry of the church, and the ushers. The altar guild sets up the altar area of the church for our Sunday morning services and special events in the life of the church. The altar guild is also responsible for the flowers that decorate the church. The music ministries of the church have been working very well. The chancel choir has approximately 101 members and is presenting music at both worship services on Sunday morning. Our ushers meet, greet, and seat those attending worship services as well as collecting the offerings. In addition, the ushers are trained to handle any emergencies that might occur during the worship services.

There was also a report from the committee on three services. Tom Dyer presented the report. Due to the construction which will begin soon and the confusion that will undoubtedly result, as well as the efforts being made to duplicate the 10:45 worship service at the 8:30 service, the committee feels that at this time three services would not be beneficial to the church. Instead all board members are encouraged to attend the 8:30 service and to encourage other members to do so. The committee will continue to study the issue.

Altar guild minutes of a meeting in March 1988 reported that Mr. and Mrs. Forrest Dowling Jr. and their daughter, Eugenia, designed, made, and donated the banners that are used for the liturgical seasons. Appreciation was expressed to them for their time, efforts, and gift to the church. Anne Miller is making a Lenten banner, planning some others, and making an album picturing each banner.

Trudy Simpson reported that her research showed that the present chapel is a completely memorial one and according to church policy, nothing can be replaced or changed during the lifetime of the family of the giver. She distributed a form that should be completed if you have donated an item to the church so that it can be properly recorded. The Property Disposition Committee has the authority to accept or reject gifts to the church. Trudy reported that the new white brocade parament, donated by Kitty Anderson and made by Aileen Adams, is ready and will be used Easter Sunday. All of the paraments were given in memory of Mr. [Jesse] Anderson, and inscriptions to that effect have been sewn on the back of the paraments, pulpit hangings, and Bible markers.

Early in 1988 the Worship Committee requested of the Building Committee to provide a more adequate sacristy for the preparation, care, and storage of worship elements of all kinds.

A special emphasis was made to purchase new Bibles and hymnals for the sanctuary. It was very successful.

Usher badges made by Karen Jetton and those given by Ella McVean were dedicated and presented on a special day chosen to honor and recruit ushers.

Minutes of a work area meeting in March 1988 report that to respond to the problem of applause during the worship services, three articles would be written and placed in the church paper. One would address the concern of "quietness in worship before the service, remaining in the sanctuary for the entire service," written by Maxie Dunnam; "applause during worship, choir direction in standing, being seated," by Jack Hearn; and "the leadership of ushers, the sanctuary hearing aids and Communion seating," by Tom Kelly.

Bookmarks given by Gene Rone picturing the sanctuary windows were in the process of being made.

In 1989 a new chapel was completed, given by Dorothy and Kemmons Wilson, and dedicated as the Wilson Chapel. Many gifts were given in memory and honor of others to furnish the chapel.

Administrative minutes in September 1989 indicate that Dr. Dunnam reminded the board of the reasons for changing the worship service format to provide for three services and that all were encouraged to be flexible. Features of the 9:45 service include an addition of a children's church. The service will take place in the new Wilson Chapel and the format will be more contemporary. Both men and women are being encouraged to act as ushers for this service.

In a report to the Council on Ministries, J. J. Doughtie reported that the attendance for the first three 9:45 A.M. worship services were 320, 259, and 439, respectively. Everyone seemed enthused by the response to the middle worship service.

The 1991 minutes of the work area on worship reported the following: better communication is needed when there is a funeral; a policy concerning loaning chancel or altar appointments was being written by Trudy Simpson; the lighting fund, to light the exterior of the sanctuary, had enough money to start getting bids but the project was referred to the Board of Trustees for further action.

THE ALTAR GUILD

In 1982, shortly after Dr. Maxie Dunnam became the minister of Christ United Methodist Church, Jewel (Mrs. William N.) Crowson, as chairperson of the worship work area, envisioned and initiated the organizational work for establishing an altar guild at Christ Church. Its duties were delineated to include working under the direction of the senior minister to provide a more beautiful and meaningful atmosphere for worship services by correctly preparing for all worship services and sacraments of the church. The care and storage of the Communion vessels, altar linens, paraments, banners, vestments, and baptismal font are part of this task in addition to the preparation of the elements of Holy Communion. The guild is responsible also for the interpretation to the congregation of the Christian symbolism, liturgical symbolism, and seasons as they are used in the worship service. Another task is the appropriate preparation of the chancel for weddings, funerals, Christmas, Easter, and candlelight services.

In 1983, Sugar (Mrs. John III) Walker succeeded Mrs. Crowson as worship work area chairperson, and at this time Kathy (Mrs. Dwight) Clark was selected to be the first chairperson of the altar guild, which would function as a committee under the auspices of the worship work area. Under her direction, the dream of an altar guild was realized. She prepared the first altar guild manual that outlined the policies, duties, and purpose of the guild and recruited the original members.

Purpose of the Altar Guild

1. To work under the direction of the minister and in cooperation with the work area on worship to provide a more beautiful and meaningful atmosphere for worship by correctly preparing for all worship services and sacraments of the church.

2. To care for and store Communion vessels, altar linens, paraments, banners, hangings, vestments, and worship equipment.

3. To care for the baptismal font, provide water in it for baptisms, and clean basins.

4. To prepare the elements of Holy Communion for the chapel and sanctuary and all other services as needed.

5. To provide proper candles of adequate length and other furnishings and arrange for flowers for the altar.

6. To keep all altar furnishings clean and polished, and to assure that the chancel area in the sanctuary and chapel are clean.

7. To advise concerning and/or prepare the chancel for any special services, weddings, funerals, Christmas, or candlelight services.

8. To assist in planning worship centers in other parts of the church.

9. To interpret Christian symbolism, liturgical colors, seasons, and elements of worship to church members and visitors.

10. Guild members' duty assignments are for one week a month. From Friday A.M. through Thursday P.M., except Communion stewards, who serve for the designated Communion service throughout the year.

Checklist to Prepare for Sunday Services
    (Paraments and acolyte robes are stored in cabinets in closet next to sacristy on west side of sanctuary.)
    (Call the church office Friday A.M. to check on services and activities for your entire week.)

For the Sanctuary
1. Check the floors and woods in chancel area altar table, pulpit, etc. and clean where needed.

2. Check the liturgical color calendar in sacristy and change paraments antependia (pulpit scarf), the lectern bookmarks, and altar cover appropriately. White fair linen cloth is always used for Communion. Plastic cover is used over the appropriate altar cloth.

3. Buff the brass candlesticks with a soft cloth or cotton gloves. Be sure candles are of height to be attractive and to burn for at least the morning services and any to be held in afternoon or evening. Place the candlesticks about six to seven inches to either end of the altar past the pedestal base and centered from side to side on the altar table.

4. Remove any wax from altar with sharp knife and candle wax remover in the cabinet. (Use remover sparingly, as it is expensive.)

5. Check and raise wicks in the candlelighters, being sure there is a lighter on each side of the choir pews, secured in holders. Replace wicks if less than three inches long. Leave candlewicks in position that is easy for acolytes to ignite the candles.

6. Leave one set of candlelighters, fully prepared with adequate wicks, behind the door of the sacristy for emergency use.

7. Check matches and scissors—two each—in the brass box in the robe cabinet in new storage room (between brides' room and sacristy). Also, check matches and candlelighter in the chapel in Communion cabinet drawer. Matches should be out of sight of children using the chapel facilities.

8. Put a small amount of water in silver bowl and place in baptismal font in sanctuary. See that the bowl is polished. There are two such revere bowls in the storage cabinet. Use the larger one, as first choice.

9. Flowers will be provided every Sunday, either from a wedding the day before or fresh from Sandy's Florist at church expense or as honoraria or memorials. Check to see that the florist or others have placed the flowers in stand centered behind the altar table unless there is a Saturday evening wedding in the sanctuary, from which you should make a check on Sunday morning to see that the flowers were properly placed for the Sunday services. Do any minor rearranging of flowers as may be needed to look balanced and attractive in our setting. If major problems occur with the flower arrangement, contact Gail King immediately. Containers should be checked for adequate water on Saturday and Sunday.

10. The janitor is to trim the candlewicks between the first and second service to assist the acolytes in lighting candles; however, altar guild members should check on this to be sure it is done. Don't leave anything to chance or someone else—check everything!

For the Chapel
1. Dust altar and polish brass furnishings that are not lacquered. Pull the cross and candleholders out toward center front of the altar and away from the tapestry; center the cross with the candleholders equally balanced.

2. Change candles to maintain one-half to two-thirds the height of the chimneys. Clean the chimneys and holders. Day school uses these candles several times during the week. Provide for this much burning.

3. Replace matches in brass box and replace wick in candlelighter as needed. Place both in drawer of the Communion cabinet next to organ, out of sight of the children.

History of Worship: 1982–1994   125

4. Set up Communion. Remember that Communion is served twice on the third Sunday. Empty one small can of grape juice into the small pewter chalice and put about 25 to 30 wafers on the small plate. Place in Communion cabinet, with clean white napkin (purificator) over the wafer plate and a white square pall over the chalice. Leave one can of grape juice in the cabinet for emergency use by the ministers. Return the small chalice and plate to the chapel cabinet after cleanup. Emmaus may have a pottery chalice and plate in the chapel cabinet that should remain there.

5. Put small amount of water in pewter bowl and place in baptismal font. After emptying it, return bowl to Communion cabinet after Sunday use. Leave jar of water in Communion cabinet.

Checklist for Cleanup after Sunday Services

1. Pour water out of chapel baptismal bowl (bowl stains and pits if water remains in it) and place bowl in small cabinet.

2. Leave water in sanctuary baptismal font bowl (for weekday use if needed) but change water every weekend.

3. Clean up Communion chalice and plate in chapel. Put wafers back in box and pour out grape juice. Return chalice and plate to chapel Communion cabinet. One can of grape juice, one box of wafers, and jar of water should always remain in Communion cabinet in chapel with chalice and plate for ministers' unexpected emergency use.

4. Extinguish candles if still lit and clean wax away. (It is easier to clean when fresh.)

5. Straighten kneeling cushions in sanctuary and everything in general. Turn out the lights, especially in chancel area, unless someone is working in the sanctuary. Light switches are on the wall beside pulpit.

6. Clean and straighten sacristy—please leave sink and counters very clean. Check floor for wax as we track it to the marble chancel floor. Dust, dirty water spots, and trash can soil the paraments and white napkins if they are laid on the counter. The sacristy should be reverenced as a place where holy work and holy articles are maintained. It should be kept clean at all times. Be sure doors are locked and keys returned.

Preparation for Holy Communion in Sanctuary
(About five times a year.) We use the intinction method—dipping the wafer/bread into the wine.

Weekly Team
Place the white linen cloth with thin fair linen cloth over it on the altar. Apply plastic cover. Change the antependia (pulpit scarf) and lectern bookmarks to white. Check candles, etc.

Communion Stewards
1. Polish the silverplate chalices, patens, bread tray, and flagon to be used. Alternate use of flagons; they were gifts from members.

2. On the altar table, place the four large chalices centered, one on either side of each brass candlestick with space left in the center for the minister to place the flagon and bread tray which he takes from the family who presents them (see photos in back of master manual in sacristy). Cover the empty chalices with a white square napkin, each called purificator. (Linens are in a box in the old sacristy cabinet.)

3. Place a lavabo towel, folded once, at the east end back corner area of the altar table for the minister's use as he pours.

4. At each end of the chancel on the lowest level against the wall (near flags) place a small table covered with a white cloth. Put a covered tray of wafers on each table as an extra for the ministers' use. Move flags to walls for worshipers to pass in front of them (return them after service).

5. Just before the service: Fill flagon with grape juice using about one-and-one-half bottles, and instruct the family that is to carry flagon and homemade bread on silver tray down aisle to the altar. Family should be advised to bring bread to sacristy earlier before the service and come there before the service for the instructions. Guild member takes flagon to narthex as service begins, placing it in cabinet there (after January) so as not to be conspicuous to any worshipers entering sanctuary.

A family who has shown leadership in the church is secured at least two weeks before Communion service. They are asked to bake the bread in a loaf shape and bring it to the sacristy as they come to Sunday school.

Instructions for the Family
As the service begins, family sits in back pews. Later, the family goes to back center door of sanctuary to start walking slowly down the center aisle as hymn begins after the Communion meditation has been given by the minister. The father carries the flagon; mother carries the silver tray of bread. Children, if under twelve to fourteen years, walk in front of parents—if older, they should walk behind parent. If children are very small and no more than two, they may

walk beside parents, possibly holding their hand. The family walks up center steps to the altar table, gives the flagon of juice and tray of bread to minister across the table as they stop in front center. They then walk inside the chancel rail to the right (east end) of the altar table, stopping inside the rail with backs to the organ and facing the ministers. They will be served Communion elements with the ministers prior to the congregation. Then they leave via the center steps and center aisle returning to their seats.

Acolytes come forward from their seats at either end of the choir when the choir is invited to come to the chancel. They kneel at front of the altar—two on west side and one on last side—and return to their same seats as the choir returns to their seats.

1. Communion stewards should remain in or near the sacristy during Communion services in case they or any supplies are needed.

2. Clean up as soon as the service is over. Pour out grape juice, put wafers in boxes, wash and dry Communion vessels, and lock them in sacristy cabinet. Wipe grape juice from chancel rails and clean around altar and chancel as needed.

Lenten and Christmas Eve Communion

Follow the same guidelines for the advance preparation and altar furnishings. With these changes: Grape juice is put directly into two large chalices and placed on the altar table with three patens (plates) of wafers—one is for reserve use. These are all placed on the altar about thirty minutes before the service begins. Bottles of grape juice are in the closet next to the sacristy room on upper shelf.

Be sure candles are lit in advance of beginning of the service and extinguished afterward, as acolytes are not used in these services. Put one large host wafer on the paten nearest the flagon. Clean up after service as usual.

After the Communion services, check the chancel rails for any money that has been left. If ushers are not collecting this, guild members or Communion stewards should collect it and put it in the bank bag in drawer in sacristy if Gynette Bennett, financial secretary, is not present to receive it. Call the church office the next morning to ask someone to take this to the office.

Maundy Thursday Service

Prepare Communion according to sanctuary Communion section of this manual and Lenten and Christmas Eve Communion above, but place the juice flagon on the altar table a little to the left of center prior to the beginning of service. Use the three patens of wafers and place one host wafer on top of the nearest paten to the flagon.

Plan ahead for two altar guild members to wear white robes (from choir room), walk out to the altar at the ending of the service, and strip the altar of all paraments and candlesticks and drape the wooden cross with black chiffon and a crown of thorns. The chiffon is on a rod in the new paraments cabinet next to the sacristy. The crown of thorns hangs in the sacristy above the sink. After this takes place, everyone leaves in silence. Marvin Budd helps with placing the cross on the altar table.

Ask Mr. Bennett to get the wooden cross for you ahead of the service—the day before, if possible. Check its condition and secure the black chiffon and place these items and robes in the sacristy ready for use.

Holy Matrimony

1. Hang the white paraments in the three places in the chancel area. A new white brocade altar cloth will be completed after Christmas to match the antependia and bookmarks. These should be used for weddings.

2. Check candles for enough height and lengthy good wicks.

3. Clean brass candlesticks with soft cloth.

4. Check candlelighters for adequate wicks and be sure matches are available.

5. See that everything is clean and in order.

6. After any wedding—in sanctuary or chapel—Myra Barksdale, the wedding hostess for the church, is responsible for cleaning up and changing the paraments from white to the color to be used for Sunday worship, returning the white cloth to the hangers, and for removing any flowers and candleholders that were used for the wedding.

7. If wedding flowers are not to be used for Sunday services, they should be removed from the altar and placed in first floor ladies' restroom until picked up. Guild members on duty should go through Sunday preparation checklist to determine if sanctuary and chapel are ready for Sunday following a wedding. Straighten kneeler cushions; clear halls. If there should be duplicate flower arrangements, place the lesser one in the narthex or east foyer. If any problems arise, call altar guild chairman.

Service Team Guidelines for Flower Distribution

It is the responsibility of the service team (Flower Distribution Committee) to insure that the altar flowers, after use during the Sunday worship services, are distributed in an efficient, economical, and caring manner each Sunday, if they are not to be claimed by their donor.

The committee member designated below for each week should contact the flower chairman, Gail King, not later than the preceding Friday, to determine if the family or organization donating the flowers wishes to take them. If not, the

History of Worship: 1982–1994 129

committee member should call the church office to ascertain whether or not there are any church activities during the first few days following her Sunday at which the altar flowers could be used. If so, she arranges use with that leader.

If the flowers are not to be used at the church, it is the responsibility of the committee member to remove the flowers from the altar at the close of the 10:45 A.M. service and divide the arrangement into two or three smaller bouquets and deliver them to homebound members of the congregation. This should be done as soon as possible after the close of the service while the flowers are still fresh. A list of the shut-ins, their addresses, and telephone numbers is kept in the window of the sacristy in a plastic cover. Choose two or three names from the list and write the current date of delivery beside the name so that a record maybe kept of who has received flowers. This is very important.

Wrap the bouquet in green florist paper and include a card and church bulletin with your delivery. Both paper and cards are kept on the lower shelf of the first cabinet as you enter the sacristy. You may desire to bring containers in which to place each or the total flower arrangement. Please write on the card: From the altar guild with love. If you can make a ten-minute visit with the shut-in, it would be an added service.

This is a very important ministry of the church to members who cannot attend worship services because of illness and a personally rewarding one, as well. If for any reason the committee member is unable to serve on the designated Sunday, please call the flower distribution service team chairman, Chris Garrett, by Friday noon, and help her locate a substitute. This is not always easy to do at the last minute.

The used oasis and flower container from the altar can be left in the sacristy.

Service Team and Designations

Chairman and Fifth Sunday	Mrs. H. Edward Garrett (Chris)
First Sunday	Mrs. Theodore W. Medlin (Mary Lou)
Second Sunday	Mrs. B. J. Kelley (Carolyn)
Third Sunday	Mrs. Robert C. Black (Sarah)
Fourth Sunday	Mrs. Jimmy M. Kelly (Delaine)
Altar Flower Chairman (Reservations and Arrangements)	Mrs. W. Scott King (Gail)
Our Florist: Sandy's	

✢ ✢ ✢

ACOLYTES

Three children are recruited by acolyte guild members from grades four, five, and six of the church school (families must be members of the church) to serve for one month at second Sunday service as two acolytes and one crossbearer. Boys and girls are alternated by the month. Parents are contacted for permission and support.

The guild member conducts a training session with each group of children on the Friday afternoon before they begin serving on Sunday. Parents are encouraged to come with the children for training.

On Sunday morning, each child is robed in a white monk's alb (robe) that hangs in the closet next to the sacristy. The acolyte guild chairman and assistant chairman have keys. A wooden emblem of the flame and cross is worn around the neck on the appropriate color ribbon that matches the altar paraments. The candlelighting acolytes walk into the chancel area before the service begins and take a seat on either side of the choir. Candlelighters are to be hanging in a holder at the end of the choir pew. Wicks should be checked each Sunday morning by the acolytes to be sure they are adequate. Additional wicks are located in the sacristy cabinet next to the sink.

On Sunday morning, the crossbearer goes to the narthex where the choir will be gathered for processional. The crossbearer will lead the processional down the aisle stopping in front center of the altar table. As the first hymn closes, the crossbearer walks to the side of the pulpit and places the cross pole in the floor stand provided for it, then goes to sit next to the acolyte at the end of the choir pews.

As the service closes, after the benediction, the crossbearer picks up the cross pole from its stand and walks to the center of the altar, then walks down center aisle to the vestibule and back down side corridor to vestment closet. Acolytes go to altar table as crossbearer starts down chancel steps to extinguish candles, then walk to either side of chancel and to vestment closet. The crossbearer should be cautioned to hold the cross pole straight, so that it does not lean forward.

✣ ✣ ✣

Banners

The banners and poles were made, designed, and donated by Mrs. Eugenia Trousdale and Mrs. Virginia Nowlin in 1977. They were expensive in money and time. Great care should be taken to protect them in their use and storage. They are stored in the attic room over the narthex.

Several days before the banners are to be used, the bases in which the poles rest and the banners should be brought down and placed along the sanctuary walls in the order to be processed, so they can be checked and repaired if needed and to allow the felt and decorations to fall in place. Each horizontal pole should have a finial on each end and should be secured with a glue gun. To secure the vertical pole, run cord through pole and tie a small knot at the back of the banner.

The banners are brought down with the blank side facing the altar, so the congregation can see the front of the banner, and placed along the side walls with the first base placed on the floor between the side door and the end of the chancel rail. The second base is placed on the other side of the door and about six to seven feet apart down the wall. High school boys who carry the banners wear white youth choir robes and line up across the back wall with the banner they carry. Two banners are carried the first Sunday of Advent. The next Sunday, those same two are carried and two more added and so on for the four Sundays until the eight have been processed on the last Sunday of Advent. Before the second carrier starts from the back, the first carrier should be a little more than halfway down the aisle, etc. The crossbearer walks behind the banner carriers.

The placement of the banners is as follows:

First Sunday:	Mary and Angels	#1 on East Side
	Lilies and a trumpet	#1 on West Side
Second Sunday: (add)	Mary and Joseph	#2 on East Side
	Brown one with tree	#2 on West Side
Third Sunday: (add)	Shepherd (dark blue)	#3 on East Side
	Manger (brick red)	#3 on West Side
Fourth Sunday: (add)	Mary with Baby (decorative)	#4 on East Side
	Chi Rho symbol (blue, white, gold)	#4 on West Side
Epiphany:	Wise Men	#5 on East Side
	Star on violet background	#5 on West Side

The plan for the addition of the banners should be discussed with the music director and organist so they can add more music.

✜ ✜ ✜

Music

February 1, 1970, Don Sanford came to the staff as director of music. He was a native of Massachusetts and a graduate of Boston University with a major in sacred music. One of the programs he introduced was the use of handbells which were to be used for special occasions. Meanwhile, Chris Mays, whose family had been active in the church from the very beginning, became interim organist. Chris was brilliant at the console but his job as a pilot with Federal Express kept him from accepting the permanent position.

Jane Gamble joined the staff as organist. She was a graduate of Lambuth College with a degree in music. In time she received her doctorate. On September 28, 1974, Jane left to become minister of music at a sister church. She returned to Christ Church October 5, 1975. She resigned again March 1, 1982, and Emily McAllister returned as organist. On September 26, 1982, Don Sanford resigned, and Tom Machen was named interim director, a position he was well qualified to fill. Tom was at that time director of opera at Memphis State University, so his duties at Christ Church were only in the area of directing the chancel choir. He did not have administrative duties. Tom's fiancée, Kallen Esperian, had a beautiful voice and her presence added immensely to the music program. They married and she eventually became an international opera star and traveled the world. Eventually, Tom resigned in order to spend more time with Kallen and to travel with her.

Michael Brewster became director of music ministry, May 8, 1983. Mike was greeted with enthusiasm by the choir. He was young and had great plans for building the choir. His wife, Julie, was a soloist and a welcome addition to the alto section. One of the highlights of his tenure was presenting the great oratorio, *Elijah*, with Tom Machen in the title role. When the Annual Conference took place at Christ Church, the chancel choir, combined with St. Luke's Methodist choir, presented special music. Circumstances caused Mike to resign in April 1986, and Tom Machen again became interim director for a short while.

Jack Hearn became director of music ministries in September of 1986. He had previously served in a Presbyterian church in Jackson, Tennessee. Jack was young, vibrant, funny, and easily endeared himself to the choir. His wife, Luanne, soon became involved in children's music. They had two children, Margaret and Paul. One of the highlights of Jack's ministry was the presentation of Mozart's *Requiem* with over six hundred in attendance. His training as a classical musician served him well in the doctrine and ritual of the Episcopal Church. Eventually he became choirmaster at an Episcopal church in Houston, Texas.

Emily McAllister had resigned the year before and Perry Redfearn, a longtime friend of Jack's became organist. When Jack left, Perry became interim director as well as organist.

The First Generation Singers. This choral group of seniors was formed in 1993 by Flo Seward for the purpose of visiting and entertaining in retirement and nursing homes. With the exception of the summer months, rehearsals are held on Thursdays in the choir room. Jack Hearn was the first director and accompanist followed by Bob McBain and then Sean Pollock. Songs selected are always upbeat and happy. If the music is familiar, the residents will often join in and the response is always gratifying as well as rewarding.

✧ ✧ ✧

1982

Work Area on Worship
Jewel Crowson,
    Chairman

Altar Guild Chairman
Kathy Clark

Ushers
Samuel Barnett
Eddins Hopps

Music
Henry Harry

House
Sewell Dunkin

Sound Booth
Milton Bennett

Communion Stewards
Lynn & Doug Cross

History of Worship: 1982–1994

At-Large Members
Patty Williams
Maxine Pyron
Norma Massey
Frances Hawthorne

Staff
Dr. Maxie D. Dunnam,
  Sr. Minister

Minister of Music
Tom Machen
Don Sanford

Organist
Emily McAllister

1983–1984

Work Area on Worship
Carolyn Walker (Mrs.
  John III), Chairman

Altar Guild Chairman
Kathy Clark

*Assistant Altar Guild
Chairman*
Jewel Crowson

1985–1986

Work Area on Worship
Eleanor Eubank,
  Chairman

Altar Guild Chairman
Kathy Clark

*Assistant Altar Guild
Chairman*
Jewel Crowson

1986

Altar Guild Chairman
Mary Louise Caldwell

*Assistant Altar Guild
Chairman*
Anne Howdeshell

Members
Myra Barksdale, Church
  Wedding Hostess
Betty Crockett, Acolyte
  Supervisor
Marilyn Crosby
Ann Curry, Banner
  Coordinator

Members
Eleanor Eubank
Mary French
Chris Garrett
Betty Harbison
Anne Howdeshell
Delaine Kelly

Flower Coordinator
Gail King

Members
Julia Kirkscey
Donna Libby
Lucy McArtor
Greene Miller
Jenny Mitchell
Courtney Sexton
Trudy Simpson

*Flower Distribution
Committee*
Chris Garrett,
  Chairman

Communion Stewards
Glenn Ragland
Mary Sue Pierce
Milton Bennett, Staff

1987

Work Area on Worship
Lynn Holloway,
  Chairman

House
Bill Crosby
Ernest Jetton
Dr. Tom Long
Glenn Ragland

Music
J. J. Doughtie
Donna Libby
Yvonne McCrary
Dr. Len Sumner

Altar Guild Chairman
Mary Louise Caldwell

*Assistant Altar Guild
Chairman*
Anne Howdeshell

Guild Members
Ellen Cockrell
Arrena Cheek
Debbie Dorman
Eleanor Eubank
Betty Harbison
Maggie Hollabaugh
Lynn Holloway
Anne Howdeshell
Carolyn Kelly
Gail King
Julia Kirkscey
Diane Land

Donna Libby
Lucy McArtor
Yvonne McCrary
Greene Miller
Jenny Mitchell
Ramona Seabold
Courtney Sexton
Mimi Steepleton

1988

Worship Work Area
Lynn Holloway,
  Chairman

Ushers
Tom Iverson
Jim Kelly

Altar Guild Chairman
Mary Louise Caldwell

Members
Ruth Carrier,
  Communion
  Steward
Kathy Farnsworth,
  Acolyte Leader
Cindy Lipscomb,
  Acolyte Leader
Anne Howdeshell,
  Assistant Guild
  Chairman
Gail King
Donna Libby
Yvonne McCrary
Sharrel McGrew
Anne Miller
Greene Miller
Mary Sue Pierce
Ramona Seabold
Trudy Simpson

Past and Present Altar Guild Members through 1988
Janie Allen (Mrs. Don)
Myra Barksdale
  (Mrs. Jack C.)
Frances Bates
  (Mrs. Oliver)
Nancy Beasley
  (Mrs. Louis)
Sarah Black
  (Mrs. Robert C.)
Jane Browndyke
  (Mrs. J. N. III)
Ruth Carrier
Arrena Cheek
  (Mrs. Richard C.)
Ellen Cockrell
  (Mrs. Richard G.)
Bobbye Crockett
  (Mrs. Harry G. Jr.)
Marilyn Crosby
  (Mrs. William J.)
Lynn & Doug Cross
Ann and Dud Curry
Debbie Dorman
  (Mrs. Paul)
J. J. Doughtie
  (Mrs. Richard III)
Janice Fly
  (Mrs. Kenneth)
Joan Fox (Mrs. David)
Mary French
  (Mrs. Dewitt C.)
Chris Garrett
  (Mrs. H. Edward)
Karla Grant
  (Mrs. Donald L.)
Sallie Grant
  (Mrs. David L.)
Betty Harbison
  (Mrs. Charles E.)
Betty and Bob Hardin

Betty Herrington
  (Mrs. Clarence C.)
Maggie Hollabaugh
  (Mrs. Robert S.)
Sheila Jayroe
  (Mrs. Jack Jr.)
Kathryn Jennings
Carolyn Kelly
  (Mrs. B. D.)
Delaine Kelly
  (Mrs. Jimmy M.)
Gail King
  (Mrs. W. Scott)
Julia Kirkscey
  (Mrs. David A.)
Diane Land
  (Mrs. Mack A.)
Donna Libby
  (Mrs. David)
Lucy McArtor
Yvonne McCrary
  (Mrs. Conrad E.)
Sharrel McGrew
  (Mrs. Frank A. III)
Robbie McQuiston
  (Mrs. Paul G.)
Mary Lou Medlin
  (Mrs. Theodore W.)
Anne Miller
  (Mrs. Jackie H.)
Greene Miller
  (Mrs. P. D.)
Jenny Mitchell
  (Mrs. John C.)
Ruth Montague
  (Mrs. Charles A. Jr.)
Julia Morrison
  (Mrs. James F.)
Mary Sue Pierce
Adair Rainey
  (Mrs. A. Jackson)
Glenn Ragland
  (Mrs. Tom)

History of Worship: 1982–1994 135

Melinda Rauscher
Ramona Seabold
  (Mrs. John S.)
Courtney Sexton
  (Mrs. Ray O.)
Trudy Simpson
  (Mrs. Warren)
Mimi Steepleton
  (Mrs. Ed)
Nancy Stephenson
  (Mrs. Robert)
Sibyl Sumner
  (Mrs. Len)
Elizabeth Turner
  (Mrs. John)
Sugar Walker
  (Mrs. John III)
Rhonda Wiedman
  (Mrs. John C.)
Patty Williams
  (Mrs. Robert J.)

1989–1990

Work Area on Worship
J. J. Doughtie, Chairman
Julie Brewster
Mary Louise Caldwell,
  Altar Guild
  Chairman
William Crosby, House
  Chairman
Dr. James C. Eoff III
Ernest A. Jetton

Ushers
Jimmy Kelly
Donna Libby
Virginia McClain
W. H. (Bill) Meadows
Fairfax Segner
Dr. Len Sumner
Elizabeth Turner

Ex Officio Members
Milton Bennett
Dr. Maxie D. Dunnam,
  Sr. Minister
Jack Hearn, Director of
  Music
Thomas Machen,
  Chancel Choir
  Director
Emily McAllister,
  Organist

1991

Work Area on Worship
Kathy Clark, Chairman

Ex Officio Staff
Dr. Maxie D. Dunnam,
  Sr. Minister
Jack Hearn, Director of
  Music
Emily McAllister,
  Organist

Members
Jewel Crowson
Debbie Dorman
Tom Iverson, Head of
  Ushers
Bruce Loveless
Virginia McClain
Bill Meadows
Frances Parsons
Ramona Seabold
Trudy Simpson
Mimi Steepleton, Altar
  Guild Chairman
Dr. Clinton Stewart

Altar Guild
Gail King, Flower
  Chairman

Anne Miller, Banner
  Chairman
Carole Watson, Acolyte
  Chairman
Pat Beeson
Arrena Cheek
Kathy Clark
Carolyn Grizzard
Maggie Hollabaugh
Delaine Kelly
Nan Landess
Sharrel McGrew
Marie Roberson
Ramona Seabold
Trudy Simpson
Mimi Steepleton

1992

Worship Work Area
Bubba Clark, Head of
  Ushers
Kathy Clark, Chairman
Jewel Crowson, Funeral
  Guild Co-Chairman
Ken Draffin, Chairman
  of 8:30 A.M. Service
  Committee
Bill Mainord, Drama
  Guild Chairman
Eugenia Trousdale, Fine
  Arts Guild
  Chairman
Virginia Hollon,
  Needlework Guild
  Co-Chairman
Jennifer Jones, Flower
  Guild Chairman
D. J. Meyer, Baptismal
  Guild Chairman
Frances Parsons,
  Needlework
  Co-Chairman

Mimi Steepleton, Altar Chairman
Sugar Walker, Funeral Guild Co-Chairman
Betty Harbison
Bruce Loveless
Bill Meadows
Anne Miller
Greene Miller
Betsy Peck
Trudy Simpson

Ex Officio Staff
Dr. Maxie D. Dunnam, Sr. Minister
Jack Hearn, Director of Music
Emily McAllister, Organist

1993

Work Area on Worship
Christie Clark, Acolyte Chairman
Kathy Clark, Chairman
William "Bubba" Clark, Head of Ushers
Ken Draffin, Chairman of 8:30 A.M. Service
Janice Fly, Banner Guild Chairman
Virginia Hollon, Co-Chairman Needlework Guild
Dianne Latimer, Altar Guild Chairman
Bill Mainord, Chairman, Drama Guild
D. J. Meyer, Baptismal Guild Chairman
Frances Parsons, Co-Chairman Needlework Guild
Dean Scott, Flower Guild Chairman
Eugenia Trousdale, Chairman Fine Art Guild
Jewel Crowson
Scott Little
Bruce Loveless
Betsy Peck
Ramona Seabold
Trudy Simpson
Sugar Walker

9:45 A.M. Worship Committee
Matt Hook, Staff
James Loftin, Staff
Jack Brown
Terry Brown
Kathy Clark
Pam McDaniel
Laura Kimbro
Jean Sproul
Susan Amsler

Ex Officio
Dr. Maxie D. Dunnam, Sr. Minister
Jack Hearn, Director of Music
Emily McAllister, Organist

1994

Work Area on Worship
Lorraine Bradford, Chairman Banner Guild
Jean Branch, Chairman Funeral Guild
Jack Brown, Chairman 9:45 Service
Christie Clark, Acolyte Chairman
Ken Draffin, Chairman 8:30 Service
Mim Duncan, Chairman Baptismal Guild
John C. Ford, Special Services Coordinator
Virginia Hollon, Chairman Needlework
Eddins Hopps, 8:30 Head Usher
Dianne Latimer, Altar Guild Chairman
Bruce Loveless, Usher
Bill Mainord, Chairman Drama Guild
Barbara Melton, Co-Chairman
Keith Parsons, Music Chairman
Trudy Simpson, Chairman
Jean Sproul, Chairman Flower Guild Seabrook
Eugenia Trousdale, Fine Arts Guild Chairman
Carole Watson, Chairman Flower Guild Sanctuary
William Bubba Clark
Jewel Crowson
Loel Hickman
Scott Little

History of Worship: 1982–1994

Staff
Dr. Maxie D. Dunnam,
  Sr. Minister
Jack Hearn, Director of
  Music
Emily McAllister,
  Organist
Matt Hook, 9:45 A.M.
  Music Assistant

Perry Redfearn,
  Associate Director of
  Music and Organist

*Saturday Night Alive
Advisory Committee*
9/10/94
Jim Bybee
Russell Day

Donna and Loel
  Hickman
Sherri Masse
Carla Thompson
Nim Underwood
Pat Whaley, Staff
Lynn White

✣ ✣ ✣

THE ARTISTIC ELEMENTS IN WILSON CHAPEL
Christ United Methodist Church

When the committee that was formed to deal with the design of and the appointments in the new chapel first met, they decided early in that meeting that the new chapel should not only be a room that is used to worship God, but also a room that in its own beauty praises and adores our Creator. They decided that, as much as possible, every element in Wilson Chapel should be a work of art, using natural materials of creation, without losing sight of the function of the chapel. With that thought in mind, the committee proceeded to work with artisans and craftsmen to create windows, chancel furniture, and other appointments for the new chapel.

The I Am Windows. Knowing that the eight windows, 19 by 6 inches in size, would set the theme for the chapel, the committee set out first to come up with a theme for the windows that would be compatible with our church and the sanctuary windows. Drawing upon the book, *Jesus Claims Our Promises* by Dr. Dunnam, they decided to center in on the nature of Christ as found in His *I Am* sayings. The theme for each window then came from the Holy Scriptures.

Looking at the chancel area from the back of the chapel, one sees the first four of the eight windows. To the left of the chancel (on the east side) one sees the first window, and their order follows in clockwise motion.

1. "I am the Resurrection and the Life: he who believes in me, though he die, yet shall he live." (John 11:25)

2. "I am the Bread of Life: he who comes to me shall not hunger, and he who believes in me shall never thirst." (John 6:35)

Mr. and Mrs. Kemmons Wilson.

3. "I am the Vine, you are the branches. He who abides in me, and I in him, he it is that bears much fruit, for apart from me you can do nothing." (John 15:5)

4. "I am come forth from the Father, and am come into the world." (John 16:28)

5. "I am the Good Shepherd. The Good Shepherd lays down his life for His sheep." (John 10:11)

6. "Lo, I am with you always, to the close of the age." (Matt. 28:20)

7. "'Who are you, Lord?' And He said to me, 'I am Jesus of Nazareth whom you are persecuting.'" (Acts 22:8)

8. "You call me 'Master' and 'Lord,' and rightly so, for that is what I am." (John 13:13 NEB)

(The last four windows were installed in January 1990.)

The Chancel Appointments. The pulpit, baptismal font, and the Communion table, symbols of the word, water, and wine, are made of solid mahogany by John Cassibry, sculptor, of Marigold, Mississippi.

The pottery candlesticks, chalice, and paten are handmade by Lee and Pup McCarty, potters, of Marigold, Mississippi. The solid mahogany offering plates were made by Dana Curtis of Memphis. The needlepoint kneelers were designed by Indie Cockerham.

The Chapel Windows of Christ United Methodist Church. There are a total of ten chapel proper windows and one narthex window consisting of over twelve hundred square feet of leaded, handblown glass. The windows were fabricated in the studios of Louisville Art Glass by craftsmen skilled in the age-old technique of hand-fitted cut glass. For seven thousand years, glass has been known as a raw material. Man has practiced the art of glass blowing for two thousand years, and for the last eight hundred years, glass for windows has been blown. The tradition lives on.

The theme for the first window, and what was to become the impetus for the remaining windows, was taken from the revelation of John, the sixteenth chapter and the twenty-eighth verse: "I am come forth from the Father, and am come into the world" (John 16:28).

✥ ✥ ✥

Window Description
This revelation given to the disciples in the latter fleeting moments of the ministry of Jesus was given not only for their benefit and comfort but also faithfully recorded to comfort generations to come.

On other occasions, Jesus had revealed fragments of his manifold nature. On one such occasion, Jesus asked his followers, "Who do you say that I am?" They had given Him several answers earlier when He asked how others identified Him. But when asked directly, Peter answered and said, "You are the Christ, the Son of the Living God!" No one word can describe the name attributed to the self-existent one, I Am; but Jesus, throughout His ministry, revealed the nature of that name through varying comparison. Of these, Jesus proclaimed, "I am the Light of the World," "I am the Way, the Truth, and the Life," "I am the resurrection," "I am the Door," "I am the Good Shepherd," as well as many others.

To fully appreciate the window designs, we must first examine the origin of the name *I Am*. Although mentioned as early as the fifteenth chapter of Genesis: "I am thy Shield, and thy exceeding Great Reward"; the most definitive account occurs in Exodus 3:14, "And God said unto Moses, I Am That I Am: and He said, Thus shalt thou say unto the children of Israel. I Am hath sent me unto you" (KJV).

It is interesting that God revealed Himself privately to Moses as I Am That I Am, yet publicly to the children of Israel as I Am only. One can draw from this that not only is God the Creator of all that is, and all that is to come, the Procreator of the beginning of all things great and small, but that He also takes interest and control in the course of events, even unto the falling of a sparrow, and thus desires a personal relationship with humankind on an individual basis.

This brings us full circle back to the thesis of the first window, "I came forth from the Father, and am come into the world" (John 16:28 KJV).

To fully illustrate this passage in visual form, we felt it absolutely necessary to draw a connection between the Old and New Testaments, such that symbols representing the Father or the law would be incorporated with symbols of the Son of Life. Jesus came to show us how to live, not by the letter of the law, but by the intent of the law.

Symbolism. There is a natural progression of symbols located within the central band of vertical warm colors. Starting at the top of the window, the first symbol is the tablet of stone, the Ten Commandments. An immediate connection is made with the Old Testament and the law. "I am the Lord thy God . . . Thou shalt have no other gods before me" (Exod. 20:2–3 KJV). Progressing downward, one is met with the outline of a descending dove. The Holy Spirit or the Spirit of God has a double connotation, denoting both the Old as well as the New Testaments. "And the Spirit of God moved upon the face of the waters" (Gen. 1:2 KJV). "And lo, the heavens were opened unto him, and he saw the Spirit of God descending like a dove, and lighting upon him" (Matt. 3:16 KJV). At this point the design, in symbolic content, starts to bridge the Old and New Testaments. One is reminded that we are to worship in spirit and in truth; as it were, the spirit of the law.

The next progressive symbol is the seven-branched candlestick. This represents the practice of the law: the lighting of the candles, the trimming of the wicks, the everyday application of what we hold to be the truth. It is through the practice of experience that new light is shed and greater understanding perceived.

At this juncture in the design, one is met with the visage of Jesus Christ. His left hand is raised, making contact with symbols of the law and of the Father. His right hand is lowered, as in reaching down to the creation of the world. The motion of this gesture serves to direct the viewer's eye from the spiraling forms at the top of the window, diagonally downward. This diagonal movement is reinforced by flowing shapes that represent a river. One is reminded of the river, which flows out from the throne of God. "And he shewed me a pure river of water of life, clear as crystal, proceeding out of the throne of God and of the Lamb" (Rev. 22:1 KJV).

The symbol of water unifies the Father and the Son further, and also alludes to baptism. If one follows this river along its course downward, one will come to a palm branch. This single branch represents the world. A palm denotes a respite in the desert, its lush foliage is pleasing in contrast with the otherwise harsh landscape. Its branches were used as a symbol of praise and honor when Jesus entered into Jerusalem. The heralding crowd cast them down in His path. This they did because they supposed that He had come to break the bondage of their Roman yoke. However, their praise was hollow. He came not to establish a kingdom among people, but rather to set up a kingdom in the hearts of men and women. In this sense, the palm branch represents the immediate concerns of the world rather than eternal concerns. The separation of the palm branch to the left of the vertical band of warm colors represents the fact that Jesus came into the world but was not of the world.

As one moves into the lower portion of the window, one finds an open Bible with the Greek letters Alpha and Omega. The primary inference of this symbol is taken from the following verse: "And the Word was made flesh, and dwelt among us. . ." (John 1:14 KJV).

Because the Word was preexisting, was made flesh and dwelt among men, the Word must necessarily be the same yesterday, today, and forever. Therefore, the beginning and the end must be the same. For this reason, the Alpha and Omega have been used to denote the Christ; the I Am which dwelt among humanity. One must also consider that the Bible is open or divided, and yet one. This represents the two Great Testaments, the giving of the letter of the law and the law revealed.

The symbol at the base of the window is a lamb. The lamb is a testimony to the fact that Jesus became our sacrificial Lamb and took upon Himself the sins of the world. Because the lamb is placed at the base of the window, it is the closest symbol to the viewer. The lamb symbolically is within the reach of even a small child and represents the ultimate sacrifice and sole reason Jesus Christ came into the world.

Secondary symbolism not readily discerned by the eye has also been incorporated into the design. The spiraling mass at the top of the window represents the

Creation, the vortex of which is the eye of God. "And God saw every thing that he had made, and, behold, it was very good" (Genesis 1:31 KJV).

Coming from this spiral is the diagonal image of a river which gives rise to the greenery at the bottom of the window. One is reminded of the seed which fell on good ground and that it had to be watered to bring forth fruit. Pictured directly behind Christ is a rectangular shape which represents a door. Jesus Christ is the Way; He is the Door to the Father. "Ask, and it shall be given you; seek, and ye shall find; knock, and it shall be opened unto you" (Matthew 7:7 KJV).

Because the shape of the door includes vertical edges that are not parallel to one another, but instead narrows at one end, one can draw inspiration from the seventh chapter of Matthew. It is mentioned that wide is the gate and broad is the way that leads to destruction, but narrow is the way that leads to life.

The final segment of symbolism rests in the flame shapes rising from the feet of the Christ figure. This draws our attention to the final book of the written word, where it is noted, "And his feet like unto fine brass, as if they burned in a furnace" (Rev. 1:15 KJV). It is in this chapter that Scripture is mentioned which pulls the symbolism of the window even closer. John writes: "And I turned to see the voice that spake with me. And being turned, I saw seven golden candlesticks; And in the midst of the seven candlesticks, one like unto the Son of man, clothed with a garment down to the foot, and girt about the paps with a golden girdle" (Rev. 1:12–13 KJV).

In conclusion, the window gives us a broad overview of John 16:28, focusing on Christ's desire to reveal the Father through His actions. The broader theme *I Am* is explored in endless variation and carried into the remaining windows. If we explore the possibility of taking the name I Am That I Am and letting the separate identities take on the connotation of promise and performance, of outward declaration and inward reconciliation, one can recognize the overall theme of the windows to be broken down as follows.

The four windows flanking the altar deal with things celestial. Communion themes are adapted by using the statements "I Am the Bread of Life" and "I Am the True Vine." These themes are explored in the windows directly facing the altar. The two windows facing the congregation deal with the Word made flesh and the Resurrection.

The remaining four windows deal with things earthly or the performance of things celestial. These windows relate to our response to the call of Christ and our relationship with Him.

Composition. The composition of the windows, when broken down into its simplest elements serves to enhance the architecture of the building. The vertical band of warm colors in the amber to red range compliments the height of the window openings. Since this band is somewhat narrower than the actual width of the window, it acts to slenderize each opening, giving them more of a lancet feel. The central image is placed strategically to pull all three sections of a window together. The swirling colors that spiral outward beyond the boundaries of the windows serves as a unifying element that will act to pull all eight openings together through the introduction, of a greater but common component. Since this element expands beyond the plane of each window, it becomes a common factor relevant to all eight, conjoining them somewhere in the viewers' imagination. This swirl flows inward in the four altar windows, representing the inflow of the Spirit to the individual. In the remaining windows, the swirl flows outward, representing the abundant outward flow of the believer to others.

Color. By keeping the color of the windows fairly purist in its approach, a scheme is set up that will be enduring and timeless. By staying away from decorator colors, we are eliminating the dated look associated with vogueness. The vivid colors give direction and impact to both the composition and the theme. Various nuances have been set up to provide ranges, from subtle shifts in color to jumps that provide directional static tension.

Style. Style is an overused generic term which has come to mean more than the word actually implies. In visual arts, style may be used to imply the presence of common characteristics associated with a certain artistic period, approach, or treatment of a concept. While the design holds similarities with the works of C. Z. Laurence and Georg Meisterman, these similarities are reflections of their influence upon the artist. In the final analysis, the design is emblazoned with an unmistakable signature. The imagery, broad outline of the figure, and color use all reflect the hand of the artist.

A review of the artist's reflections is included at the close. But, first let us consider the remaining windows.

I Am the Resurrection and the Life. As this title (taken from John 11:25) suggests, this window deals with the promise of life eternal. Other references are found in John 10:17–18, 27–28 (KJV).

John 10:17	"Therefore doth my Father love me, because I lay down my life, that I might take it again."
John 10:18	"No man taketh it from me, but I lay it down of myself. I have power to lay it down, and I have power to take it again. This commandment have I received of my Father."
John 10:27	"My sheep hear my voice, and I know them, and they follow me:"
John 10:28	"And I give unto them eternal life; and they shall never perish, neither shall any man pluck them out of my hand."

Starting at the top of the window, one first notices the form of a pillar. This recalls that moment when Jesus rebuked the money changers and sellers of sacrificial animals at the temple and in reply to their question regarding His authority, he stated, "Destroy this temple, and in three days I will raise it up" (John 2:19 KJV). They supposed that he was speaking of the temple, but he was foretelling his death and resurrection. Just below the pillar's capital is the form of a butterfly intertwined with the shape of flames. As a butterfly emerges from a cocoon, its form changed, so also is the resurrection. The flames represent the power of this mystery. Paul wrote in his epistle to the Philippians: "That I may know him, and the power of his resurrection," Paul continues; however, "and the fellowship of his sufferings, being made conformable unto his death; If by any means I might attain unto the resurrection of the dead" (3:10–11 KJV).

To express this connection between the power of the Resurrection and the fellowship of his sufferings, the next two images have been drawn upon. To the left of the butterfly are three crosses, speaking of the crucifixion—two of which are amber in color, the third is a cool blue. The blue cross represents the thief who rejected Christ. The amber cross in the foreground is the cross of Christ's crucifixion, and the amber cross in the background speaks of the thief who accepted Christ. This thief received the promise, "To day, shalt thou be with me in paradise" (Luke 23:43 KJV). The next image that deals with Christ's suffering is the crown of thorns. The thorns have been illustrated in a form such that they create a halo around the head of Christ. The thorns also take on the shape of a laurel wreath, a crown given to a victor.

The Christ figure stands, both arms downstretched, the nail prints of the

I Am the Resurrection and the Life.

Crucifixion visible in the palms. Regardless of where the viewer stands, the figure appears to focus its gaze elsewhere. The expression is one of blamelessness. The symmetry of the figure speaks of the ease of the soul passing from mortality to immortality. The left hand and right hand are counterbalanced against one another. Dropping from the right shoulder of the figure is a garment. It appears to wrap around behind the figure and reemerge, dropping diagonally across the knees. This garment represents a shroud, and because it changes color from red to almost transparent, it reinforces the fact that corruption must put on incorruption.

At the feet of Christ is a circular form. This alludes to the stone, which was rolled away from the tomb. Because it is at Christ's feet, we must observe that death is just a stepping stone to a higher existence. Following the circumference of this stone are the arched wings of a phoenix. The phoenix is a mythical creature which is said to have raised to new life out of its own ashes. In its talons is a serpent, representing that death has lost its sting.

The final symbol in this window is found at its lower left corner. There is a small branch supporting a bud and a pomegranate. The bud represents the promise of immortality; the pomegranate, because of its many seeds, speaks of the surety of rejuvenation. The fact that the pomegranate, in pagan mythology, was attributed to Proserpina and symbolized her return to earth in the spring, further defines its use in Christian symbolism as representing the Resurrection. The fact that it is an adopted symbol from paganism adds a little insight to this closing quote, speaking of the Resurrection, "It is sown in dishonour; it is raised in glory"(1 Cor. 15:43 KJV).

I Am the True Vine. The title of this window is taken from John, the fifteenth chapter and verse one: "I am the true vine, and my Father is the husbandman" (KJV).

The obvious connotation of the vine would be to allude to Communion; therefore we have started the imagery with that in mind. At the top of the window is a descending dove, representing the Holy Spirit. At the Last Supper in the Upper Room, Christ exhorted the disciples "this do in remembrance of me," speaking of the act of Communion. Jesus also stated, "But the Comforter, which is the Holy Ghost, whom the Father will send in my name, he shall teach you all things, and bring all things to your remembrance, whatsoever I have said unto you" (John 14:26 KJV). The Holy Spirit overshadows the Holy Sacrament of Communion, and the Spirit's presence is essential to Christian beliefs.

The next major image is that of a vine with fruit. If one looks carefully, you can see the ingrafting of a small branch held in place by bindings. To the left of the vine is a pruning hook. We are reminded of Christ's words, "Abide in me, and I in you. As the branch cannot bear fruit of itself, except it abide in the vine; no more can ye, except ye abide in me" (John 15:4 KJV). The apostle Paul further expanded in Romans 11:20, 23: "because of unbelief they were broken off" and further, "and they also, if they abide not still in unbelief, shall be grafted in." God's severity is tempered by His mercy toward those who reject Him. If they would but turn from their unbelief, they will surely be received anew. The image of the vine springs forth from an open Bible. As it were, the roots of the vine are the living Word. Located in front of the Bible is a chalice and host completing the imagery of wine and bread, relative to Communion.

But the vine encompasses more than just Communion. The vine also denotes the life of the Church. Every plant bears fruit after its own kind. The vines of a grape vineyard do not produce cucumbers. Likewise, the believer engrafted into the Church must bear fruit of the name of Jesus Christ. Also, as the vine experiences pruning and the cutting back of dead branches in winter, likewise Christ deals with His Church. Finally, one must consider spring and new life. Therefore, a shell, the symbol of baptism, has been placed to the upper left of the Bible. Through baptism we are made one with the experience of His name, death, and life. Through Communion we experience the mystery of His sacrifice.

Christ being the true vine came forth to reveal the love of the Father and to reveal the true intent of the law. Without the revelation of the true intent of the law, sin was covered by a cloak. That Christ could prove Himself the true vine, miracles were done in the sight of men. Jesus said, "If I had not done among them the works which none other man did, they had not had sin: but now have they both seen and hated both me and my Father" (John 15:24 KJV). Because miracles of a necessity were given to justify His claim, Christ's first miracle seemed suitable for inclusion in the artwork. Is it a coincidence that as a confirmation of Christ as the true vine

I Am the True Vine.

the first miracle performed by Jesus was the changing of water into wine? To illustrate this miracle, six water pots have been pictured along with a wreath of flowers normally worn by the bride and bridegroom. For it was at the marriage at Cana that Jesus performed the first miracle.

At the base of the window there is illustrated a pile of burning branches. This speaks of those who are pruned from the vine and cast into the fire. The design could well have ended here but for the remembrance of the verse of Scripture that states "Moreover the law entered, that the offence might abound. But where sin abounded, grace did much more abound" (Rom. 5:20 KJV). That the mercies of the living God be justified, there is a final symbol, and that of a gourd. Through the image of a gourd the viewer is reminded of the story of Jonah, how Jonah prophesied destruction against Nineveh and went without the city to wait and see. The people of Nineveh repented and God withheld his judgment which greatly displeased Jonah. Therefore, God caused a vine, a gourd, to grow up to give Jonah shade and then destroyed it. Jonah had pity on the gourd and God spoke to him out of that example:

> Then said the Lord, Thou hast had pity on the gourd, for which thou hast not laboured, neither madest it grow; which came up in a night, and perished in a night: And should not I spare Nineveh, that great city, wherein are more than sixscore thousand persons that cannot discern between their right hand and their left hand; and also much cattle? (Jon. 4:10–11 KJV).

Jesus Christ, the true vine, is a vine of pity and forgiveness. As God went to a great extent to send Jonah to provoke Nineveh to repentance, how much more so will He deal with those who are knowledgeable of His mercies, those who can discern between their right and left hands.

I Am the Bread of Life. The basis for this theme is taken from John 6:35 KJV: "I am the bread of life: he that cometh to me shall never hunger; and he that believeth on me shall never thirst." Jesus upbraided the multitude because they sought Him for the sake of bread whereby they might be filled. He further exhorted them not to seek after sustenance which perishes, but rather to seek after that which is eternal. The crowd desired to know what they must do to work the works of God, or rather to labor for this bread. Jesus replied, "This is the work of God, that ye believe on him whom he hath sent" (John 6:29 KJV). Man's labor therefore is to believe, and this act of belief must be a daily one. The act of believing must be nurtured and labored after, just as a seed must be nurtured and labored after to produce bread. Therefore this window depicts the natural cycle of seed from sowing to the finished product.

The first image is that of a hand sowing seed. When one sows seed, one is actually sowing a promise that the seed will mature and produce grain. Likewise we must believe in the promises of God, and it is this very act that causes us to partake of the Bread of Life. The second image is one of a stalk of grain, of mature fruit. This denotes the fact that whatsoever God promises He is well able to perform. If one follows this stalk downward, it becomes obvious that the plant arises from an open Bible. The symbolism of the plant rooted in the word of God, however, will be discussed later. Let us first consider the scythe, the next symbol in the series. God gives to all people liberally; it rains on the just and the unjust alike. But the revelation of His Word is given to those who seek after knowledge and wisdom. No one appreciates the harvest quite like those who labored in the reaping. Therefore, the scythe stands for the believer who is diligent to study and show himself or herself approved. "Study to shew thyself approved unto God, a workman that needeth not to be ashamed, rightly dividing the word of truth" (2 Tim. 2:15 KJV).

The next image is that of a winnowing basket. It is through the tossing of the grain that the chaff is blown away by the wind. In a Christian's walk, it is often the upheavals in life that bring out that within us that is not Christlike. By allowing this chaff to be blown away we are putting off the "old man" and are putting on the new.

> That ye put off concerning the former conversation the old man, which is corrupt according to the deceitful lusts; And be renewed in the spirit of your mind; And that ye put on the new man, which after God is created in righteousness and true holiness (Eph. 4:22–24 KJV).

Having discussed the significance of the imagery of the scythe and the winnowing basket we return to the

I Am the Bread of Life.

stalk of grain which visually connects those symbols to the central image of the window. This is the pictorial representation of an open Bible. The root of all of our sustenance is the Word, and the Word is Christ. The Bible is pictured open denoting the fact that the call to come is to "whosoever will." It displays a red bookmark indicating the first step of faith required of the believer. It is a simple act recorded in the Book of Romans. "That if thou shalt confess with thy mouth the Lord Jesus, and shalt believe in thine heart that God hath raised him from the dead, thou shalt be saved" (Rom. 10:9 KJV). This small seed act of faith will give rise to the full revelation of God.

If the viewer looks closely, it can be seen that the open Bible is superimposed in front of the Ten Commandments. It obscures all but four of the commandments and these are the first, fifth, sixth, and tenth. The first commandment declares that we should have no other gods before God. The fifth requires us to honor father and mother. The sixth instructs us not to kill. The tenth exhorts us not to covet our neighbor's possessions.

These four commandments could be paraphrased as the love commandments; love God, love family, love life, and love our neighbor as ourselves. Jesus extolled these virtues. If we are to partake of the Bread of Life, then we must follow in His example.

Located just below the open Bible is a millstone. A millstone is used to grind grain into flour, to break the grain down to a digestible form. The Word, the Bread, likewise comes to us in small quantities.

> Whom shall he teach knowledge? and whom shall he make to understand doctrine? them that are weaned from the milk, and drawn from the breasts. For precept must be upon precept, precept upon precept; line upon line, line upon line; here a little, and there a little: (Isa. 28:9–10 KJV).

The next image is that of a loaf of bread. It represents the final phase in the cycle of grain. In Communion the bread is broken and each believer partakes of a small portion of that broken bread. We fellowship with the suffering of Christ and are renewed through meditating on Him. The suffering which we partake of is minute when compared to His. The Bread of Life is twofold. It has a sacrificial side represented by the unleavened bread, as well as joy represented by bread which has been leavened. Therefore the loaf as pictured is actually a composite illustration of a leavened loaf of bread and a flat, unleavened bread. The idea of two types of bread is further alluded to by the depiction of an olive branch to the lower right of the loaf. From olives is derived oil, and oil is a biblical reference to gladness. "Thou lovest righteousness, and hatest wickedness; therefore God, thy God, hath anointed thee with the oil of gladness above thy fellows" (Ps. 45:7 KJV).

The last bit of symbolism in the window returns the viewer to the parable of the sower. In that parable some seed fell on rocky ground and some on thorny ground, but some fell on good ground and sprang forth and remained fruitful.

The rocky ground is literally pictured by the round rock-like forms in the lower left corner. The thorny ground is represented by thorn forms surrounded by flames, which ties in the parable of the tares and the punishment of the wicked. The good ground is represented by the green leaf forms springing up at the lower right corner of the window. Segments of the green spiral upward through the design returning the viewer to the origin of the design, a hand sowing seeds.

I Am the Good Shepherd. The title of this window is taken from John 10:14; "I am the good shepherd, and know my sheep, and am known of mine" (KJV). The purpose of this window is to show the nature of Jesus Christ which is loving and caring.

The first symbol in this window is a shape of which recalls the outline of a crescent moon. The moon speaks of the night season. The fact that it is a crescent moon illustrates the point that outside factors affect its appearance. The sun lights half of the moon, and the earth casts a shadow on the remaining half. Christians are sinners saved by grace. Christians do have the light of Christ but are also influenced by the shadow of their own earthly nature. When one considers that the devil "as a roaring lion, walketh about, seeking whom he may devour"; (1 Pet. 5:8 KJV) and that by our very nature we are bound to humanity and carnality: "For I know that in me (that is, in my flesh,) dwelleth no good thing: for to will is present with me; but how to perform that which is good I find not" (Rom. 7:18 KJV); then one can understand the exasperated words of Paul,

I Am the Good Shepherd.

"O wretched man that I am! who shall deliver me from the body of this death?" (Rom. 7:24 KJV).

We have all felt the same when faced with our shortcomings, but we do have consolation and refuge in Jesus Christ the Good Shepherd. That crescent moon represents the struggle between our own flesh and our will to do good. The devil as a roaring lion is depicted by the stars in the background that make up the constellation of Leo the lion. In the forefront of it all stands Christ holding a small lamb. His attention is not diverted by the flesh or the devil; He sees only the innocent and helpless lamb. Jesus cradles the lamb in His left arm holding it close to His heart. In His right hand He holds a staff, an instrument used for guiding and retrieving lost sheep. The Shepherd is ever vigilant to protect and nurture His flock.

Kneeling at the feet of Jesus is a small child. The viewer is reminded of Christ's command, "Suffer the little children to come unto me" (Mark 10:14 KJV). Except we become as a small child we shall not enter into the kingdom. The Shepherd's will is to protect those that are vulnerable; we must therefore take on the nature of a child in order to invoke his protection. In the face of adversity we have two options. We can attempt to stand on our own reasoning or we can humble ourselves before Christ as a child and allow Him to be the redeemer.

Just below the central figure of Christ and the child are a yoke and a cross superimposed one against the other. If we will take up our cross and follow after Him then He will be there to be yoked together with us, to see us through. A prized team of oxen is said to be composed of one strong spirited ox and one that is slow and steady. If we will but take life's circumstances one step at a time and be steady and faithful in all that we do, then He will be there to be the strong one to bear the brunt of the load.

The next image is that of a fish. The fish has been used to symbolize Christ because the five Greek letters that form the word "fish" are the initial letters of the five words "Jesus Christ God's Son Savior." The fish was often used in early Christian art and was the method of identifying other believers in times of persecution. A Christian, when meeting others who were strangers, would draw an arc in the dirt. If the strangers bisected this arc with one of their own, the resulting image was a crude fish; this was a sign that they were among believers. The flame shapes at the base of the window represent the persecution of believers throughout the ages. Even through the bright red and amber color of the flame shapes, the arcs of the fish stand out. One is reminded that whenever two or more are gathered in His name that He is in their midst. The Shepherd knows His sheep. He hears their cry in times of trouble.

I Am Jesus of Nazareth. This window draws its inspiration from the twenty-second chapter of Acts. This chapter deals with Paul's account of his own conversion. His journey to Damascus was interrupted by a wondrous visitation. A great light shown upon him such that he was blinded by its brightness; and he heard the voice of our Lord speaking "Saul, Saul why persecutest thou me?" When Paul inquired as to the person speaking the reply was given "I am Jesus of

Nazareth, whom thou persecutest." It seems odd that Christ would identify His name with His home prior to His ministry. Could He not have replied that He was the Christ or the Jesus who was crucified in Jerusalem? His definitive reply, however, was to identify Himself to Paul as a Man of humble beginnings. Obviously, this persona as Jesus of Nazareth is descriptive in part of the greater "I Am That I Am." It is reassuring to know that the Christ is very much connected to and, in fact, is conjoined to the humble beginnings of Jesus of Nazareth.

Little is known about the life Jesus experienced prior to his ministry except that He was a carpenter. Since Jesus received no formal training such as Paul received at the feet of Gamaliel, His teachings were drawn from everyday experiences. It is from these teachings that we can receive an insight concerning His early years. Specifically, the parables were stories that illustrated a point on a very practical level. One can imagine when considering the story of the rich man, who was increased in goods and had need of nothing, that Jesus drew this story from life's experience. The story states that this man planned to have his barns torn down and have larger ones built to accommodate his increase; however, his life was taken suddenly and his earthly labors were for naught. One can imagine a wealthy man with such plans discussing the details of the project with a local carpenter to contract a portion of the work and then suddenly death interrupts his plans. Could Jesus have been this carpenter? Could the story have some basis in real life? We can only

I Am Jesus of Nazareth.

speculate. However, it is easy to see how the parables could have been drawn from Jesus' own experiences prior to His ministry. Therefore, these simple stories have been drawn upon to illustrate the earthly, human connotation of Jesus of Nazareth.

The first symbol is that of the pearl of great price. Jesus likened the kingdom of heaven to a merchant seeking pearls. When he found one pearl of great price he sold all that he had and purchased it. The next image is that of a sparrow. Jesus taught that if a sparrow falls in a field that the Father knows it and that the very hairs of our head are numbered. How much more then are we worth than a sparrow? Following this image is that of a fig tree. Jesus used this common tree to impress the point that if it is easy to foretell the coming of spring by the leaves of the fig tree that His coming will be preceded by signs as well.

At the base of the fig tree are two lamps. One has a flame indicating that it is full of oil; the other is without. These two lamps refer to the parable of the ten virgins, five with oil in their lamps and five without. The parable of the virgins is drawn from a Jewish marriage ritual. By tradition, the bridegroom was to come during the night to steal away with his bride and escort her to the feast. The bride's virgins were to keep watch with lamps to herald the coming of the bridegroom. Jesus used this common tradition which He had most assuredly seen on occasion to emphasize the fact that believers should be ever diligent in their service.

Just below the lamps are ten circular shapes. These round forms represent coins and are symbolic of the parable of the ten talents. The wise servants increased their masters' profit by investing and trading the money wherewith they were entrusted; however, the foolish servant hid the coin which he had been given and received no increase. This is a simple story dealing with the principle of working with what you have perchance to increase it rather then letting what you have lie idle. To the right of these coins is a depiction of a small village, which represents Nazareth. Nazareth was a hill-set village that overlooked the plain of Jezreel. One can almost imagine a reference to Nazareth when Jesus spoke, "Ye are the light of the world. A city that is set on a hill cannot be hid" (Matt. 5:14 KJV).

It was in this city that Jesus practiced His trade as a carpenter. People came to Him to make ox yokes, to hew beams, for plows, and all manner of woodwork. The tools He would have used include the bow saw and mallet, among others. Pictured in the upper section of the lower panel are these two instruments. They represent the fact that Jesus was a man acquainted with hard work; He earned His living with His hands. Surely His hands were rough and callused, but yet, they were gentle enough to caress a small child, to comfort the sick, to touch the eyes of the blind, to minister to others.

At the lower section of the window is a lamb. One is reminded of the parable of the man who had one hundred sheep but one was lost. He left the ninety-nine to seek that which was lost, and when he had recovered it he called his friends together to rejoice with him. Jesus used this parable to express the joy in the presence of the angels of God over one sinner that comes to repentance.

The least of all of the images but perhaps the most important is that of a reed or cattail. Jesus used the minimization of a reed shaken by the wind to chide the multitude concerning John. If they followed John, who was more than a reed shaken by the wind, then of what was John worthy? He was more than a prophet; he was the messenger of Christ. If John were indeed a messenger of God, the forerunner of Christ, then why did they not believe him concerning Jesus? Why did John, himself, while in prison, send his disciples saying, "Art thou he that should come? or look we for another?" (Luke 7:19 KJV). We all have the potential to doubt, especially under desperate circumstances. We can experience unbelief and become as a reed shaken by the wind, turning wherever the wind would blow.

As Jesus looked out over the multitude one can imagine that His memories as a young boy sitting on a hillside overlooking the grasses of the plain shaking and waving in the wind would come to mind. Jesus stated that if the works that were done in Judea and Galilee were done among the gentiles then they would have repented. The nation of Israel as a whole confessed godliness with their mouths but failed to believe in their hearts. As Christians, our fervent prayer when faced with barriers of unbelief should be to follow the example of the father that came to Jesus distraught over the illness of his son. Jesus said, "If thou canst believe, all things are possible to him that believeth." The father of the child cried out with tears in his eyes, "Lord, I believe; help thou mine unbelief" (Mark 9:23–24 KJV). This Jesus of Nazareth was a man acquainted with the common suffering and hardship of everyday life. He didn't present treatises and complex dissertations to comfort and instruct but rather chose the commonplace, the things of home, and presented them as jewels of revelation.

I Am Master and Lord. "Ye call me Master and Lord: and ye say well; for so I am" (John 13:13 KJV). Jesus made this definitive statement concerning himself at the Passover feast of the Last Supper. He made it prior to washing the disciples' feet and stated that "if I then, your Lord and Master, have washed your feet; ye also ought to wash one another's feet." This example was important, for it expressed, in real terms, that the greatest should be the servant of all. Likewise, the servant is not greater than his Lord. This declaration of equality among believers and in the eyes of God came hundreds of years before our own Declaration of Independence which states, "All men are created equal."

Philippians 2:5–7 states: "Let this mind be in you, which was also in Christ Jesus: Who being in the form of God, thought it not robbery to be equal with God: But made himself of no reputation, and took upon him the form of a servant, and was made in the likeness of men" (KJV).

That Jesus Christ could be equal with God and yet equal with humankind makes Him the sole mediator of our faith, and further, that he, "being found in fashion as a man, he humbled himself, and became obedient unto death, even the death of the cross" (Phil. 2:8 KJV), through His surrender, became the sole propitiation for our sins.

The first symbol at the top of the window is that of a lamb holding a crossed staff. This image directly relates to Jesus as the slain Lamb who was obedient unto death. The next central image is that of a regal crown which is interlaced with a crown of thorns. Suffering and exaltation go hand in hand, and Christ is our chief example. He was Master and Lord when He entered triumphantly into Jerusalem and He was Master and Lord when He hung suspended between earth and sky on the cross.

In the original Greek the word translated Master is *Didaskoalos* which literally means instructor or teacher; the word translated Lord is *Kurios* which means supreme controller. Jesus Christ is the supreme controller of our lives and He does so to teach and instruct. For this reason, the Christ figure has been posed such that one hand reaches upward toward a mass of swirling stars and the other hand reaches downward to man. This gesture is as if the figure is crying out, "If I the Master and Lord of the universe can keep the planets in their orbits and can arrange the stars, can I not also be the Master and Lord of the lives of men?" This figure stands still stretched between heaven and earth and His hands bear the scars of His sacrifice. If the viewer looks carefully, there are circular marks in the palms of the figure's hands.

At the feet of the figure are a water pitcher and a basin recalling that the Master washed the feet of His disciples. Foot washing is an Eastern custom intended to refresh a weary traveler by cleansing soiled feet. Today something as

I Am Master and Lord.

simple as a kind word can have the same effect. We can wash one another's feet symbolically by uplifting them, encouraging them, and refreshing them with kind words. Sometimes the everyday worries we face settle upon our hearts and minds like dust physically affecting our composure and our health. Just a single word spoken in season could be all that is needed to refresh someone weary and soiled with life's dust.

At the base of the window is a rooster. This signifies the denial of Peter the night that Jesus was taken. In the midst of the turmoil of the arrest, Peter denied Jesus three times even to the extent of cursing His name. But what is significant is the fact that our failure does not affect God's master plan. Jesus Christ is still Master and Lord regardless of how many times we fail.

I Am with You Always. "Go ye therefore, and teach all nations, baptizing them in the name of the Father, and of the Son, and of the Holy Ghost: Teaching them to observe all things whatsoever I have commanded you: and, lo, I am with you alway, even unto the end of the world. Amen" (Matt. 28:19–20 KJV).

This window deals with the omnipresence of Christ and His influence on the Church through the ages.

The descending dove interlaced with the shape of a flame represents Pentecost and the birth of the Church. Below the dove is a circular form with four crosses each pointing to different compass points. This represents Christ's command to spread the gospel to the four corners of the earth. Next is a scroll that signifies the giving of the written gospel through the inspiration of the Holy Spirit. These three images represent the early history of the Church.

The center of the window deals with the Reformation and the rise of Protestantism. The major image is that of Gutenberg's printing press which was the starting point of making the written word available to all people. If one looks carefully, the center vertical arm and top beam of the press conform to the image of a cross. Attached to the top of that cross is a small rectangular plate that represents Pilate's declaration in jest, "Jesus Christ, King of the Jews." This first declaration by the Gentiles may have been in jest, but it heralded the movement of the Church away from Judaism and recalls another declaration made by a Gentile centuries later—Martin Luther's declaration of faith nailed to the door of the Wittenburg castle church. Behind this cross is pictured the tables of stone, the Ten Commandments. We must recall that the first tables of stone were carved by the hand of God. This set was broken by Moses when he saw that the children of Israel worshiped the golden calf. The second set was carved by Moses himself. "And the Lord said unto Moses, Write thou these words . . . and he wrote upon the tables the words of the covenant, the ten commandments" (Exod. 34:27–28 KJV).

The giving of the written word through writings of the apostles as led by the Holy Spirit can be likened to the first set of commandments. It was by the inspiration of God that Gutenburg developed the printing press, and thus the printed word can be likened to the second set of commandments. Was the sin of the church during the dark ages any less than the sin of Israel and the golden calf? Because of the sin of the church, God raised up a new generation through the Reformation. This included the founders of Methodism. The cross of the printing press is flanked on the left by two flames duplicating the logo of the Methodist movement.

Just below the press is an outline of the State of Tennessee and below that a horse and rider. This represents the spread of the gospel in the new world and gives recognition to early circuit rider preachers who braved untold hardships to further the gospel. The next image is that of an open book. This book with blank pages represents the continuing presence of Christ within the Church and that which is yet to be accomplished in His will. At the base of the window is a depiction of the building of Christ United Methodist Church. Its spire stands as a monumental testament to all that see it that Christ is with us always.

The Narthex Window. The theme of this window is based on Malachi 4:2: "But unto you that fear my name shall the Sun of righteousness arise with healing in his wings" (KJV).

It was necessary that the narthex window have similarities with the chapel windows but that it should also exhibit a uniqueness of its own. It has a similar movement to the chapel windows, including a spiral with strong diagonal lines. However, this movement is not reinforced with color; it is emphasized with light only. It is appropriate that the window that deals with the "Sun of righteousness" is emphatic in its interplay with light. The facets and

I Am with You Always.

History of Worship: 1982–1994

textures of the glass were intended to capture light and express its energy and form from every angle. The window literally transforms exterior light into hundreds of independent flashes, glinting with illumination a source thousands of miles away. Likewise Christ, whose presence can only be seen as glimpses through the lives of believers, is the source of light. Those who call upon His name are able to experience the healing light of His word and, as followers, have the responsibility to reflect His light and love to others.

✣ ✣ ✣

A Note from the Artist

Working with the committee responsible for the stained glass was an opportunity rather than a task. Their direction and encouragement were major influences in the development of the art for the windows. Without their support and guidance, the windows would not have obtained the level of artistic expression evident in their final form. Their requests for change and modification during the preliminary design phase were rational and expressed sensitivity to the art form. Beset by their expectations, as well as my own, the designs began to exhibit a wealth of inspiration; inspiration drawn from the camaraderie of the committee as well as my own experience with Christ. The theme of the windows, based on the *I Am* sayings of Christ, seemed to explode with possibilities. Just as I thought I had a grasp on the implications of a certain Scripture or visual form, it would take a tangent and erupt in a thousand different directions. Due

The Narthex Window.

to the infinite revelation of the word of God, the major task was not where to start but rather where to stop. When dealing with a specific theme, there was a wealth of Christian art and symbolism from which to draw. However, in most cases the images or symbols that were standard lacked the impact needed to express the full embodiment of the Scriptures. Nevertheless, they were starting points from which to build.

Once the basic form of a window was laid out, and certain given images sketched in, the design would take on the appearance of a shadow of something greater. The forms would lose their immediate significance and would take on new meaning. A perfect example would be the sketch of Gutenburg's printing press. Once the basic form was drafted it became a minimal composition of lines and surfaces. By reducing its form to its simplest terms one could allow its elements to reestablish lines of importance giving rise to new surfaces. It was amazing how the horizontal and vertical surfaces of the press leaped out to form a cross, a separate form with its own importance. I encourage the viewers to seek their own reconciliation between the visual forms and their own experience with Christ. The interpretation of the work must find its basis in that part of the viewer where heart and mind and the senses merge to form a single experience.

It is my hope that the windows exhibit the same sense of growth and transformation to the viewer as they did for me during their design.

Wilson Chapel Windows Information
The designer and person who made and cut the pieces for the stained-glass windows:

Louisville Art Glass Studio
1110 Baxter Avenue
P.O. Box 4665
Louisville, KY 40204

Mr. Mickael McCarty

Committee for Wilson Chapel stained-glass windows:

Lynn Holloway, Chairman	Emily McAllister	Kathy Clark
Dr. Maxie D. Dunnam	David Libby	Jack Hearn

The Wilson Chapel windows were given in honor or memory of the following:

Given in Honor of Our Families by Cindy and Mat Lipscomb
"I am the Resurrection and the Life; he who believes in me, though he die, yet shall he live" (John 11:25 RSV).

History of Worship: 1982–1994

Given in Memory of Jesse Andrew Anderson by His Family
"I am the Bread of Life; he who comes to me shall not hunger, and he who believes in me shall never thirst" (John 6:35 RSV).

Given in Honor of Dr. Charles W. Grant and in Memory of Dr. J. Harold Beaty by Mr. & Mrs. Jack Renshaw
"I am the vine, you are the branches. He who abides in me, and I in him, he it is that bears much fruit, for apart from me you can do nothing" (John 15:5 RSV).

Given in Memory of John Alden Parsons by Mrs. John A. Parsons and son, Frank Parsons
"I came from the Father, and have come into the world" (John 16:28 RSV).

Given in Honor of Our Family by Mr. & Mrs. C. Winston Hoover Jr.
"I am the Good Shepherd. The Good Shepherd lays down his life for the sheep" (John 10:11 RSV).

Given in Honor of Erie Sanson Henrich by His Wife, Margaret Y. Henrich
"Lo, I am with you always, to the close of the age" (Matt. 28:20 RSV).

Given in Memory of Charles Robert Tate by Eloise Garrison Tate; Eloise Tate and Joseph Holt Foster Jr; Allison, Angelique, and Holt Foster
"'Who are you, Lord?' And He said to me, 'I am Jesus of Nazareth whom you are persecuting'" (Acts 22:8 RSV).

Given in Memory of Fred Miller Ridolphi by Mrs. Fred Miller Ridolphi
"You call me 'Master' and 'Lord,' and rightly so, for that is what I am" (John 13:13 NEB).

Narthex Window: "But for you who fear my name, the sun of righteousness shall rise, with healing in its wings" (Mal. 4:2 RSV).

✜ ✜ ✜

Chapel Altar Tapestry

The needlepoint tapestry hanging above the chapel altar was designed and created by Mr. Charles Roma and made by him and other members of Christ United Methodist Church. It was dedicated to the glory of God and in honor of the Reverend Howard W. Rash.

Reverend Howard Rash became an appointed clergy to Christ Church in 1963 and served faithfully in that position until his retirement in 1971. He has continued to serve the church since his retirement as a visitor to the shut-ins, hospitalized, and troubled.

The symbols on the tapestry are significant and tell their story as follows. Facing this work of art, the top squares going left to right are the same as the symbols in the stainedglass windows on your right. They remind us of highlights in the life of Jesus Christ.

The first is the star of Bethlehem, telling us of the long expected and desired birth. The second block is the descending dove, symbolizing the Holy Spirit, which came from heaven at the time of His baptism along with the voice telling us of His Messiahship as it said, "This is my beloved Son in whom I am well pleased."

The third block denotes the work or ministry of Christ, with the symbols of the cross and Alpha and Omega reminding us that He is first and last, all things to the believer.

The fourth is the cross and dove, symbols of the Crucifixion and the presence of God.

The final block is the lily, symbol of resurrection and victory over death.

The four blocks on the left going down are the symbols of the four evangelists, Matthew, Mark, Luke, and John, the authors of the four New Testament Gospels. These are of early origin and are four winged creatures based on Ezekiel 10:14 and Revelation 4:7. The winged man is used to represent Matthew because his Gospel deals with the human genealogy of our Lord and throughout emphasizes His manhood. The winged lion is used to represent Mark because of the allusion in Mark 1:3 to "the voice of one crying in the wilderness," symbolized by a lion. The lion is said to signify royalty, alluding to the kingly office of Christ.

The winged calf represents Luke, whose Gospel treats very fully the atoning sacrifice of Christ, a calf or an ox being the most common symbol of sacrifice. The eagle, believed to soar higher than any other bird, is the emblem of John because in his Gospel he expresses the divine nature of Christ in the most exalted terms to be found in the New Testament.

It is sometimes said that these four figures signify, respectively, humanity, royalty, sacrifice, and divinity.

On the right-hand side are four symbols of the Church. The ship is the symbol of the Church and emphasizes its going forth, its missionary outreach. Below is an open book, the Bible, wherein humankind is instructed in God's word. The chalice and wafer, the third symbol of the Church, signify Holy Communion, wherein the Church remembers the sacrifice of Christ in giving His body and blood for our salvation. The final Church panel is the flame symbolizing Pentecost and the gift from God to the Church of the Holy Spirit.

The three remaining panels on the bottom of the hanging symbolize the work of the members of the Church. The shell has always been associated with baptism. The one to be baptized would walk into the water about waist deep and would be baptized by the Church as a believer as the clergy dipped the shell in the water and poured this over the head. The lamp symbolizes the light that comes to the believer through Christ: "I am the light of the world." The towel and basin symbolize servanthood and remind us of our example as Christ washed the feet of the disciples.

The center of the tapestry has symbols that are meaningful, too. The triangle symbolizes the Trinity. The central triangle is called the trefoil. It is a modification of the three circles of equal size with the overlapping parts cut out. Inside the Trinity symbol is an Alpha and Omega, the first and last letters in the Greek alphabet. It means Jesus Christ, the beginning and the end. Above it is a crown, symbolizing Jesus Christ as King of kings.

Worship Chairman: Mrs. John R. Walker III
Altar Guild Chairman: Mrs. Dwight Clark

RECOLLECTIONS OF FOURTEEN YEARS AT CHRIST UNITED METHODIST CHURCH

Rev. James L. Loftin

Carolyn and I moved to Memphis in June 1983. We had two children at that time—Jonathan at three months, Ashley at four years of age. Dr. Maxie Dunnam and the Staff-Parish Relations Committee had asked me to consider working with the teenagers at Christ Church. After the bishops agreed, we left Meridian, Mississippi, and moved to Memphis.

These were hard times for the church. Dr. Beaty had died less than two years earlier, and the church was still reeling from the Stubblefield nightmare. Dale Brady was directing the recreation department and his wife, Sandra, had been working with the teenagers. She was suffering with cancer and died shortly after I arrived. Sandra loved the teenagers. She regretted leaving them and feared that her replacement would not be found in a timely manner. Upon hearing of my arrival, I was told that she said, "Good. Now I can die in peace." She died a few days later. Another tragedy at Christ Church. As I prepared to move to Memphis, I wondered about this string of crises that Christ Church was experiencing. I wondered what would be next.

In the seventies and early eighties, local churches in Memphis were not being very intentional about youth ministry. However, Young Life, a parachurch organization that focuses on high school students, was growing wildly. Scores of Christ Church teens faithfully attended these Young Life meetings in homes though they never attended anything at their own church. Parent after parent asked me to create a ministry at Christ Church that would make their child want to be a part of our church, instead of going off to Young Life. Some of the first adult volunteers to help with the youth program were Jean Branch, Debbie Williams, Shiree Charles, and Ann and Richard Zambetti. Tom and Jana Marino joined the church the first Sunday I was on staff at Christ Church. They began as youth group volunteers that very night. Tom soon became a major factor in our youth ministry. The kids loved him and he loved them.

I clearly remember the church staff in those days—Milton and Gynette Bennett, Mike Brewster, Earl Johnston, Jewel Crowson, Sam Drash, Thomas Mungen, Dale Brady, Donna Thomas, Jan Conder, Shirley Lynn, Mary Ann Thurmond, Marvin Budd, and dear Maxie. Denice Hampton was my first secretary, though I have gone through many during the last fourteen years. Jan was famous for her ability to recall information. She had a miraculous ability to remember names, addresses, and telephone numbers. She could give you data on most church members without looking at their records.

Here are some of the important moments in the life of our church, as I remember them:

1. In 1983 the two-story white-frame parsonage on the back of the property was destined for destruction. All the plumbing fixtures had already been salvaged. The trustees decided to hold off the bulldozers and allow the youth to have the house. The youth raised money and recruited labor to rehab the house. The house was named the Timothy House. The name refers to the goal of the youth ministry as seen in Paul's words to his young disciple in 2 Timothy 2:2. The purpose of the house was twofold. The upstairs would house youth ministry interns, and the downstairs would provide warm space for youth Bible studies and other events. The den was once filled with a truckload of sand as part of a "Beach Bash." Raccoons have invaded the house more than once. To my knowledge there has never been a burglary. Amazing.

2. The first person to reside in the Timothy House was a young woman from Meridian, Mississippi. She was the first youth ministry intern. Her name was Kim Callahan. She lived in the house for one year. There has been a constant stream of interns since Kim left for seminary in 1985. This aspect has had a powerful impact on our teenagers, and it has helped train many young adults for ministries around the world.

3. In the early eighties the church had a series of revival services led by the world-famous preacher, Dr. Lloyd John Ogilvie. Though we have had preaching events since then, I don't remember anything similar to the evangelistic nature of these meetings. I took part in training a team of laity to assist in counseling those who we felt would respond to the altar calls. Scores of people responded to Dr. Ogilvie's invitations. I clearly remember the altar being full. For the next few weeks, I spent a major portion of my time counseling and encouraging teenagers who had given their lives to Christ during the services.

4. The construction of the Rogers Youth Center was another big step for the youth ministry. It put our youth ministry on the map. Though the space seemed so large after construction, it was soon filled with teenagers. The backlit stained-glass focal center in the fellowship room was designed by Jerry Dunnam.

5. After working with me as a volunteer and then as part-time staff, Tom Marino took over the youth ministry position in the spring of 1988. Maxie and the Staff-Parish Relations Committee called me to establish a ministry to young adults and to young married couples. They also asked me to develop our small group ministry and expand our missions ministry. My title was minister of discipleship. As these ministries matured, each was passed off to newly hired staff. In 1991 I finally became full-time in missions. The decision of Staff-Parish to invest in missions in this way was a radical step toward reaching the congregation's long-voiced desire to "do as much for others as we do for ourselves."

6. The Volunteers in Missions (VIM) program has had a dynamic impact on our congregation. Approximately four hundred people have taken part in one or more international trips during the past ten years—Brazil, Costa Rica, El Salvador, Dominican Republic, Czech Republic, Russia. Most of the people providing leadership for our missions ministry are VIM veterans. These trips inspire people to reach out at home as well as abroad.

7. After a great deal of discussion but very little research, Maxie and I started the 9:45 worship service. I don't remember the Worship Committee being very involved at first. Many people were skeptical. Soon after the completion of Wilson Chapel, we had our first service. The pews had not been delivered yet. Maxie felt that we should only set up one hundred chairs. I asked maintenance to set up two hundred. However, three hundred people showed up. We naively began this service never realizing the impact that it would have in the community and in our church. Though many churches in Memphis now have similar services, no one was doing this in 1992. For the first three or four years the only musical accompaniment was piano (the marvelous Jeremy Ramey) and a bass guitar.

8. Maxie had tried to start a service of healing shortly after he became the pastor of Christ Church. I understand that the idea was rejected with some people being concerned that the church had hired a Pentecostal. After ten years Maxie was ready to try again. The Sunday evening service of prayer, healing, and Holy Communion is a powerful and unique ministry at Christ Church. It was never intended to reach masses. However, the people who attend each week come because there is a crisis in their lives. The crowd changes each week, but needs are being met and prayers are being answered. I can't imagine us not having this service.

9. Since I became full-time in missions, the church has hired two other full-time missions staff. Rev. Don Burford and Tom Marino are both urban missions staff at our church. They are paid by our church and held accountable by our leaders, but the focus of their ministry is in the inner city. This was a bold step. Here again, Christ Church was blazing new trails. At that time no other church in Memphis was willing to make such a move. Very few churches around the nation have displayed such a commitment to the renewal of their cities. Hundreds of volunteers from Christ Church have been mobilized because of the work of these two men.

10. The "Up with Christ" Capital Funds Program was a dramatic effort. From the beginning, I felt that if God was calling Christ Church to put that much

money into property at 4488 Poplar, then surely He was calling us to do something equally radical for people beyond our membership—missions. I shared these feelings at one of the Charge Conference meetings leading up to the beginning of the fund-raising campaign. Within four days I received a memo from Bill Bouknight. He affirmed my idea and suggested that we tithe to missions from the capital campaign. That could have meant $2.5 million for missions. That was even more radical than I had dared to dream. I worked hard in the preparation of a plan to present to the church, but I was only slightly optimistic. One of the highlights of my ministry at Christ Church was the night that the Administrative Board voted on adding this missions component to the capital funds campaign. The plan presented by the Missions Committee included four local projects and two foreign projects. The board enthusiastically affirmed the plan. After the meeting more than one person mentioned that they had never been more proud of Christ Church.

11. The hiring of Anthony Anderson was another step forward by Christ Church. I feel that this marked a new day for Christ Church. Though it had been decades perhaps since any official representative of our church had demonstrated blatant racism, we are not blatantly demonstrating reconciliation.

APPENDIX

The Official Boards, Commissions, and Committees

Board Chairmen and Lay Leaders 1982–1994

Dr. Howard McClain
Chairman
1982–1983

Thomas Dyer
Lay Leader, 1982–1983
Chairman, 1986–1990

Jack Morris
Chairman, 1984–1985
Lay Leader, 1988

Dr. Richard Ross
Lay Leader, 1984–1987
Chairman, 1993–1994

BOARD CHAIRMEN AND LAY LEADERS 1982–1994

Bert Ferguson
Lay Leader
1989–1992

William Watkins
Chairman
1991–1992

Wayne Pyeatt
Lay Leader
1993

Randall D. Noel
Lay Leader
1994

The Administrative Board
1982

Dr. Howard McClain, Chairman
Thomas Dyer, Lay Leader
Bert Alexander
Avis Allen
Kitty Anderson
Myra Antwine
Frances Barnard
Samuel V. Barnett
Dr. Leonard M. Batey
W. S. Beckwith III
Gynette Bennett
Ben F. Birdwell
Richard G. Bolks
Dr. Howard Boone
Stanley Booth
Donald E. Bourland
Helen Boyd
Dale Brady
Dr. Howard Bragg III
Alan Broyles
Joseph N. Browndyke
Larry Bryant
Marvin Budd
Dr. George A. Burghen
Ben Carpenter
Jack Caskey
Armistead F. Clay
Margaret Colby
Ray Conder
Mary Condra
Rev. Jerry F. Corlew
Harry Cost
Becky Craig
Harry G. Crockett Jr.
William J. Crosby
Mr. & Mrs. Douglas Cross
Jewel Crowson
R. C. Cunningham
James D. Curry
Dr. William Dobbs
Faye Daniel
Howard Davenport
James Davenport
C. A. Davis Jr.
J. J. Doughtie
Sam Drash
Dan S. Duncan
Sewell Dunkin
Durelle Durham
Tom Dyer
J. A. Edwards
Tom England
Dr. Jim Eoff
Robert B. Erskine
Howard Estes
Eleanor Eubank
Dr. John Y. Eubank
Henry Farmer
Dr. Turley Farrar
Ernest T. Felts
Bert Ferguson
Frank W. Fisher
R. Byron Fisher
Ned French
J. Albert Fulmer
Dr. Edward Garrett
Charles Gilliland
James A. Gordon Jr.
David Grant
Don Grant
Dr. Tom Grizzard
W. L. Gully
Clarence Hampton
Dr. O. B. Harrington
Charles L. Harris
Henry Harry
Larry Hawkins
Erie Henrich
Margaret Henrich
Dr. Clarence Herrington
Nancy Higgason
Virginia Hollon
Lynn Holloway
James H. Holmes Jr.
Eddins Hopps
W. E. Horton
Henry Hottum
Anne Howdeshell
Don Howdeshell
Warner Howe
Toni Huddleston
John P. Huggins
Grace Hutchison
C. S. Jasper
Jack Jayroe Sr.
Karen Jetton
Harry A. Johnson Jr.
Orin R. Johnson
Charles H. Johnston
Dr. Albert Jones
Mike Jones
William T. Jordan
Kate Joyner
Jimmy M. Kelly
William Kennon
Dwight Koenig
Dr. Susan Ruby Lamb
Dr. Wayne Lamb
Dr. Andrew Lasslo
Shirley Lynn
James B. Markham
Kenneth Markwell Jr.
Emmett Marston
Edmund C. Massey
James A. Massey Jr.
Samuel H. Mays

Appendix: The Official Boards, Commissions, and Committees 171

Ralph McCool
Lee B. McCormick
Dr. Frank A. McGrew
Rozan McKnatt
Paul McQuiston
J. Marion Meadows
William Meadows
Mary Lou Medlin
Theodore Medlin
Dr. Robert M. Miles
Mr. & Mrs. Jackie Miller
Dr. P. D. Miller
Betty Moore
John H. Morris III
Gary Morse
Harry Murchison
Dennis Neenan
Dallas Nelson
Dr. Charles Newman
D. A. Noel
Charles Ogan
Frances Parsons
Jack L. Perry
Judge H. LeRoy Pope
Rev. Howard W. Rash
Melinda Rauseher
Jack Renshaw
Boyd Rhodes
E. R. Richmond Sr.
George T. Roberts
Patsy Roberts
C. K. Robinson
Dr. Richard T. Ross
J. P. Rutledge
Donald S. Sanford
G. Duke Schaeffer
Ralph B. Scherr
Dr. Dan Scott
James H. Seabrook
Dr. Ray Sexton
H. Clay Shelton Jr.
Henry C. Shelton III

Dr. Thomas H. Shipmon
Gordon B. Slappey Jr.
Frances Smith
William Cazy Smith
William Loyd Smith
Maurice E. Stanley
Coni Stevens
Harold W. Stewart
Dr. W. J. Templeton
Don Thomas
H. Edward Thomas
Mary Elizabeth Thomas
Mary Ann Thurmond
J. P. Tucker
George Vanek
William Watkins Jr.
Roger D. Watson
Henry Weber
Martha Weber
Keith Weisinger
John C. Whitsitt
Neal D. Whitten
Gene Williams
John Williams
Patty Williams
Dr. Sid Wilroy
Dr. James L. Wiygul
C. Lasseter Woodard
Daniel Yacoubian

Lay Members, Annual Conference
Avis Allen
Larry Hawkins
Anne Howdeshell
Don Howdeshell
Kate Joyner
Dr. Susan Ruby Lamb
Henry Weber
Martha Weber
John Williams

Chairman, Council on Ministries
H. Edward Thomas

Chairpersons of Work Areas

Education
Dr. James C. Eoff III

Evangelism
Eleanor Eubank

Outreach
Donald A. Thomas

Worship
Jewel Crowson

Age-Level Coordinators

Children's Ministries
Karen Jetton

Youth Ministries
Dr. Tom Grizzard

Adult Ministries
Bert Ferguson

Family Ministries
Ann & Jackie Miller

Youth Members of the Council on Ministries
Lauren Miller
Lauren Thurmond

Young Adult Members of the Council on Ministries
Ann Duncan
Jack G. Moore

Recording Secretary
Don Grant

*Secretary of Career
Planning and Counseling*
Marvin Budd

*Health and Welfare
Representative*
Dr. Dan Scott

*Honorary Members,
Administrative Board*
Howard Davenport

*Committee on Pastor-
Parish Relations*
D. A. Noel, Chairman
Tom Dyer
Kate Joyner
James A. Massey Jr.
R. Bradley Martin
Lee McCormick
H. Clay Shelton Jr.
Keith Weisinger
Gene Williams

Consultants
Bert Ferguson
Charles Harris

Committee on Finance
Roy Thurmond,
    Chairman
Bert Alexander
R. W. Ashley
Don Bourland
William Dismuke
Ned French
Albert Fulmer
Charles L. Harris
Lynn Holloway
Ernest Jetton

Harry A. Johnson Jr.
Dwight Koenig
James Markham
Dr. Howard McClain
Lee McCormick
J. Marion Meadows
John H. Morris III
Wayne Pyeatt
Tom Ragland
Jack Renshaw
E. R. Richmond Sr.
H. Clay Shelton Jr.
Keith Weisinger
John Whitsitt

Ex Officio
Margaret Colby
Jewel Crowson
Sewell Dunkin
Tom Dyer
Dr. James C. Eoff III
Eleanor Eubank
Emmett Marston
Ralph McCool
Mary Lou Medlin
Dr. P. D. Miller
Don Thomas
H. Edward Thomas
Gene Williams
John Williams

District Steward
James Seabrook Sr.

Trustees
Robert B. Erskine
Winston Hoover
Orin R. Johnson
Emmett Marston
Jack Renshaw
George Roberts
H. Edward Thomas

John Whitsitt
Gene Williams

Financial Secretary
Gynette Bennett

*Church School
Superintendent*
Dr. James C. Eoff III

*Representative United
Methodist Youth
Ministries*
Mike Jones

*Representative United
Methodist Neighborhood
Centers*
Tom Huddleston

*Representative Lambuth
College*
Larry Bryant

*Representative
Metropolitan Missionary
Society*
Dr. Howard Bragg

*Representative Lakeshore
Assembly*
Don Bourland

*Coordinator of
Communications*
Grace Hutchison

Nominating Committee
Avis Allen
J. J. Doughtie
Don Howdeshell
Burns Landess
Dr. Howard McClain

Appendix: The Official Boards, Commissions, and Committees

Henry C. Shelton III
H. Edward Thomas
Mary Ann Thurmond
Gene Williams

Other Officers and Committee Chairpersons

Audit
Mary Lou Medlin

Collectors and Ushers
Samuel V. Barnett
Eddins Hopps

Communion
Mr. & Mrs. Douglas Cross

Dietetics
Margaret Colby

House
Sewell Dunkin

Insurance
Frank W. Fisher

Legal Counsel
Emmett Marston

Music
Henry Harry

Pension Plan
E. R. Richmond Sr.

Property Use
Ralph McCool

Policy Committee
Jerry F. Corlew

Records and History
Frances Smith

Recreation
Dr. P. D. Miller

Wills and Legacies
Harry A. Johnson Jr.

Administrative Board
Dr. Howard McClain, Chairman
H. Edward Thomas, Vice Chairman
Don Grant, Secretary

Officers Reported though Elected Otherwise

UMW President
Margaret Henrich

Day School Board Chairman
Bill Watkins

THE ADMINISTRATIVE BOARD
1983

Dr. Howard McClain, Chairman
Thomas Dyer, Lay Leader

Class of 1985
Julia Atkinson
Martha Barta
Louis K. Beasley
Dr. Joyce Bittle
Charles E. Black
Robert A. Blackmon Jr.
Rosa Bourland
J. Barry Brindley
Mary Louise Caldwell
Ann Chambers

Kathy Clark
Bea Crofford
Dr. Carol Crown
Jewel Crowson
Lottie Dabbs
Nancy Detling
Joe Dial
William Dismuke
Dianne Duncan
Dr. Thad H. Ferrell
J. Robert Gatlin
Robert E. Gentry
Donald L. Hawkins
James R. Hillis
Hugh H. Hogue
Pauline Hord

Elisabeth Horton
Dr. Alvin J. Ingram
Dr. Howard M. Jernigan
Thomas F. Jones
Thomas H. Jones Jr.
Dr. B. J. Kelley
Edward Langdon
Weston G. Lawson
Donald W. Lewis
Mary Lou Liming
Dr. Frank W. Ling
R. Bradley Martin
C. R. McDaniel
Ella McVean
Edward W. Miller
George D. Miller

Dr. S. Meade Moore III
Ann Orr
Elizabeth Poole
Nancy Poore
Andrew A. Sippel Jr.
Ronald B. Thomas Jr.
Judy Van Steenberg
J. D. Weatherford
Ruth Woodard

Class of 1984
Bert Alexander
Kitty Anderson
W. S. Beckwith III
Dr. Howard Boone
Donald E. Bourland
Helen Boyd
Ben M. Carpenter
Harry Cost
Faye Daniel
Joe A. Edwards
Henry Farmer
Ernest T. Felts
Frank W. Fisher
Charles A. Gilliland III
David L. Grant
W. L. Gully
Nancy Higgason
Virginia Hollon
Lynn Holloway
Jack Jayroe Sr.
Charles H. Johnston
Theodore W. Medlin
Betty Moore
John H. Morris III
Frances Parsons
Jack Renshaw
Boyd L. Rhodes
E. R. Richmond Sr.
J. P. Rutledge
G. Duke Schaeffer
Dr. Ray Sexton
H. Clay Shelton Jr.

William Cazy Smith
George J. Vanek
Gene C. Williams

Class of 1983
Dr. Leonard M. Batey
Joseph N. Browndyke
Dr. George A. Burghen
Armistead Clay
Mary Condra
Harry G. Crockett Jr.
B. C. Cunningham
James Davenport
Dan Duncan
Durelle Durham
Howard Estes
Dr. John Y. Eubank
Dr. Turley Farrar
J. Albert Fulmer
James A. Gordon Jr.
Charles L. Harris
Dr. C. G. Herrington
William T. Jordan
Jimmy M. Kelly
Dr. Andrew Lasslo
James B. Markham
Kenneth Markwell Jr.
Edmond C. Massey III
Dr. Frank A. McGrew
Dr. Robert M. Miles
Harry Murchison
Dr. Charles Newman
Charles Ogan
Jack L. Perry
Judge H. LeRoy Pope
Patsy Roberts
George T. Roberts
C. K. Robinson
Dr. Richard T. Ross
Ralph B. Scherr
William Loyd Smith
Maurice E. Stanley
Harold W. Stewart

Mary Elizabeth Thomas
Mary Ann Thurmond
J. P. Tucker
Roger D. Watson
Dr. James L. Wiygul

Lay Members, Annual Conference
Avis Allen
Clarence Hampton
Larry Hawkins
Don Howdeshell
Kate Joyner
Dr. Susan Ruby Lamb
Shirley Lynn
Henry Weber
Martha Weber
John Williams

Chairman, Council on Ministries
H. Edward Thomas

Chairpersons on Work Areas

Education
Dr. James C. Eoff III

Evangelism
Eleanor Eubank

Outreach
Eloise Mays

Worship
Carolyn Walker

Age-Level Coordinators

Children's Ministries
J. J. Doughtie

Appendix: The Official Boards Commissions, and Committees 175

Youth Ministries
Dr. Tom Grizzard

Adult Ministries
Tom F. Jones

Family Ministries
Ann & Jackie Miller

Youth Members of the Council on Ministries
Lauren Miller
Lauren Thurmond

Young Adult Members of the Council on Ministries
Jeffrey Brannen
Mary Stigall

Recording Secretary
Don Grant

Secretary of Career Planning and Counseling
Marvin Budd

Health and Welfare Representative
Dr. Dan Scott

Honorary Members, Administrative Board
Howard Davenport

Committee on Pastor-Parish Relations
D. A. Noel, Chairman

Class of 1983
James A. Massey Jr.
Gene Williams

Class of 1984
Tom Dyer
Kate Joyner
Lee McCormick

Class of 1985
Don Grant
Ted Medlin
Mildred Whitsitt

Committee on Finance
Roy Thurmond,
    Chairman

Class of 1983
Charles L. Harris
Harry A. Johnson Jr.
Dwight Koenig
Dr. Howard McClain
Tom Ragland
Jack Renshaw
John Whitsitt

Class of 1984
Don Bourland
William Dismuke
Lynn Holloway
Ernest Jetton
Lee McCormick
E. R. Richmond Sr.
Keith Weisinger

Class of 1985
Harry Crockett
Sewell Dunkin
Ken Markwell
Frances Parsons
Dr. Thomas H. Shipmon
Mimi Steepleton
Don Thomas
Bill Watkins

Ex Officio
Margaret Colby
Dan Duncan
Tom Dyer
Dr. James C. Eoff III
Eleanor Eubank
Winston Hoover
Emmett Marston
Eloise Mays
Dr. Howard McClain
Ralph McCool
Dr. P. D. Miller
H. Edward Thomas
Carolyn Walker
John Williams

Representative Lambuth College
Larry Bryant

Representative Metro Missionary Society
Dr. Howard Bragg

Representative Lakeshore Assembly
Don Bourland

Coordinator of Communications
Grace Hutchison

Nominating Committee

Class of 1983
Avis Allen
Don Howdeshell
Gene Williams

Class of 1984
J. J. Doughtie
Dr. Howard McClain
Henry C. Shelton III

Class of 1985
Ernest Felts
John Walker

Curriculum Committee
Bill Crosby, Chairman
Don Bourland
L. C. Daniel
Dee Dyer
Karen Jetton
Dorris Smith
Anne Howdeshell

Ex Officio
Judy Dixon
J. J. Doughtie
Dr. James C. Eoff III
Miriam Handorf
Nancy Poore

Other Officers and Committee Chairpersons

Audit
Dan Duncan

Bicentennial
Tom F. Jones

Collectors and Ushers
Samuel V. Barnett
Eddins Hopps

Communion
Mr. & Mrs. Douglas Cross

Dietetics
Margaret Colby

House
Winston Hoover

Insurance
Frank W. Fisher

Legal Counsel
Emmett Marston

Music
Lynn Holloway

Pension Plan
E. R. Richmond Sr.

Property Use
Ralph McCool

Policy Committee
Dr. Maxie D. Dunnam

Publicity
Ray Conder

Records and History
Frances Smith

Recreation
Dr. P. D. Miller

Wills and Legacies
Harry A. Johnson Jr.

Administrative Board
Dr. Howard McClain, Chairman
H. Edward Thomas, Vice Chairman
Don Grant, Secretary

Officers Reported though Elected Otherwise

UMW President
Trudy Simpson

Day School Board Chairman
Bill Watkins

THE ADMINISTRATIVE BOARD
1984

Jack Morris, Chairman
Dr. Richard Ross, Lay Leader
Bert Alexander
Avis Allen
Kitty Anderson
Rev. Myra B. Antwine
James B. Arnette

Julia Atkinson
Gary Barta
Martha Barta
Louis Beasley
W. S. Beckwith
Gynette Bennett
Dr. Joyce Bittle
Charles E. Black

Joe Dial
William O. Dismuke
J. J. Doughtie
Sam Drash
Dan Duncan
Dianne Duncan
Sewell Dunkin
Dr. Maxie D. Dunnam

Appendix: The Official Boards, Commissions, and Committees 177

Dr. Frank M. Dyer Jr.
Tom Dyer
Joe A. Edwards
Dr. James C. Eoff III
Henry Farmer
Ernest Felts
Bert Ferguson
Dr. Thad H. Ferrell
John Ford
Steve Fransioli
Mary French
Grady Frisby
Robert Gatlin
Robert Gentry
Alice Gibson
Charles Gilliland
Louis Goke
David Grant
W. L. Gully
Clarence Hampton
Dr. Howard Jernigan
Ernest A. Jetton
Harry A. Johnson Jr.
Charles Johnston
Rev. Earl Johnston
Melanie Jones
Thomas F. Jones
Thomas H. Jones Jr.
Kate Joyner
Dr. B. J. Kelley
Dwight Koenig
Dr. Susan Ruby Lamb
Dr. Wayne Lamb
Dr. Mack Land
Wes Lawson
Donald W. Lewis
Dr. David Libby
Mary Lou Liming
Dr. Frank W. Ling
Rev. James L. Loftin
Shirley Lynn
Dr. Howard McClain
Lee McCormick

Paul Permar
Elizabeth Poole
Nancy Poore
Tom Ragland
Rev. Howard W. Rash
Jack Renshaw
Boyd Rhodes
Ed Richmond Sr.
Dr. Richard Ross
J. P. Rutledge
G. Duke Schaeffer
James Seabrook Sr.
Dr. Ray Sexton
H. Clay Shelton Jr.
Ruthann Shelton
Trudy Simpson
Warren L. Simpson
Andrew A. Sippel Jr.
Gordon B. Slappey Jr.
William Cazy Smith
Dorris Smith
Frances Smith
Phoebe Smith
Coni Stevens
John Stone
Don Sutch
Dr. Len Sumner
Dr. W. J. Templeton
H. Ed Thomas
Don Thomas
Ron Thomas
Ed Thorn
George Vanek
John Van Steenberg
Sugar Walker
Albert Walton
Bill Watkins
Jerry Weatherford
Ken Weatherford
Nancy Webb
Henry Weber
Martha Weber
Tom White

Gene Williams
Ruth Woodard

Lay Members, Annual Conference
Avis Allen
Marvin Budd
Mary Louise Caldwell
Clarence Hampton
Larry Hawkins
Don Howdeshell
Thomas F. Jones
Kate Joyner
Dr. Susan Ruby Lamb
Shirley Lynn
Henry Weber
Martha Weber

Chairman, Council on Ministries
Boyd L. Rhodes Jr.

Chairpersons of Work Areas

Education
Jackie H. Miller

Evangelism
Gary Barta

Missions
Thomas B. Dyer

Church and Society
Eloise Mays

Stewardship
Donald A. Thomas

Worship
Sugar Walker

Age-Level Coordinators

Children's Ministries
J. J. Doughtie

Youth Ministries
James F. Morrison

Adult Ministries
Thomas F. Jones

Youth Members of the Council on Ministries
Janet Holloway
Dorree Jane Smith
Brandon Webb

Young Adult Members of the Council on Ministries
Jeff Brannen
Julie Sutch

Recording Secretary
Mary Louise Caldwell

Secretary of Career Planning and Counseling
Marvin Budd

Health and Welfare Representative
C. Henry Hottum

Honorary Members, Administrative Board
Howard L. Davenport, Chairman

Committee on Staff-Parish Relations
H. Ed Thomas, Chairman

Margaret Colby
Thomas R. Dyer
Don Grant
Kate Joyner
Paul McQuiston
Lee McCormick
Ted Medlin
Mildred Whitsitt

Committee on Finance
Don Thomas, Chairman
Don Bourland
Barry Brindley
Harry Crockett
William Dismuke
Sewell Donkin
Ann Duncan
Bert Ferguson
Lynn Holloway
Ernest Jetton
Ken Markwell
Dr. Howard McClain
Lee McCormick
Dr. P. D. Miller
Jackson W. Moore
Jack Morris
Frances Parsons
Ed Richmond Sr.
George Roberts
Dr. Thomas H. Shipmon
Mimi Steepleton
Bill Watkins
Keith Weisinger

Ex Officio
James B. Arnette
Gary Barta
Gynette Bennett
Dan Duncan
Dr. Maxie D. Dunnam
Winston Hoover

Don Howdeshell
Harry A. Johnson Jr.
Rev. Earl Johnston
Dr. Frank Ling
Emmett Marston
Eloise Mays
Jackie Miller
Boyd Rhodes
Dr. Dick Ross
Sugar Walker

District Steward
James Seabrook Sr.

Trustees
Harry A. Johnson Jr., Chairman
Clarence Colby
Ray Cummins
Dr. Tom Gizzard
Erie Henrich
Winston Hoover
Dr. Alvin J. Ingram
James A. Massey
Gene Williams

Membership Secretary
Jan Conder

Church Treasurer and Financial Secretary
Gynette Bennett

Church School Superintendent
Jackie Miller

Representative, United Methodist Youth Ministries
Janet Holloway

Appendix: The Official Boards, Commissions, and Committees

Representative, United Methodist Neighborhood Centers
Tom Huddleston

Representative, Lambuth College
Jack Morris

Representative, Metro Missionary Society
Dr. Howard Bragg

Representative, Lakeshore Assembly
Don Bourland

Status and Role of Women
Avis Allen

Nominations and Personnel
Bill Crosby
Dr. Maxie D. Dunnam
J. J. Doughtie
Ernest Felts
Dr. Howard McClain
Vivian Murchison
Mike Rauscher
Henry C. Shelton III
John Walker
John Whitsitt

Curriculum Committee
Sarah Black
Don Bourland
Skip Daniel
Dr. James C. Eoff III
Judy Hogue
Elisabeth Horton
Dorris Smith

Ex Officio
Marvin Budd
Judy Dixon
J. J. Doughtie
Miriam Handorf
Jackie Miller
Nancy Poore

Other Officers and Committee Chairpersons

Audit
Dan Duncan

Bicentennial
Don Howdeshell

Collectors and Ushers
Eddins Hopps
Warren Simpson

Day School Board
Bill Watkins

Dietetics
James B. Arnette

House and Grounds
Winston Hoover

Insurance
Don Bourland

Legal Counsel
Emmett Marston

Music
Lynn Holloway

Pension Plan
E. B. Richmond Sr.

Planned Giving
Lee McCormick

Property Use
Dwight Koenig

Policy Committee
Dr. Maxie D. Dunnam

Publicity
Ray Condor

Records and History
Frances Smith

Recreation
Dr. Frank Ling

Administrative Board
Jack Morris, Chairman
Boyd Rhodes, Vice Chairman
Mary Louise Caldwell, Secretary

Officers Reported though Elected Otherwise

UMW President
Harriet Shelton

Day School Board Chairman
William W. Watkins

Policy Committee
Dr. Maxie D. Dunnam, Chairman
Winston Hoover
Harry A. Johnson Jr.
Jackie Miller
Jack Morris
Boyd Rhodes

Dr. Dick Ross
Don Thomas

Insurance
Don Bourland
James D. Curry
Fran Fisher
Grady Frisby
Jack Jayroe
Jack Rainey
Roy Thurmond

Records and History
Mary Louis Caldwell
Ben Carpenter
Becky Craig
Frances Smith

Dietetics
James B. Arnette
Becky Craig
Frances Harris

House and Grounds
Robert Crouch
Winston Hoover
Warner Howe
C. S. Jasper
Ralph McCool
Kenneth W. Rash
Ed Thorn

Property Use
Dwight Koenig, Chairman
Winston Hoover
Boyd Rhodes

Day School Board
Bill Watkins, Chairman

Class of 1984
Dr. Leonard Batey
Bill Crosby

Class of 1985
Walter Howell
Larry Miller
Jeff Morrison
Nancy Poore
Adair Rainey
Elizabeth Turner

Class of 1986
Skip Daniel
Courtney Sexton
Henry C. Shelton III

Class of 1987
Richard Cook
Lowell Hays
Robert Thomas

Ex Officio Day School Board
Sam Drash
Rev. Earl Johnston

THE ADMINISTRATIVE BOARD
1985

Jack Morris, Chairman
Dr. Richard Ross, Lay Leader

Class of 1985
Julia Atkinson
Dr. Joyce Bittle
Charles E. Black
Rosa Bourland
Bea Crofford
Lottie Dabbs
Nancy Detling
William Dismuke
Dianne Duncan
Dr. Thad Ferrell
Don Hawkins
Hank Hogue

Pauline Hord
Elizabeth Horton
Dr. Alvin J. Ingram
Dr. Howard Jernigan
Dr. B. J. Kelley
Wes Lawson
Don Lewis
Mary Lou Liming
C. R. McDaniel
Ed Miller
Dr. Meade Moore
Ann Orr
Nancy Poore
Andrew A. Sippel Jr.
Ron Thomas
Jenny Weatherford
Ruth Woodard

Class of 1986
Jean Branch
Dot Brannen
Claud Brown Sr.
Mike Butler
Mary Louise Caldwell
Clarence Colby
Edyth DeMauro
Sewell Dunkin
Dr. Frank Dyer
John S. Ford
Steve Fransioli
Grady Frisby
Mary French
Louis Goke
Lowell Hays
Don Helm

Appendix: The Official Boards, Commissions, and Committees 181

Jack Hurdle
C. S. Jasper
Ernest Jetton
Dr. Mack Land
Dr. David Libby
Dr. Howard McClain
Preston McDaniel
Larry Miller
Fred Mills
Colby S. Morgan Jr.
Randy Noel
Virginia Nowlin
Alton Orr
Ruthann Shelton
Trudy Simpson
Dorris Smith
Phoebe Smith
John Stone
Dr. Len Sumner
Don Sutch
Ed Thorn
Albert Walton
Bill Watkins
Ken Weatherford
Nancy Webb
Tom White

Class of 1987
Jim Bordon
Dr. George Cook
Ray Cummins
Byron Fisher
Jac Gates
Betty Grant
Karla Grant
Tom Guinn
Dr. Charles E. Harbison
Shelton Harrison
Flicky Hartman
Tom Iverson
Harry A. Johnson III

Orin R. Johnson
Martha Anne Johnston
Bill Kennon
Dr. Warren Lesmeister
Mat Lipscomb
James Mason
Phil Mischke
Troy O'Brien
Watts Parrish
Lou Payne
Glenn Ragland
Mike Rauscher
Irma Roberts
Robert Rogers
Dr. Ed Segner
Florence Seward
Charles Shaphard
Robert Sharpe
Mike Sheahan
Harriett Shelton
Dr. Thomas H. Shipmon
Bettye Smith
Dr. Bruder Stapleton
Brenda Tate
Gene Stigall
John Turner
Marge Utterback
Nash Vickers
John Walker
Keith Weisinger
Leslie Weldon
Allen Whitsitt
Neal Whitten
Hoot Wilder
Brady Wilson
Sam Wilson
Ann Zambetti

Officers and Ex Officio
James B. Arnette
Gary Barta
Gynette Bennett

Don Bourland
Mike Brewster
Barry Brindley
Marvin Budd
Mary Louise Caldwell
Kathy Clark
Bill Crosby
Howard Davenport
Dan Duncan
Dr. Maxie D. Dunnam
Durelle Durham
Tom Dyer
Dr. James C. Eoff III
Eleanor Eubank
Bert Ferguson
Charles Glascock
Dr. Charles W. Grant
Clarence Hampton
Don Helm
Eddins Hopps
Henry Hottum
Rev. W. Edward Horton
Don Howdeshell
Ernest Jetton
Harry A. Johnson Jr.
Rev. Earl A. Johnston
Martha A. Johnston
Jana Jones
Dwight Koenig
Dr. Wayne A. Lamb
Dr. Warren Lesmeister
Dr. Frank Ling
Rev. James L. Loftin
Shirley Lynn
Jackie Miller
Fred Mills
Jack Morris
Jeff Morrison
Julia Morrison
Rev. Dennis Neenan
Nancy Poore
Rev. Howard W. Rash
Boyd Rhodes

E. R. Richmond Sr.
Dr. Richard T. Ross
James H. Seabrook Sr.
Henry C. Shelton III
Warren Simpson
Frances Smith
Don Thomas
H. Edward Thomas
Mary Elizabeth Thomas
William H. Watkins
Henry Weber
Beth Whitsitt

Trustees
Don Thomas, Chairman
Clarence Colby
Erie Henrich
Art Massey
Gloria McDaniel
Beth Moore
Tom Quinn
Harriet Shelton
L. M. Wilson

Lay Members, Annual Conference
Mary Louise Caldwell
Bert Ferguson
Clarence Hampton
Don Howdeshell
Martha Anne Johnston
Shirley Lynn
Jack Morris
Henry C. Shelton III
Mary Elizabeth Thomas
Henry Weber

Reserves
Mrs. J. J. Doughtie
Byron Fisher
Dr. Dick Ross
H. Clay Shelton Jr.
John Whitsitt

Chairman, Council on Ministries
Boyd Rhodes

Chairpersons of Work Areas

Education
Jackie Miller

Evangelism
Gary Bass

Missions
Tom Dyer

Church and Society
Fred Mills

Stewardship
Dr. Clarence Herrington

Worship
Eleanor Eubank

Age-Level Coordinators

Children's Ministries
Beth Whitsitt

Youth Ministries
Jeff & Julia Morrison

Council on Ministries

Youth Member
Jana Jones

Young Adult Members
Jeff Brannen
Julie Sutch

Recording Secretary
Mary Louise Caldwell

Secretary of Career Planning and Counseling
Marvin Budd

Representative, Lambuth College
Jack Morris

Representative, Metro Missionary Society
Dr. Warren Lesmeister

Representative, Lakeshore Assembly
Clarence Hampton

Status and Role of Women
Nancy Poore

Nominations and Personnel

Class of 1985
Ernest Felts
Mike Rauscher
John Walker

Class of 1986
Bill Crosby
Vivian Murchison
John Whitsitt

Class of 1987
Paula Bourland
Jack Morris
Ann Orr

Appendix: The Official Boards, Commissions, and Committees

Curriculum Committee
Dr. James C. Eoff III, Chairman
Margaret Hickey
Judy Hogue
Elizabeth Horton
Watts Parrish
John Seabold
June Whithead

Ex Officio
Marvin Budd
Janice Fly
Jackie Miller
Betty Ridenhour
Ruthann Shelton
Beth Whitsitt

Other Officers and Committee Chairpersons

Policy Committee
Dr. Maxie D. Dunnam, Chairman
Bill Crosby
Harry A. Johnson Jr.
Dwight Koenig
Jackie Miller
Jack Morris
Boyd Rhodes
Dr. Dick Ross
Don Thomas

Insurance
Don Bourland
James D. Curry
Byron Fisher
Grady Frisby
Jack Jayroe Jr.
Jack Rainey
Roy Thurmond

Ex Officio
C. Henry Hottum
Rev. Earl Johnston

Records and History
Frances Smith, Chairman
Mary Louise Caldwell
Ben Carpenter
Becky Craig

Dietetics
James B. Arnette, Chairman
Becky Craig
Eddins Hopps
Eloise Mays
Jeanette Watkins

House and Grounds
Bill Crosby, Chairman
Robert Crouch
Ray Henley
Warner Howe
C. S. Jasper
Kenneth W. Rash

Ex Officio
Rev. Earl Johnston
Milton Bennett

Recreation
Dr. Frank Ling, Chairman
Sue Berry
Jim Borden
Scott Brewster
David Joiner
Scott King
Shirley Moore
Dave Ralston
John Russell
Dr. Bruder Stapleton

Ex Officio Staff
Marvin Budd
Rev. James Loftin
Donna Thomas

Work Area on Education
Jackie Miller, Chairman
Dr. Jeff Bigger
Dr. Joyce Bittle
Sarah Black
Horace & Jean Branch
Brad Conder
Mary Condra
Janice Fly
David Fox
Preston McDaniel
Jeff Morrison
Ann Orr
Elizabeth Poole
Melinda Rauscher
Amy Rhodes
Betty Ridenhour
Ruthann Shelton
Andrew A. Sippel Jr.
John Turner
Beth Whitsitt

Ex Officio Staff
Marvin Budd
Rev. James Loftin

Children's Ministry Council
Beth Whitsitt, Chairman
Dr. & Mrs. George Cook
Janice Fly
Jean Higdon
Dr. Mack & Diane Land
Betty Ridenhour
Ruthann Shelton

Coni Stevens
Al & Jo Ann Walton

Ex Officio Staff
Marvin Budd

Audit
Dan Duncan, Chairman
Harry Crockett
C. Henry Hottum
Dr. P. D. Miller

Planned Giving
Barry Brindley,
    Chairman
Kitty Anderson
Peggy Harwell
Erie Henrich
Harry A. Johnson Jr.
Anita I. Lotz
Lee McCormick
Jackson W. Moore
Don Thomas
Keith Weisinger
John Whitsitt

Ex Officio Staff
Dr. Maxie D. Dunnam
Rev. Earl Johnston

Christ Counseling Center Board
Julia Atkinson,
    Chairman
Erie Henrich

Orin R. Johnson
Ted Medlin
Vivian Murchison
Robert Sharpe
Dr. Thomas H. Shipmon
Martha Vandervoort
Carole West

Ex Officio Staff
Rev. W. Edward Horton

Youth Ministry Council
Jana Jones, President
Horace & Jean Branch
Karen Clark
Rachel Cook
Brad Conder
John Crockett
Matthew Crosby
Beth Crowson
John Duncan
Jenny Dyer
Ellen Eubank
Ashley Grizzard
Lowell Hays
Lara Hemington
Tonia Light
Tom & Jana Marino
Tom McAllister
Lauren Miller
Jeff & Julia Morrison
John Russell
Elizabeth Ryan
Trip Smith
Brandon Webb

Ex Officio Staff
Mike Brewster
Kim Callahan
Rev. James Loftin
Donna Thomas

Council on Ministries
Boyd Rhodes, Chairman
Gary Barta
Jeff Brannen
Kathy Clark
Faye Daniel
Tom Dyer
Eleanor Eubank
Ernest Jetton
Peggy Hampshire
Janet Holloway
C. Henry Hottum
C. S. Jasper
Dr. Frank Ling
Jackie Miller
Fred Mills
Jack Morris
Jeff & Julia Morrison
Dr. Dick Ross
Dorree Jane Smith
Julie Sutch
Don Thomas
Brandon Webb
Beth Whitsitt

THE ADMINISTRATIVE BOARD
1986

Tom Dyer, Chairman
Dr. Richard Ross, Lay
    Leader

Class of 1986
Jean Branch
Claud Brown Sr.

Mike Butler
Clarence Colby
Sewell Dunkin

Appendix: The Official Boards, Commissions, and Committees

Dr. Frank Dyer
John S. Ford
Steve Fransioli
Mary French
Grady Frisby
Louis Goke
Lowell Hays
Jack Hurdle
C. S. Jasper
Dr. Mack Land
Dr. David Libby
Dr. Howard McClain
Preston McDaniel
Larry Miller
Colby S. Morgan Jr.
Randy Noel
Virginia Nowlin
Alton Orr
Ruthann Shelton
Dr. Thomas H. Shipmon
Trudy Simpson
Dorris Smith
Phoebe Smith
John Stone
Dr. Len Sumner
Don Sutch
Ed Thorn
Albert Walton
Bill Watkins
Ken Weatherford
Nancy Webb
Tom White

Class of 1987
Jim Borden
Dr. George Cook
Ray Cummins
Byron Fisher
Jac Gates
Betty Grant
Karla Grant
Dr. Charles E. Harbison
Shelton Harrison

Flicky Hartman
Tom Iverson
Harry A. Johnson III
Orin R. Johnson
Bill Kennon
Mat Lipscomb
James Mason
Phil Mischke
Tiny O'Brien
Watts Parrish
Lou Payne
Tom Guinn
Glenn Ragland
Irma Roberts
Robert Rogers
Dr. Ed Segner
Florence Seward
Charles Shaphard
Robert Sharpe
Mike Sheahan
Harriett Shelton
Bettye Smith
Dr. Bruder Stapleton
Gene Stigall
Brenda Tate
John Turner
Marge Utterback
Nash Vickers
John Walker
Keith Weisinger
Leslie Weldon
Allen Whitsitt
John Whitsitt
Neal Whitten
Hoot Wilder
Brandy Wilson
Sam Wilson

Class of 1988
A. Y. Brown
Dr. Richard Cheek
William Cossett

Ann Curry
William W. Dunlap
John Elkington
Charles Gadd
John C. Harris
Margaret Henrich
Amanda Herstoff
Dr. Walter Hughes
Kay Jones
Dr. Thomas Long
Dr. Frank McGrew
Ed Meyer
Jackson W. Moore
Don W. Morgan
Price Morrison
Charles Norvel
Charles Patton
Linda Richmond
George Roberts
David Rogers
Steve Shular
Roy Thurmond
Dr. J. D. Upshaw
Ben Walton
Dr. James Wiygul

Officers and Ex Officio
Gynette Bennett
Robert C. Black
Don Bourland
Paula Bourland
Mike Brewster
Dr. Hal C. Brunt
Marvin Budd
Mary Louise Caldwell
Kathy Clark
Jan Conder
William J. Crosby
Ray Cummins
Howard Davenport
J. J. Doughtie
Dr. Maxie D. Dunnam

Durelle Durham
Tom Dyer
Eleanor Eubank
Ernest Felts
Bert Ferguson
Byron Fisher
Frank Fisher
David Fox
Charles Glascock
Dr. Charles W. Grant
E. C. Handorf
Jane Isbell Haynes
Don Helm
Dr. Clarence Herrington
Hank Hogue
C. Henry Hottum
Don Howdeshell
Ernest Jetton
Rev. Earl A. Johnston
Martha Anne Johnston
Dr. Wayne A. Lamb
Dr. Warren Lesmeister
Rev. James L. Loftin
Shirley Lynn
Tom Manno
Sam Mays
J. W. McAllister
Lee McCormick
Yvonne McCrary
Dr. P. D. Miller
Fred Mills
Jack Morris
Dr. Archie C. Morrison
Rev. Fred C. Morton
D. A. Noel
Ann Orr
Charles Patton
Rev. Howard W. Rash
Amy Rhodes
Fred Ridolphi
James H. Seabrook Sr.
Dr. E. P. Segner Jr.
Steve Shular
Henry C. Shelton III
Warren Simpson
Dr. Len Sumner
Don Thomas
Donna Thomas
Marge Utterback
Martha Vandervoort
John Walker
William H. Watkins
Henry Weber
Beth Whitsitt
Gene Williams
Sam Wilson

Honorary Lifetime Members
H. L. Davenport
E. C. Handorf
Sam Mays
Lee McCormick
Fred Ridolphi
James H. Seabrook Sr.

Audit
J. W. McAllister, Chairman
Harry Crockett
C. Henry Hottum
Mary Lou Medlin

Budget Committee
William Watkins, Chairman
John Brannen
William Dunlap
Martha Helm
Dr. Scott King
Mat Lipscomb
Mildred Orr
Jack Renshaw
Dr. Edmund Segner
Tom White

Ex Officio Staff
Gynette Bennett
Dr. Maxie D. Dunnam
Rev. Earl Johnston

Building Committee
D. A. Noel, Chairman
Kathy Clark
Winston Hoover
Ken Markwell
Charles Shapard

Communications
Durelle Durham, Chairman
Nancy Chase
Steve Shular

Council on Adult Ministry
Steve Shular, Chairman
Steve Fransioli
Don Grant
Vikki Roberts
Joan Sigman
Leslie Sigman
Ed Thomas
Mary Elizabeth Thomas

Ex Officio Staff
Marvin Budd

Council on Children's Ministry
Beth Whitsitt, Chairman
Dr. & Mrs. George Cook
Grady Frisby
Patty Johnson
Lucy McArtor

Appendix: The Official Boards, Commissions, and Committees

Janet Mitchell
Christine Munson
Coni Stevens
Anne Wilder

Ex Officio Staff
Paula Bourland
Marvin Budd

Council on Ministries
Robert Black
Don Bourland
Faye Daniel
Tom Dyer
C. Henry Hottum
Ernest Jetton
Yvonne McCrary
Dr. P. D. Miller
Jack Morris

Work Area Chairpersons

Missions
Dr. Hal C. Brunt

Worship
Eleanor Eubank

Stewardship
Dr. Clarence Herrington

Church and Society
Kathy Clark

Higher Education
Dr. Edmund Segner

Education
Dr. Len Sumner

Evangelism
John Walker

Age-Level Coordinators
Hank Hogue
Leslie Sigman
Joan Sigman
Beth Whitsitt

At-Large Members
Kelli Charles
Brad Conder
Peggy Hampshire
C. S. Jasper
Leslie Weldon
Hoot Wilder

Ex Officio Staff
Paula Bourland
Mike Brewster
Marvin Budd
Dr. Maxie D. Dunnam
David Fox
Rev. Earl Johnston
Rev. James Loftin
Shirley Lynn
Tom Marino
Donna Thomas

Council on Youth Ministry
Lauren Brewster
Kelli Charles
Brad Conder
Heather Conder
Ross Dyer
Matt Fox
Frank McGrew
Elizabeth Middlecoff
Lauren Miller
Carrie Morgan
Andy Rambo
Peter Rayburn
Amy Rhodes
Shannon Rhodes
John Russell

Elizabeth Ryan
Trip Slappey
Debbie Thurmond
Brandon Webb

Ex Officio Staff
Horace Branch
Jean Branch
Mike Brewster
Beth Crowson
Rev. James Loftin
Tom Marino
Donna Thomas

Counseling and Family Life Committee
Martha Vandervoort, Chairman
Martha Barta
Erie Henrich
Orin R. Johnson
Ted Medlin
Dr. Thomas H. Shipmon
Dorris Smith
Carole West

Ex Officio Staff
Dr. Maxie D. Dunnam
Rev. Earl Johnston
Rev. Fred C. Morton

Finance
Helen Boyd
A. Y. Brown
Dr. John Eubank
Robert Gatlin
Lowell Hays
Winston Hoover
Harry A. Johnson Jr.
Burns Landess
Eloise Mays
Dr. Howard McClain

Dr. P. D. Miller
Jackson W. Moore
Harry Murshison
Harry Orr
Jack Renshaw
George Roberts
Robert Rogers
Dr. Ray Sexton
John Turner
Tom White
Dr. Charles Wilkinson

Ex Officio
Bob Black
Don Bourland
Dr. Hal C. Brunt
Kathy Clark
William Crosby
Tom Dyer
Eleanor Eubank
Ernest Felts
Charles Glascock
Dr. Clarence Herrington
Hank Hogue
Don Howdeshell
J. W. McAllister
Jack Morris
Dr. Len Sumner
Don Thomas
John Walker
Sam Wilson

Ex Officio Staff
Gynette Bennett
Dr. Maxie D. Dunnam
C. Henry Hottum
Rev. Earl Johnston

House and Grounds
William Crosby,
　Chairman
Ray Henley

C. S. Jasper
Elizabeth Foole
Kenneth W. Rash
Don Sutch

Ex Officio Staff
Milton Bennett
Rev. Earl Johnston

Insurance
Sam Wilson, Chairman
James D. Curry
Charles Johnston
Mat Lipscomb
Ralph McCool
Jack Rainey
Roy Thurmond

Ex Officio Staff
C. Henry Hottum
Rev. Earl Johnston

Kitchen
Hank Hogue, Chairman
Sallie Granz
Doris Hawkins
Eddins Hopps
Eloise Mays

Staff
Rev. Earl Johnston

*Lay Delegates, Annual
Conference*
Mary Louise Caldwell
J. J. Doughtie
Bert Ferguson
Don Howdeshell
Martha Anne Johnston
Jack Morris
Ann Orr
H. Clay Shelton Jr.
Henry Weber

Reserves
Byron Fisher
Dr. Dick Ross
H. Clay Shelton Jr.
John Whitsitt

Music
Ernest Jetton, Chairman
Carla Baylor
Julie Brewster
Lauren Brewster
Becky Dunlap
Mat Lipscomb
Mike Sheahan
Hoot Wilder
Ruth Woodard

Ex Officio
Mike Brewster
Ann Curry
Nancy Greenwood
Susie Hillis
Emily McAllister
Cathy Meisner

*Nominations and
Personnel*
Dr. Maxie D. Dunnam,
　Chairman
Bill Crosby
Earl Johnston
Jack Morris
Vivian Murchison
Ann Orr
John Whitsitt

*Pension Trust Fund
Committee*
Don Howdeshell,
　Chairman
Charles Harris
Keith Weisinger

Appendix: The Official Boards, Commissions, and Committees

Planned Giving
Charles Patton, Chairman
Kitty Anderson
Bert Ferguson
Harry A. Johnson Jr.
Anita I. Lotz
Jackson W. Moore
George Roberts
Roy Thurmond
Keith Weisinger
John Whitsitt

Policy Committee
Dr. Maxie D. Dunnam, Chairman
Don Bourland
Bill Crosby
Tom Dyer
Frank Fisher
Dr. P. D. Miller
Jack Morris
Dr. Len Sumner
Don Thomas

Property Disposition Committee
Ray Cummins, Chairman
Jerry Dunnam
Randy Jones
Ben Madden
Mary Glynne Massey
J. W. McAllister
Charles Patton

Ex Officio Staff
Earl A. Johnston

Property Use
Frank Fisher, Chairman
Don Bourland
Bill Crosby

Records and History
Jane Isbell Haynes, Chairman
Mary Louise Caldwell
Ben Carpenter
Dr. Susan Ruby Lamb
Lou Payne

Ex Officio Staff
Dr. Maxie D. Dunnam

Recreation
Robert Black, Chairman
Jan Averwater
Sue Berry
Jim Borden
Scott Brewster
David Joiner
Scott King
Lauren Miller
Shirley Moore
Bill Patrick
Dave Ralston
Dr. Bruder Stapleton

Ex Officio Staff
Marvin Budd
Rev. James Loftin
Donna Thomas

Staff-Parish Relations Committee
Gene Williams, Chairman
Margaret Colby
Bert Ferguson
Lee McCormick
Paul McQuiston
Betty Moore
Dr. Dick Ross
Trudy Simpson
Ed Thomas

Trustees
Don Thomas, Chairman
Clarence Colby
Erie Henrich
James A. Massey
Gloria McDaniel
Beth Marston Moore
Tom Quinn
Harriett Shelton
L. M. Wilson

Day School Board
H. Clay Shelton Jr., Chairman
Bruce Bury
Tom Butterick
Lowell Hays
David Joiner
Adair Rainey
Dr. Richard Ross
Frank Schriner Jr.
Ramona Seabold
Al Walton

THE ADMINISTRATIVE BOARD
1987

Tom Dyer, Chairman
Dr. Richard Ross, Lay Leader

Class of 1987
Jim Borden
Dr. George Cook

Ray Cummins
Byron Fisher
Jac Gates

Betty Grant
Karla Grant
Dr. Charles E. Harbison
Flicky Hartman
Tom Iverson
Harry A. Johnson III
Orin R. Johnson
Bill Kennon
Mat Lipscomb
James Mason
Phil Mischke
Troy O'Brien
Watts Parrish
Lou Payne
Glenn Ragland
Irma Roberts
Robert Rogers
Dr. Ed Segner
Florence Seward
Charles Shapard
Robert Sharpe
Mike Sheahan
Harriett Shelton
Brenda Sippel
Bettye Smith
Gene Stigall
John Turner
Marge Utterback
Nash Vickers
John Walker
Keith Weisinger
Leslie Weldon
John Whitsitt
Neal Whitten
Hoot Wilder
Brady Wilson
Sam Wilson

Class of 1988
A. Y. Brown
Dr. Richard Cheek
Ann Curry

William W. Dunlap
John Elkington
Charles Gadd
William Gossett
Dr. O. B. Harrington
John C. Harris
Margaret Henrich
Amanda Herstof
Dr. Walter Hughes
Kay Jones
Dr. Thomas Long
Dr. Frank McGrew
Ed Meyer
Don W. Morgan
Price Morrison
Charles Norvel
Charles Patton
Lola Patton
Linda Richmond
George Roberts
David Rogers
Steve Shular
Roy Thurmond
Dr. J. D. Upshaw
Ben Walton

Class of 1989
George Allen
Sam Barnett
Charles Echols
Dr. Turley Farrar
Mary Jane Fransioli
Ed Gatlin
Jim Gordon
Wade Gowan
Marshall Harrison
Shelton Harrison
Henry Harry
James Hayden
Karla Hefty
Virginia Hollon
Larry Karban
Dr. Scott King

Tommy Land
Anita I. Lotz
Emmett Marston
George Martin
Pat McClain
Yvonne McCrary
Ted Medlin
Richard Middlecoff
Burt Milam
Robert Montgomery
Jackson W. Moore
Jack G. Moore
Joe Neeley
Bill Patrick
Mary Sue Pierce
Ed R. Richmond Sr.
John Seabold
Carol Stricklin
Tom Watson
Bob Whitsitt

Officers and Ex Officio
Gynette Bennett
Robert C. Black
Don Bourland
Paula Bourland
Dr. Hal C. Brunt
Marvin Budd
Mary Louise Caldwell
Margaret Colby
Jan Conder
Rev. Bruce Crill
William J. Crosby

Finance
Dr. P. D. Miller,
   Chairman
Helen Boyd
A. Y. Brown
Harry Crockett
Paul Dorman
Ernest Felts
Al Fulmer

Appendix: The Official Boards, Commissions, and Committees 191

Robert Gatlin
David Grant
Grace Hayden
Lowell Hays
Harry A. Johnson Jr.
Harry A. Johnson III
Burns Landess
James Lee
Dr. David Libby
Dr. Howard McClain
Harry Murchison
Jonathan Page
Ed Richmond
G. Duke Schaeffer
Mike Sheahan
Tom Watson
Carol Yochem

Ex Officio
Bob Black
Don Bourland
Dr. George Cook
Bill Crosby
Durrell Durham
Tom Dyer
Robert Hardin
Lynn Holloway
Burns Landess
J. W. McAllister
Dick Middlecoff
Jack Morris
J. P. Rutledge
Saralene Thomas
John Walker
William Watkins
John Whitsitt
Sam Wilson

Ex Officio Staff
Charles Bagley
Gynette Bennett
Dr. Maxie D. Dunnam
Rev. Earl Johnston

Recreation
Robert Black, Chairman
Dr. Richard Cheek
Dr. George Cook
Bill Dunlap
Alan Greer
Flicky Hartman
Jean Martin
Phil Mischke
Dr. Mike Mitchell
Don W. Morgan
Charles Norvel
Watts Parrish

Staff-Parish Relations
Gene Williams,
    Chairman
Julia Atkinson
Dr. Thad Ferrell
Dr. Charles E. Harbison
Virginia Hollon
Beth Marston Moore
Wayne Pyeatt
Dr. Dick Ross
Don Thomas

Trustees
John Whitsitt,
    Chairman
Ken Markwell
Ralph McCool
Yvonne McCrary
Beth Marston Moore
Janet N. Sheahan
John Turner
Sugar Walker
L. M. Wilson

Delegates, Annual Conference
Margaret Colby
Kate Davenport
J. J. Doughtie

Tom Dyer
Harry A. Johnson Jr.
Ann Orr
Dr. Richard Ross
Henry C. Shelton III
Gordon B. Slappey Jr.

Reserves
H. Clay Shelton Jr.
Jane Isbell Haynes
E. C. Handorf
Dr. Susan Ruby Lamb

Work Area on Church and Society
Jean Sharpe, Chairman
Dick Bolks
Bob Gatlin
Chris Garrett
Mona Hoover
Anita I. Lotz
Eloise Mays
Gloria McDaniel
Betty Pyeatt
Bob Sharpe
Phoebe Smith
Sybil Tucker
Ben Watson
Terry Whitsitt
Chuck Wilkinson

Ex Officio Staff
Marvin Budd

Work Area on Education
Dr. Len Sumner,
    Chairman
Gary Barta
Becky Coleman
Mary Condra
Martha Helm
Hank Hogue

Patty Johnson
Debbie Kelly
Mary Lou Medlin
Janet Mitchell
Carol Morgan
Colby S. Morgan Jr.
Molly Morgan
Christine Munson
Steve Shular
Carol Stricklin

Ex Officio
Paula Bourland
Marvin Budd
David Fox
Rev. James L. Loftin

Work Area on Worship
Lynn Holloway,
　Chairman
Mary Louise Caldwell

Bill Crosby
J. J. Doughtie
Ernest Jetton
Donna Libby
Dr. Tom Long
Yvonne McCrary
Glenn Ragland
Dr. Len Sumner

Ex Officio Staff
Dr. Maxie D. Dunnam
Milton Bennett
Jack Hearn
Emily McAllister
Tom Machen

Council on Children's Ministry
Debbie Kelly, Chairman
Ellen Cockrell
David Goodwin
Mike Henning

Diane Osborne
Trudy Rhodes
Debbie Starr
Bob Whitsitt

Ex Officio Staff
Paula Bourland
Marvin Budd

House and Grounds
Bill Crosby, Chairman
Clarence Colby
John Ford
Elizabeth Poole
Kenneth W. Rash
Ken Robinson
Don Sutch

Ex Officio Staff
Charles Bagley
Milton Bennett
Rev. Earl Johnston

The Administrative Board
1988

Tom Dyer, Chairman
Jack Morris, Lay Leader

Class of 1988
A. Y. Brown
Dr. Richard Cheek
Ann Curry
William W. Dunlap
John Elkington
Charles Gadd
Dr. O. B. Harrington
John C. Harris
Margaret Henrich
Amanda Herstoff
Dr. Walter Hughes
Kay Jones
Dr. Thomas Long

Dr. Frank McGrew
Ed Meyer
Don W. Morgan
Price Morrison
Charles Norvel
Charles Patton
Lela Patton
Linda Richmond
George Roberts
David Rogers
Steve Shular
Roy Thurmond
Dr. J. D. Upshaw
Ben Walton

Class of 1989
George Allen

Sam Barnett
Charles Echols
Dr. Turley Farrar
Mary Jane Fransioli
Ed Gatlin
Jim Gordon
Wade Gowan
Marshall Harrison
Shelton Harrison
Henry Harry
James Hayden
Karla Hefty
Virginia Hollon
Larry Karban
Dr. Scott King
Tommy Land
Anita I. Lotz

Appendix: The Official Boards, Commissions, and Committees 193

Emmett Marston
George Martin
Pat McClain
Yvonne McCrary
Ted Medlin
Richard Middlecoff
Burt Milam
Robert Montgomery
Jackson W. Moore
Jack G. Moore
Joe Neely
Ball Patrick
Mary Sue Pierce
Ed R. Richmond Sr.
John Seabold
Carol Stricklin
Tom Watson
Bob Whitsitt

Class of 1990
Byrd Baggett
W. S. Beckwith
Dr. Jeff Bigger
Robert Blackmon Jr.
Richard L. Cheek
Richard Cockrell
R. J. Duncan
Dr. Mary Dundas
  Deeter
Jo Dupree
Kathy Farnsworth
Ernest Felts
Millie Gedney
Jane Goodhue
Clarence Hampton
Charles Holmes
Roger Hoover
Eddins Hopps
Dr. Alvin J. Ingram
C. S. Jasper
Kate Joyner
Jim Kelly

Ben Landess
Dr. Andrew Lasslo
James Lee
R. Bradley Martin
Art Massey
Dr. Howard McClain
Ralph McCool
Paul McQuiston
Mark Melton
Dick Middlecoff
Dr. P. D. Miller
Jack Morris
Dr. Archie C. Morrision
Jeff Morrison
Rev. Fred Morton
D. A. Noel
Ann Orr
Mildred Orr
Charles Patton
Connie Peebles
Andrew Rambo
Rev. Howard W. Rash
Fred Ridolphi
Ed Roberson
J. P. Rutledge
James H. Seabrook Sr.
Dr. Ed Segner
Florence Seward
Jane Sharpe
Dr. Thomas H. Shipmon
Gordon B. Slappey Jr.
Kathy St. John
Elizabeth Stevens
Donna Thomas
Saralene Thomas
David Tichenor
Kathy Tuberville
John Walker
William Watkins
John Whitsitt
Gene Williams
Sam Wilson

Ervin Wright Jr.
Linda Wright

Honorary Administrative Board Members
Howard Davenport
E. C. Handorf
Sam Mays
Lee McCormick
Fred Ridolphi
Jimmy Seabrook Sr.

Finance
Dr. P. D. Miller,
  Chairman
Helen Boyd
A. Y. Brown
Harry Crockett
Paul Dorman
Ernest Felts
Al Fulmer
Robert Gatlin
David Grant
Grace Hayden
Lowell Hays
Harry A. Johnson Jr.
Harry A. Johnson III
Burns Landess
James Lee
Dr. David Libby
Dr. Howard McClain
Harry Murchison
Jonathan Page
Ed Richmond
G. Duke Schaeffer
Mike Sheahan
Tom Watson
Carol Yochem

Ex Officio
Bob Black
Don Bourland
Dr. George Cook

Bill Crosby
Durelle Durham
Tom Dyer
Robert Hardin
Lynn Holloway
Burns Landess
J. W. McAllister
Dick Middlecoff
Jack Morris
J. P. Rutledge
Saralene Thomas
John Walker
William Watkins
John Whitsitt
Sam Wilson

Ex Officio Staff
Charles Bagley
Gynette Bennett
Dr. Maxie D. Dunnam
Rev. Earl Johnston

Recreation
Robert Black, Chairman
Dr. Richard Cheek
Dr. George Cook
Bill Dunlap
Alan Greer
Flicky Hartman
Jean Martin
Phil Mischke
Dr. Mike Mitchell
Don W. Morgan
Charles Norvel
Watts Parrish

Staff-Parish Relations
Gene Williams,
    Chairman
Julia Atkinson
Dr. Thad Ferrell
Dr. Charles E. Harbison

Virginia Hollon
Beth Marston Moore
Wayne Pyeatt
Dr. Dick Ross
Don Thomas

Trustees
John Whitsitt,
    Chairman
Ken Markwell
Ralph McCool
Yvonne McCrary
Beth Marston Moore
Janet N. Shehan
John Turner
Sugar Walker
L. M. Wilson

Delegates, Annual Conference
Margaret Colby
Kate Davenport
J. J. Doughtie
Tom Dyer
Harry A. Johnson Jr.
Ann Orr
Dr. Richard Ross
Henry C. Shelton III
Gordon B. Slappey Jr.

Reserves
E. C. Handorf
Jane Isbell Haynes
Dr. Susan Ruby Lamb
H. Clay Shelton Jr.

Work Area on Church and Society
Jane Sharpe, Chairman
Dick Bolks
Bob Gatlin
Chris Garrett
Mona Hoover

Anita I. Lotz
Eloise Mays
Gloria McDaniel
Betty Pyeatt
Bob Sharpe
Phoebe Smith
Sybil Tucker
Ben Watson
Terry Whitsitt
Chuck Wilkinson

Ex Officio Staff
Marvin Budd

Work Area on Education
Jim Brubbs
Robert Hardin,
    Chairman
Mary Louise Caldwell
Mary Condra
Dee Dyer
Millie Gedney
Ray Henley
Hank Hogue
Maggie Hollabaugh
Patty Johnson
Debbie Kelly
Delores Kinsolving
Mary Lou Medlin
Dr. Matthew Ochs
Nancy Perrine
Leslie Sigman
Doris Smith
Carol Stricklin
Jeanette Watkins
Ken Weatherford

Ex Officio Staff
Paula Bourland
Marvin Budd
David Fox
Rev. James L. Loftin

Appendix: The Official Boards, Commissions, and Committees

Work Area on Worship
Mary Louis Caldwell
Bill Crosby
J. J. Doughtie
Lynn Holloway
Ernest Jetton
Donna Libby
Dr. Tom Long
Yvonne McCrary
Glenn Ragland
Dr. Len Sumner

Ex Officio Staff
Dr. Maxie D. Dunnam
Milton Bennett
Jack Hearn
Emily McAllister
Tom Machen

House and Grounds
Bill Crosby, Chairman
Clarence Colby
John Ford
Elizabeth Poole
Kenneth W. Rash
Ken Robinson
Don Sutch

Ex Officio Staff
Rev. Earl Johnston
Charles Bagley
Milton Bennett

Administrative Board, Honorary Lifetime Members
H. L. Davenport
E. E. Handorf
Sam Mays
Lee McCormick
Fred Ridolphi
James H. Seabrook Sr.

Audit
J. W. McAllister, Chairman
Rick Cook
Charles Harris
Mary Lou Medlin

Budget Committee
William Watkins, Chairman
John Brannen
Dud Curry
William Dunlap
Martha Helm
Don Howdeshell
Ernest A. Jetton
Dr. Scott King
Dr. Howard McClain
George Roberts

Ex Officio Staff
Gynette Bennett
Dr. Maxie D. Dunnam
Rev. Earl Johnston

Building Committee
D. A. Noel, Chairman
Kathy Clark
Winston Hoover
Ken Markwell
Charles Shapard

Ex Officio Staff
Dr. Maxie D. Dunnam
Earl Johnston

Communications
Durelle Durham, Chairman
Steve Shular
Trudy Simpson
Bob Whitsitt

Council on Adult Ministry
Steve Shular, Chairman
Dot Brannen
Julia Morrison
Troy O'Brien
Leslie Sigman
Joan Sigman

Ex Officio Staff
Marvin Budd

Council on Children's Ministry
Debbie Kelly, Chairman
Ellen Cockrell
Grady Frisby
David Goodwin
Mike Henning
Lucy McArtor
Bob Whitsitt
Ann Wilder

Ex Officio Staff
Marvin Budd
Paula Bourland

Council on Ministries
Don Bourland
Robert Black
J. J. Doughtie
Durelle Durham
Tom Dyer
C. Henry Hottum
Helen Markwell
Dr. P. D. Miller
Jack Morris

Work Area Chairpersons
Dr. Hal C. Brunt
Dr. John Eubank
Paul Dorman

Lynn Holloway
Dr. David Libby
Dr. Len Sumner
John Walker

Age-Level Coordinators
Hank Hogue
Debbie Kelly
Joan Sigman
Leslie Sigman
Martha Vandervoort

At-Large Members
Heather Conder
Steve Farnsworth
Connie Peebles
Amy Rhodes

Ex Officio Staff
Paula Bourland
Marvin Budd
Dr. Maxie D. Dunnam
David Fox

Jack Hearn
Rev. Earl Johnston
Rev. James L. Loftin
Shirley Lynn
Tom Marino
Fred Morton
Donna Thomas

The Administrative Board
1989

Tom Dyer, Chairman
Bert Ferguson, Lay Leader

Class of 1989
George C. Allen
Samuel V. Barnett
Charles A. Echols
Dr. Turley Farrar
Mary Jane Fransioli
Ed H. Gatlin
James A. Gordon Jr.
Wade Gowan
Marshall G. Harrison
Shelton E. Harrison
Henry H. Harry
James M. Hayden
Karla Hefty
Virginia Hollon
Larry W. Karban
Dr. William Scott King Jr.
Thomas L. Land
Anita I. Lotz
Emmett W. Marston
George D. Martin
Pat McClain
Yvonne McCrary
Theodore W. Medlin

Richard H. Middlecoff
Robert Montgomery
Jack G. Moore
Jackson W. Moore
Joe P. Neely
Bill W. Patrick
Mary Sue Pierce
Ed R. Richmond Sr.
John S. Seabold
Carol Stricklin
Tom Watson
Robert E. Whitsitt

Class of 1990
W. S. Beckwith III
Dr. J. F. Bigger
Robert A. Blackmon Jr.
Richard Cockrell
Richard L. Cheek
Dr. Mary L. Dundas Deeter
R. J. Duncan
Jo Dupree
Kathy Farnsworth
Ernest T. Felts
Millie Gedney
Jane Goodhue
Clarence D. Hampton
Charles V. Holmes

Roger A. Hoover
Eddins L. Hopps
Dr. Alvin J. Ingram
C. S. Jasper
Kate Joyner
Jimmy M. Kelly
Ben Landess
Dr. Andrew Lasslo
James A. Lee
R. Bradley Martin
James A. Massey III
Dr. J. H. McClain
Ralph A. McCool
Paul McQuiston
Mark C. Melton
James F. Morrison
Mildred Orr
Dr. Ed P. Segner Jr.
Dr. Thomas H. Shipmon
Kathy St. John
David R. Tichenor
Kathy Tuberville
Ervin H. Wright Jr.
Linda Wright

Class of 1991
Dr. David W. Bell
J. E. Bobbitt
Scott K. Burgess

Appendix: The Official Boards, Commissions, and Committees

Rubye Carlile
James H. Cook
James A. Davenport
James F. Duncan Jr.
Joann Farrar
Mary French
James K. Grubbs
C. Lawrence Hawkins
Erie S. Henrich
C. Henry Hottum
Anne Howdeshell
John P. Huggins
Dr. David R. Libby
Elva Lyles
Lucy McArtor
Philip E. Mischke
Dr. Michael Mitchell
Glenn Ragland
A. Jackson Rainey
Robert M. Rogers
G. Duke Schaeffer
Dr. Thomas B. Shelton
Roderick O. Shreve
Carlos Smith
Dr. Vaughn E. Stimbert
Dr. William H. West
Beth Whitsitt

Officers and Ex Officio
Charles Bagley
E. H. Barnes
Martha H. Barta
Gynette Bennett
Robert C. Black
Donald E. Bourland
Paula S. Bourland
Marvin H. Budd
Mary Louise Caldwell
Clarence Colby
Margaret Colby
Dr. George A. Cook
Rev. Bruce Crill

William J. Crosby
Kate Davenport
Angela Donahue
J. J. Doughtie
William W. Dunlap Jr.
Dr. Maxie D. Dunnam
Dee Dyer
Thomas R. Dyer
Bert Ferguson
Rev. Ray Fitzgerald
David W. Fox
Charles W. Gadd
Betty Gossett
William Gossett
Dr. Charles W. Grant
Everett C. Handorf
Jack Hearn
Harry A. Johnson Jr.
Harry A. Johnson III
Rev. Earl A. Johnston
Thomas P. Kelly III
Dr. Wayne A. Lamb
Rev. James L. Loftin
Anita I. Lotz
Rev. Shirley G. Lynn
John Thomas Marino
James A. Massey III
Samuel H. Mays Sr.
Lee B. McCormick
Don W. Morgan
John H. Morris III
Dr. Archie Morrison Jr.
Rev. Fred C. Morton
D. A. Noel
Charles Andrew Rambo
Rev. Howard W. Rash
Edwin S. Roberson
Cooper Robinson
James H. Seabrook Sr.
Florence K. Seward
Gordon B. Slappey Jr.
Elizabeth Stevens
Donna C. Thomas

Saralene Thomas
Roy H. Thurmond Jr.
Sybil Tucker
Liz Wagner
Carolyn Walker
John C. Whitsitt Sr.
Pat Wilson
John S. Wilson

Honorary Administrative Board Members
Everett C. Handorf
Samuel H. Mays Sr.
Lee B. McCormick
James H. Seabrook

Lay Delegates, Annual Conference
Margaret Colby
Kate Davenport
Thomas K. Dyer
Jane Isbell Haynes
Harry A. Johnson Jr.
Randall D. Noel
Dr. Richard T. Ross
Gordon B. Slappey Jr.

Reserves
Penny Johnson
John S. Ford
Becky Ford
Charles H. Johnston
Martha Anne Johnston
Ann Ross

Council on Ministries
Donald E. Bourland, Chairman
Robert C. Black
Joan Doyle
Thomas R. Dyer
Bert Ferguson

Betty Gossett
Deborah D. Pope
Liz Wagner
Laura West
Pat Wilson
John S. Wilson

Work Area Chairpersons
George A. Cook
H. G. Crockett Jr.
J. J. Doughtie
Charles W. Gadd
William G. Gossett
Thomas P. Kelly III
James A. Massey III
Roy H. Thurmond Jr.
Sybil Tucker

Age-Level Coordinators
Martha H. Barta
Angela Donahue
Dee Dyer
Cooper Robinson

Ex Officio Staff
Paula S. Bourland
Marvin H. Budd
Dr. Maxie D. Dunnam
David W. Fox
Jack Hearn
Rev. Earl A. Johnston
Rev. James L. Loftin
Rev. Shirley G. Lynn
Tom Marino
Rev. Fred C. Morton
Donna C. Thomas

Audit
H. B. Landess Jr.

Budget Committee
Edwin S. Roberson,
 Chairman

Robert L. Hardin
Anita I. Lotz
Jack Renshaw
Harold Stewart
Jeanette Watkins

Capital Maintenance Endowment Trust
Harry A. Johnson Jr.,
 Chairman
Donald A. Thomas
Gene C. Williams

Communications
Liz Wagner, Chairman
Michael J. Barts
Dallas E. Nelson
Donna R. Simmons
Trudy Simpson

Ex Officio Staff
Dr. Maxie D. Dunnam

Council on Adult Ministry
Dee Dyer, Chairman
Dorothy Brannen
Robert E. Darmody
Hazel B. DeHaan
Donald W. Tucker

Ex Officio Staff
Marvin H Budd
Rev. Earl A. Johnston

Council on Children's Ministry
Angela Donahue,
 Chairman
Melissa Bell
Deborah A. Kelly
Melissa Neyland
Liza Ozier

Pattie Parris
Trudy Rhodes
Mary Spangler
Deborah H. Starr
Carol Stricklin

Ex Officio Staff
Paula S. Bourland
Marvin H. Budd

Counseling and Family Life
Martha H. Beets,
 Chairman
Dr. Hal C. Brunt
Raymond Cummins
Dr. Richard Dodd
Judy Hogue
Sara Sanders
Courtney Sexton
Louis Smith
Lynn Wilroy

Ex Officio Staff
Dr. Maxie D. Dunnam
Rev. Fred C. Morton

Day School Board
William W. Dunlap,
 Chairman
Donald J. Helm
Harry A. Johnson III
Rick Linder
Jean Martin
Colby S. Morgan Jr.
Ann Orr
Steve Reynolds
Melissa Robinson

Ex Officio Staff
David W. Fox
Rev. James L. Loftin

Appendix: The Official Boards, Commissions, and Committees 199

Finance
John S. Wilson, Chairman
Mary Condra
H. Crockett Jr.
J. Paul Dorman Jr.
Ernest T. Felts
David L. Grant
Grace Hayden
Harry A. Johnson III
James A. Lee
George P. Lewis
Dr. David R. Libby
Jean Maier
Dr. J. Howard McClain
Jonathan Page
J. Albert Palmer Jr.
E. R. Richmond Sr.
G. Duke Schaeffer
Michael F. Sheahan
T. L. Smith Sr.
Robin Taylor
Tom Watson
Dr. Philip E. Wright
Carol Yochem

Ex Officio Staff
Charles Bagley
Gynette Bennett
Robert C. Black
Donald E. Bourland
Dr. George A. Cook
William J. Crosby
J. J. Doughtie
Dr. Maxie D. Dunnam
Thomas R. Dyer
Bert Ferguson
Charles W. Gadd
C. Henry Hottum
Harry A. Johnson III
Rev. Earl A. Johnston
Thomas P. Kelly III
James A. Massey III

Saralene Thomas
Roy H. Thurmond Jr.
Liz Wagner
William H. Watkins Jr.
John C. Whitsitt Sr.

House and Grounds
William J. Crosby, Chairman
Ben M. Carpenter
Clarence Colby
John S. Ford
William P. Poole
Kenneth W. Rash
Charles K. Robinson
Kent C. Stratton
Roger D. Watson

Ex Officio Staff
Charles Bagley
Bennett J. Milton
Rev. Earl A. Johnston

Insurance
Michael F. Sheahan, Chairman
J. Stephen Beale
Richard Bolks
Larry M. Bryant
C. Winston Hoover Jr.
George T. Roberts

Ex Officio Staff
Charles Bagley
Rev. Earl A. Johnston

Kitchen
Saralene Thomas, Chairman
Horace B. Branch
Eddins L. Hopps
Eloise Mays

Charles E. Parnell Sr.
Tom Ragland

Ex Officio Staff
Charles Bagley
Rev. Earl A. Johnston

Music
Betty Gossett, Chairman
Arrena Cheek
Margaret Colby
Karla Hefty
Christopher M. Howdeshell
Vivian Murchison
Frances Parsons
Jack W. Sanders
Dee Wright

Ex Officio Staff
Jack Hearn
Susie Hillis
Thomas M. Machen
Emily McAllister

Nomination and Personnel
Dr. Maxie D. Dunnam, Chairman
Nick Clark
Mary Condra
Ray Henley
Rev. Earl A. Johnston
Anita I. Lotz
Theodore W. Medlin
Jackson W. Moore
Michael F. Sheahan
Trudy Simpson
John R. Turner

Pension and Trust Fund
William H. Watkins, Chairman

Ernest A. Jetton
John H. Morris III

Ex Officio Staff
Charles Bagley
Rev. Earl A. Johnston

Planned Giving
Don W. Morgan,
　Chairman
Ned M. French
Robert L. Hardin
Alvin R. Hartman
Lowell Hays Jr.
Donald M. Howdeshell
James A. Massey III
Samuel H. Mays Sr.
Mary Lou Medlin

Ex Officio Staff
Rev. Earl A. Johnston

Policy Committee
Dr. Maxie D. Dunnam,
　Chairman
Donald E. Bourland
Thomas R. Dyer
Charles W. Gadd
Carolyn Walker
John C. Whitsitt Sr.
John S. Wilson

Property Disposition
Charles Colby,
　Chairman
Harry A. Johnson III
Betty Marston
Mary Glynne Massey
Minor Murrah
Marjorie Phelan

Ex Officio Staff
Rev. Earl A. Johnston

Property Use
Carolyn Walker,
　Chairman
Donald E. Bourland
William J. Crosby

Records and History
Florence K. Seward,
　Chairman
Avis D. Allen
Jane Goodhue
Dr. Susan Ruby Lamb
Troy E. O'Brien
James W. Sanders Jr.

Ex Officio Staff
Dr. Maxie D. Dunnam
Jane Isbell Haynes
Rev. Earl A. Johnston

Recreation
Robert C. Black,
　Chairman
A. Alan Greer
Linda Hays
David R. Heckel
Jana L. Jones
Larry W. Karban
Jean Martin
Mark C. Melton
Dr. Michael Mitchell
Katherine W. Patrick
Calvin B. Ridenhour
Bettye Slappey

Ex Officio Staff
Donna C. Thomas

Staff-Parish Relations
John H. Morris III,
　Chairman
Julia Atkinson

Dr. Thad H. Ferrell
Dr. Charles E. Harbison
Virginia Hollon
Wayne Pyeatt
Warren L. Simpson
Donald A. Thomas
Carole West

Ex Officio Staff
Thomas R. Dyer
Bert Ferguson

Trustees
John C. Whitsitt,
　Chairman
Kenneth Markwell Jr.
Ralph A. McCool
Yvonne McCrary
P. D. Miller Jr.
Jackson W. Moore
Carolyn Rogers
Janet N. Sheahan
John B. Turner

Work Area on Church and Society
Sybil Tucker, Chairman
Amy Ford
J. Robert Gatlin
Anita I. Lotz
Gloria D. McDaniel
Betty Pyeatt
Marie Roberson
Robert F. Sharpe
Marita Walton
K. M. Weatherford Jr.
Beth Whitsitt
Charles E. Wilkinson Jr.

Ex Officio Staff
Marvin H. Budd

Appendix: The Official Boards, Commissions, and Committees

Work Area on Education
Charles W. Gadd,
　Chairman
Mark Bankston
　Guenther
Mary Louise Caldwell
Millie Gedney
James K. Grubbs
Ray Henley
Joy Jaqua
Karen Jetton
Delores Kinsolving
Ben Landess
　Barbara Melton
Kathy Mitchell
Melissa Neyland
Dr. Matthew E. Ochs
Leslie B. Sigman
Doris Smith
Mary Spangler
Carol Stricklin
Marylyn Walker
Jeannette Watkins

Ex Officio Staff
Paula S. Bourland
Marvin H. Budd
Melissa Bell
Angela Donahue
Dee Dyer

Work Area on Evangelism
Thomas P. Kelly,
　Chairman
Gary E. Barta
Richard Bolks
Lorraine Bradford
Jeffrey D. Brannen
Richard Coker
Sherry Coker
Marilyn Crosby

William J. Crosby
David M. Crow
Dianne Duncan
Donald L. Grant
Karla Grant
Mary Guraki
Beth Harbison
Lee R. Harkness
Grace Hayden
Jean Higdon
Jerry R. Hinson
Paula Hinson
Charles V. Holmes
Brenda Lafferty
James Lafferty
Connie McIntyre
Steve M. McIntyre
Paul McQuiston
Mark A. Medford
Suzanne Medford
Phillip E. Mischke
Betty Moore
Colby S. Morgan Jr.
Melissa Neyland
R. Nash Neyland
Carrie Norwood
Walter S. Norwood
Melanie Paige Pacheco
Cindy Rapp
W. Roger Rapp
Anthony Rutz
Marianna Rutz
John S. Seabold
Stephen E. Shular
J. Mac Stricklin
Robin Taylor
William M. J. Taylor
Cindy Tupis
William T. Tupis
Nelle Weddington
Mildred Whitsitt
Howard Whitsitt

Ex Officio Staff
Rev. E. H. Barnes
Rev. Shirley G. Lynn

Work Area on Higher Education and Campus Ministry
William Gossett,
　Chairman
Joyce Bittle
Henry H. Harry
C. Henry Hottum
Richard T. Ross
Ed Rutz
E. P. Segner Jr.
Clinton F. Stewart
Donald W. Tucker

Ex Officio Staff
Rev. James L. Loftin

Work Area on Missions Outreach
Dr. George A. Cook,
　Chairman
Mary Louis Caldwell
Richard Cockrell
Ann Curry
John A. Elkington
Joanne Farrar
Ernest T. Felts
Roger A. Hoover
Thomas D. Iverson
Thomas L. Land
H. B. Landess Jr.
M. W. Lipscomb III
Janet Mitchell
Betty Moore
Michael F. Sheahan
Amelia Shreve
Brenda Sippel
Dawn M. Smith

Mary Elizabeth Thomas
David R. Tichenor
Dr. R. Sidney Wilroy

Ex Officio Staff
Marvin H. Budd
Dr. Maxie D. Dunnam
Rev. James L. Loftin

Work Area on Stewardship
James A. Massey III, Chairman
Robert A. Blackmon Jr.
J. E. Bobbitt
Louis P. Goke
Betty Grant
Mark Neil Gunn

Margaret Henrich
Troy E. O'Brien
Edwin S. Roberson
Ann Ross
Andrew A. Sippel Jr.
William M. J. Taylor
John B. Turner

Ex Officio Staff
Rev. Earl A. Johnston

Work Area on Worship
J. J. Doughtie, Chairman
Julie Brewster
Mary Louis Caldwell
William J. Crosby
Dr. James C. Eoff III
Ernest A. Jetton

Jimmy M. Kelly
Donna Libby
Virginia McClain
W. H. Meadows Jr.
Fairfax Segner
Dr. Len Sumner
Elizabeth Turner

Ex Officio Staff
J. Milton Bennett
Dr. Maxie D. Dunnam
Jack Hearn
Thomas M. Machen
Emily McAllister

The Administrative Board
1990

Tom Dyer, Chairman
Bert Ferguson, Lay Leader

Class of 1990
W. S. Beckwith III
Dr. J. F. Bigger
Robert A. Blackmon Jr.
Richard Cockrell
Mary Condra
Richard L. Cheek
Dr. Mary L. Dundas Deeter
R. J. Duncan
Jo Dupree
Kathy Farnsworth
Ernest T. Felts
Jane Goodhue
Clarence D. Hampton
Charles V. Holmes

Roger A. Hoover
Eddins L. Hopps
Dr. Alvin J. Ingram
C. S. Jasper
Kate Joyner
Jimmy M. Kelly
Ben Landess
Dr. Andrew Lasslo
James A. Lee
R. Bradley Martin
James A. Massey III
Dr. J. H. McClain
Ralph A. McCool
Paul McQuiston
Mark C. Melton
James F. Morrison
Mildred Orr
Dr. Ed P. Segner Jr.
Dr. Thomas H. Shipmon
Kathy St. John

Kathy Tuberville
Ervin H. Wright Jr.
Linda Wright

Class of 1991
Dr. David W. Bell
J. E. Babbitt
Rubye Carlile
James H. Cook
James A. Davenport
James F. Duncan Jr.
Joanne Farrar
Mary French
James K. Grubbs
C. Lawrence Hawkins
C. Henry Hottum
Anne Howdeshell
John P. Huggins
Ernest A. Jetton
Rob Keener

Appendix: The Official Boards, Commissions, and Committees 203

Dr. David R. Libby
Elva Lyles
Lucy McArtor
Philip E. Mischke
Dr. Michael Mitchell
Glenn Ragland
A. Jackson Rainey
Robert M. Rogers
G. Duke Schaeffer
Dr. Thomas B. Shelton
Roderick Shreve
Carlos Smith
Dr. Vaughn E. Stimbert
Dr. William H. West
Beth Whitsitt

Class of 1992
V. Hugo Akin
Gary E. Barta
Larry Bryant
Fannie Belle Burnett
John DeCell
William W. Dunlap Jr.
R. Byron Fisher
Evelyn Fondren
Jack W. Foster
Steve Fransioli Jr.
Ned M. French
Mark N. Gunn
Maggie Hollabaugh
Orin R. Johnson
Fran Lewis
Richard M. Marsh
Mark Medford
Anne Miller
Steve Mitchener
Ray Moore
Dallas E. Nelson
R. Nash Neyland
Carla Parris
Paul Rogers
Roger Rutledge
Ramona Seabold

Janet N. Sheahan
Michael F. Sheahan
H. Clay Shelton Jr.
Henry C. Shelton III
Leslie B. Sigman
Andrew A. Sippel Jr.
Tommy L. Smith Sr.
William M. J. Taylor
William V. Thompson
Dick W. Thompson Jr.
John B. Turner
John C. Whitsitt Jr.
Dr. James L. Wiygul

Honorary Administrative Board Members
Everett C. Handorf
Samuel H. Mays Sr.
Lee B. McCormick
Ed Richmond
James H. Seabrook Sr.

Lay Delegates, Annual Conference
Kate Davenport
Thomas R. Dyer
John C. Ford
Jane Isbell Haynes
Harry A. Johnson Jr.
Randall D. Noel
Dr. Richard T. Ross
Phoebe Smith

Reserves for Lay Delegates, Annual Conference
Mary Condra
Becky Ford
Penny Johnson
Charles H. Johnston
Martha Anne Johnston
Ann Ross

Council on Ministries
William Watkins Jr., Chairman
Dr. Hal C. Brunt
Bert Ferguson
Betty Gossett
Karen Jetton
Bill W. Patrick
Liz Wagner
John S. Wilson

Work Area Chairpersons
George A. Cook
J. J. Doughtie
Charles W. Gadd
William Gossett
Thomas P. Kelly III
Dick Ross
Sybil Tucker

Work Area of Church and Society
Sybil Tucker, Chairman
Amy Ford
Mona Hoover
Tim Joyce
Anita I. Lotz
Carol Malone
Eloise Mays
Gloria D. McDaniel
Marie Roberson
Beth Whitsitt
Charles E. Wilkinson Jr.

Ex Officio Staff
Marvin H. Budd

Work Area on Discipleship and Small Groups
Robin Taylor, Chairman
David H. Montague
Leslie Morgan

Melissa Neyland
Lissa Noel
Mark Sistrunk
William M. J. Taylor
Terry Whitsitt

Ex Officio Staff
Rev. James L. Loftin

Work Area on Education
Charles W. Gadd,
  Chairman
Carmen Brown
James K. Grubbs
Mark Guenther
Ray Henley
Julie Holliday
Marilyn Holmes
Joy Jaqua
Delores Kinsolving
Barbara Melton
Dr. Matthew E. Ochs
Leslie B. Sigman
Dorris Smith
Marilyn Walker
Jeanette Watkins
Dr. William H. West

Counseling and Family Life
Dr. Ken Robinson,
  Chairman
C. Hal Brunt
Raymond Cummins
Byron Fisher
Judy Hague
Paula Middleton
Courtney Sexton
Louise Smith
Lynn Wilroy

Ex Officio Staff
Dr. Maxie D. Dunnam
Rev. Fred C. Morton

Day School Board
Harry A. Johnson III,
  Chairman
Donald J. Helm
Rick Linder
John McCall
Janet Mitchell
Colby S. Morgan Jr.
Steve Reynolds
Melissa Robinson
H. Allen Whitsitt III

Ex Officio Staff
David W. Fox
Rev. James L. Loftin

Records and History
Flo Seward, Chairman
Gynette Bennett
Myrtle Curry
Jane Goochue
Troy E. O'Brien
Frances Smith
James W. Sanders Jr.

Ex Officio Staff
Dr. Maxie D. Dunnam
Rev. Earl Johnston
Jane Isbell Haynes

Recreation
Bill W. Patrick,
  Chairman
Richard Burt Jr.
Kathy Farnsworth
Alan Greer
Linda Hays
David R. Heckel
James L. Jones
Larry W. Karban
Jean Martin
Mark C. Melton

Dr. Michael Mitchell
Katherine W. Patrick
Calvin B. Ridenhour
Mary Lynn Rote
Bettye Slappey

Ex Officio Staff
Donna C. Thomas

Staff-Parish Relations
John H. Morris III,
  Chairman
Julie Atkinson
Thomas R. Dyer
Dr. James C. Eoff III
Dr. Charles E. Harbison
Warren L. Simpson
Donald A. Thomas
Mary Elizabeth Thomas
Carole West

Ex Officio Staff
Bert Ferguson
William H. Watkins

House and Grounds
Ben M. Carpenter,
  Chairman
John S. Ford
James A. Massey Jr.
William P. Poole
Kenneth W. Rash
Bill Smith
Kent C. Stratton
Roger D. Watson

Ex Officio Staff
Charles Bagley
Richard Bode
Rev. Earl A. Johnston

Insurance
Michael F. Sheahan,
  Chairman

Appendix: The Official Boards, Commissions, and Committees

Gene Bailey
J. Stephen Beale
Larry M. Bryant
Steve Mitchener
George T. Roberts

Ex Officio Staff
Charles Bagley
Rev. Earl A. Johnston

Kitchen
Saralene Thomas,
　Chairman
Virginia Darmody
Mary French
Eddins L. Hopps
Eloise Mays
Charles E. Parnell Sr.

Ex Officio Staff
Charles Bagley
Rev. Earl A. Johnston

Investment Committee
Donald A. Thomas,
　Chairman
John C. Whitsitt Sr.
Gene C. Williams

Music
Betty Gossett,
　Chairman
Eddie Bobbitt
Jeff Capwell Jr.
Arrena Cheek
Margaret Colby
Karla Hefty
Chris Howdeshell
Colby S. Morgan Jr.
Frances Parsons
Jack W. Sanders
Dee Wright
Joy Weisinger

Ex Officio Staff
Jack Hearn
Susie Hillis
Thomas M. Machen
Emily McAllister

Nomination and Personnel
Dr. Maxie D. Dunnam,
　Chairman
Rev. Earl A. Johnston
Nick Clark
Ray Henley
Anita I. Lotz
Theodore W. Medlin
Jack W. Moore
Trudy Simpson

Pension and Trust Fund
William H. Watkins Jr.,
　Chairman
Mark Medford
Preston McDaniel
Trudy Simpson
Ernest A. Jetton
John H. Morris III

Work Area on Higher Education and Campus Ministry
William Gossett,
　Chairman
Joyce Bittle
Henry H. Harry
Richard T. Ross
Ed Rutz
E. P. Segner Jr.
Clinton F. Stewart
Donald W. Tucker

Ex Officio Staff
Rev. James L. Loftin

Work Area on Missions/Outreach
Dr. George A. Cook,
　Chairman
W. S. Beckwith III
Ed Bobbitt
Richard Cockrell
Jewel Crowson
John A. Elkington
Joann Farrar
Ernest T. Felts
Karla Hefty
Roger A. Hoover
Thomas D. Iverson
Marcia Krenen
Thomas L. Land
H. B. Landess Jr.
M. W. Lipscomb III
Kelli May
Janet Mitchell
Betty Moore
Wayne Pyeatt
Michael F. Sheahan
Amelia Shreve
Brenda Sippel
Missy Sistrunk
Mary Elizabeth Thomas
David R. Tichenor
Sara Williams
Dr. R. Sidney Wilroy

Ex Officio Staff
Dr. Maxie D. Dunnam
Rev. James L. Loftin

Planned Giving
Don W. Morgan,
　Chairman
Fannie Belle Burnett
Alvin R. Hartman
Margaret Henrich
Lowell G. Hays Jr.
Donald M. Howdeshell

James A. Massey III
Mary Lou Medlin
Edwin S. Roberson

Ex Officio Staff
Rev. Earl A. Johnston

Policy Committee
Dr. Maxie D. Dunnam,
 Chairman
Dr. Hal C. Brunt
Charles W. Gadd
Carolyn Walker
John C. Whitsitt Sr.
John S. Wilson

Property Disposition
Clarence Colby,
 Chairman
Julia DeBardeleben
Harry A. Johnson III
Betty Marston
Bert McCool
Minor Murrah
Majorie Phelan

Ex Officio Staff
Rev. Earl A. Johnston

Property Use
Carolyn Walker,
 Chairman
Dr. Hal C. Brunt
Ben Carpenter

Finance
John S. Wilson,
 Chairman
Phillip Brodnax III
Mary Condra
Harry G. Crockett Jr.
John DeCell
J. Paul Dorman Jr.

Ernest T. Felts
David L. Grant
Grace Hayden
Orin R. Johnson
James A. Lee
George P. Lewis
Dr. David R. Libby
Anita I. Lotz
Jean Maier
Dr. J. Howard McClain
Jonathan G. Page
G. Duke Schaeffer
Michael F. Sheahan
T. L. Smith Jr.
Bill Thompson
John C. Whitsitt
Dr. Phillip E. Wright
Carol Yochem

Ex Officio Staff
Charles Bagley
Ben Carpenter
 Dr. George A. Cook
J. J. Doughtie
Dr. Maxie D. Dunnam
Bert Ferguson
Charles W. Gadd
Charles V. Holmes
C. Henry Hottum
Harry A. Johnson III
Rev. Earl A. Johnston
Thomas P. Kelly III
Jamie Smith
Robin Taylor
Saralene Thomas
Roy H. Thurmond
Liz Wagner
William Watkins Jr.
John C. Whitsitt Sr.

Trustees
John C. Whitsitt Sr.,
 Chairman

Mary Lou Medlin
P. D. Miller Jr.
Jackson W. Moore
George T. Roberts
Carolyn Rogers
Janet N. Sheahan
John B. Turner
R. Keith Weisinger

*Work Area on
Assimilation*
Charles V. Holmes,
 Chairman
Larry Biggert
Lorraine Bradford
Jeffrey D. Brannen
Larry O. Brooks
Marilyn Crosby
William J. Crosby
Dianne Duncan
Beth Harbison
Robert L. Hardin
Kay Jones
Kizer Jones
Larry W. Karban
Brenda Lafferty
James T. Lafferty
Mark Medford
Suzanne Medford
Kathy Mitchener
Steve Mitchener
Julia Morrison
Cindy Rapp
Roger Rapp
Marty Redding
Dr. Richard T. Ross
Anthony Rutz
Marianna Rutz
Stephen E. Shular
Dennis Starr
Robin Taylor
William M. J. Taylor
Nelle Weddington

Appendix: The Official Boards, Commissions, and Committees 207

Ex Officio Staff
Rev. Shirley G. Lynn

Communications
Liz Wagner, Chairman
Michael J. Bartz
Robert Manuel III
Dallas Nelson
Michael F. Sheahan
Donna R. Simmons

Ex Officio Staff
Dr. Maxie D. Dunnam

Council on Children's Ministry
Angela Donahue, Chairman
Melissa Bell
Christie Manuel
Melissa Neyland
Liza Ozier
Patti Parris
Trudy Rhodes
Joan Sigman
Mary Spangler
Deborah H. Starr
Carol Stricklin
Laura West
Ann Zambetti

Ex Officio Staff
Paula S. Bourland
Marvin H. Budd

Work Area on Education
Melissa Bell, Chairman
Angela Donahue
Dee Dyer
Karen Jetton
Ben Landess
Melissa Neyland

Mary Spangler
Carol Stricklin

Ex Officio Staff
Paula S. Bourland
Marvin H. Budd

Work Area on Evangelism
Thomas P. Kelly III, Chairman
Gary E. Barta
Harry V. Cost
Cathy Dalfume
Tim Dalfume
Donald L. Grant
Karla Grant
Jerry R. Hinson
Paula Hinson
C. S. Jasper
Ramona Jasper
Rob Keener
Tina Keener
Connie McIntyre
Steve McIntyre
Paul McQuiston
D. J. Meyer
C. Edward Meyer
Philip E. Mischke
James Mulroy Jr.
Nancy Mulroy
Beth Ramsey
Allen Whitsitt III

Ex Officio Staff
Rev. E. H. Barnes
Dr. James R. Mulroy

Age-Level Coordinators
Angela Donahue
Dee Dyer
Charles V. Holmes
Cooper Robinson

Dr. Ken Robinson
Robin Taylor

Ex Officio Staff
Paula S. Bourland
Marvin H. Budd
Dr. Maxie D. Dunnam
David W. Fox
Jack Hearn
Rev. Earl A. Johnston
Rev. James L. Loftin
Rev. Shirley G. Lynn
Thomas M. Marino
Rev. Fred C. Morton
Dr. James R. Mulroy
Donna C. Thomas

Audit
Henry H. Harry, Chairman
H. B. Landess Jr.
Roy H. Thurmond

Budget
Edwin S. Roberson, Chairman
Robert L. Hardin
Anita I. Lotz
Theodore W. Medlin
Jack Renshaw
Harold Stewart
John B. Turner
Lee Ann Walker
Jeanette Watkins

Capital Maintenance Endowment Trust
Harry A. Johnson Jr., Chairman
David P. Rogers
Gene C. Williams

Work Area on Stewardship
Dick Ross, Chairman
Robert A. Blackmon Jr.
J. E. Bobbitt
John Eubank Jr.
Ned M. French
Louis P. Goke
Betty Grant
Mark Neil Gunn
Margaret Henrich
Dr. Mack A. Land
Dr. J. H. McClain
Troy E. O'Brien
Edwin S. Roberson
Ann Ross
Andrew A. Sippel Jr.
William M. J. Taylor
Dr. Donald Tucker
John B. Turner
Tom Watson

Ex Officio Staff
Rev. Earl A. Johnston
George P. Lewis

Work Area on Worship
J. J. Doughtie, Chairman
Julie Brewster
Debbie Dorman
Dr. James C. Eoff III
Betty Harbison
Eddins L. Hopps
Ernest A. Jetton
Jimmy M. Kelly
Donna Libby
Greene Miller
Virginia McClain
W. H. Meadows Jr.
Fairfax Segner
Mimi Steepleton
Dr. Clinton F. Stewart
Dr. Len Sumner
Elizabeth Turner

Ex Officio Staff
Dr. Maxie D. Dunnam
Jack Hearn
Thomas M. Machen
Emily McAllister

Officers and Ex-Officio Administrative Board
Charles Bagley
E. H. Barnes
Paula S. Bourland
Dr. C. Hal Brunt
Marvin H. Budd
Ben M. Carpenter
Clarence Colby
Dr. George A. Cook
Kate Davenport
Angela Donahue
J. J. Doughtie
Dr. Maxie D. Dunnam
Dee Dyer
Bert Ferguson
Rev. Ray Fitzgerald
John C. Ford
David W. Fox
Charles W. Gadd
Betty Gossett
William O. Gossett

Dr. Charles W. Grant
Everett C. Handorf
Jack Hearn
Charles V. Holmes
Harry A. Johnson Jr.
Harry A. Johnson III
Rev. Earl A. Johnston
Thomas P. Kelly III
Dr. Wayne A. Lamb
Rev. James L. Loftin
Rev. Shirley G. Lynn
Thomas Marino
Samuel H. Mays Sr.
Lee B. McCormick
Beth Moore
Don W. Morgan
John H. Morris III
Rev. Fred C. Morton
Dr. James R. Mulroy
D. A. Noel
Bill W. Patrick
Rev. Howard W. Rash
Ed Richmond
Edwin S. Roberson
Cooper Robinson
Dr. Ken Robinson
Dick Ross
James H. Seabrook Sr.
Florence K. Seward
Suzanne Schaeffer
Elizabeth Stevens
Jamie Smith
Phoebe Smith
Robin Taylor
Donna C. Thomas
Saralene Thomas
Roy H. Thurmond Jr.

THE ADMINISTRATIVE BOARD
1991

William Watkins, Chairman
Bert Ferguson, Lay Leader

Class of 1991
Dr. David W. Bell
J. E. Bobbitt
Rubye Carlile

James H. Cook
James A. Davenport
James F. Duncan Jr.
Joann Farrar

Appendix: The Official Boards, Commissions, and Committees

Mary French
James K. Grubbs
C. Lawrence Hawkins
C. Henry Hottum
Anne Howdeshell
John P. Huggins
Ernest A. Jetton
Rob Keener
Dr. David R. Libby
Lucy McArtor
Philip E. Mischke
Dr. Michael Mitchell
Glenn Ragland
A. Jackson Rainey
Robert M. Rogers
G. Duke Schaeffer
Dr. Thomas B. Shelton
Roderick G. Shreve
Carlos Smith
Dr. Vaughn E. Stimbert
Dr. William H. West
Beth Whitsitt

Class of 1992
V. Hugo Akin
Larry M. Bryant
Fannie Belle Burnett
Mary Condra
John DeCell
William W. Dunlap Jr.
Byron R. Fisher
Evelyn Fondren
Jack W. Foster
Steve Fransioli Jr.
Ned W. French
Mark N. Gunn
Maggie Hollabaugh
Orin R. Johnson
Fran Lewis
Richard M. Marsh
Mark Medford
Anne Miller
Steve Mitchener

Ray Moore
Dallas E. Nelson
R. Nash Neyland
Carla Parris
Paul Rogers
Roger Rutledge
Ramona Seabold
Janet N. Sheahan
Michael F. Sheahan
H. Clay Shelton Jr.
Henry C. Shelton III
Leslie B. Sigman
Andrew A. Sippel Jr.
Tommy L. Smith Sr.
William Taylor
William V. Thompson
Dick W. Thompson Jr.
John C. Whitsitt Jr.
Dr. James L. Wiygul

Class of 1993
Myra Barksdale
Bruce Berry
Betty Cook
Bill Crosby
Russell Day
Deborah Dorman
Jill Ellis
Dr. James C. Eoff III
Steve Farnsworth
Jay Ford
Chuck Gadd
Lewis Goke
James Gordon
Gary Greer
Betty Harbison
David Harris
Don Helm
Margaret Henrich
Linda Hubbard
Tom Iverson
Tom Kelly
Cindy Lipscomb

Dr. Diane Long
D. J. Meyer
David Montague
Ed Mullikin
Cooper Robinson
Edward Rutz
Jim Sanders
Kay Sears
John Stone
Roy Thurmond
Paul Tuberville
John Walker
Dr. Mark Wiygul
Buddy Wright
Katherine Young

Officers and Ex-Officio, Administrative Board
Jan Averwater
E. H. Barnes
Don Bourland
Dr. C. Hal Brunt
Marvin H. Budd
Ben M. Carpenter
Kathy Clark
David Compton
Dr. Maxie D. Dunnam
Dee Dyer
Bert Ferguson
Rev. Ray Fitzgerald
John C. Ford
David W. Fox
Betty Gossett
Dr. Charles W. Grant
Everett C. Handorf
Jack Hearn
Lynn Holloway
Charles V. Holmes
Harry A. Johnson III
Rev. Ron Johnson
Rev. Earl A. Johnston
Harry Cost

Dr. Wayne A. Lamb
Rev. James L. Loftin
Rev. Shirley G. Lynn
Thomas Marino
Chris Marshburn
Emmett Marston
Samuel H. Mays Sr.
Lee B. McCormick
Barbara Melton
P. D. Miller
Don W. Morgan
John H. Morris III
Rev. Fred C. Morton
Dr. James R. Mulroy
Minor Murrah
Charles Parnell
Bill W. Patrick
Rev. Howard W. Rash
Ed Richmond
Edwin S. Roberson
Cooper Robinson
Dr. Ken Robinson
David Rogers
James H. Seabrook Sr.
Mimi Steepleton
Elizabeth Stevens
Jamie Smith
Louise Smith
Phoebe Smith
Robin Taylor
Roy H. Thurmond Jr.
Adam Webster
Patrick D. Whaley
Sam Wilson

Honorary Administrative Board Members
Everett C. Handorf
Samuel H. Mays Sr.
Lee B. McCormick
Ed Richmond
James H. Seabrook Sr.

Lay Delegates, Annual Conference
John C. Ford
Jane Isbell Haynes
Preston McDaniel
Philip Mischke
Jack Morris
Randall D. Noel
Lou Payne
Phoebe Smith
Don Wood

Reserves for Lay Delegates, Annual Conference
Mary Condra
Becky Ford
Penny Johnson
Charles H. Johnston
Martha Anne Johnston
Ann Ross

Council on Ministries
William Watkins Jr., Chairman
Dr. Hal C. Brunt
Bill W. Patrick
Bert Ferguson
Betty Gossett
Lynn Holloway
Liz Wagner
John S. Wilson

Work Area Chairpersons
Don Bourland
Kathy Clark
Harry Cost
Dee Dyer
Chris Marshburn
Ed Roberson
Adam Webster

Age-Level Coordinators
Charles V. Holmes
Barbara Melton
Steve Mitchener
Cooper Robinson
Dr. Ken Robinson
Robin Taylor
Sybil Tucker

Ex Officio Staff
Jan Averwater
Marvin H. Budd
Dr. Maxie D. Dunnam
David W. Fox
Jack Hearn
Rev. Earl A. Johnston
Lynn Koeneman
Rev. James L. Loftin
Rev. Shirley G. Lynn
Thomas M. Marino
Lisa Mischke
Rev. Fred C. Morton
Dr. James R. Mulroy
Patrick D. Whaley

Audit
Roy H. Thurmond Jr., Chairman
Jerry Davis
Henry H. Harry

Budget
David Rogers, Chairman
Robert L. Hardin
Anita L. Ramsey
Theodore W. Medlin
Jack Renshaw
Harold Stewart
Lee Ann Walker
Jeanette Watkins

Appendix: The Official Boards, Commissions, and Committees   211

Capital Maintenance Endowment Trust
Ed Richmond Sr., Chairman
David Rogers
Gene C. Williams

Communications
Liz Wagner, Chairman
Michael J. Bartz
Carol Coletta
Ray Henley
Robert Manuel III
Michael F. Sheahan

Ex Officio Staff
Dr. Maxie D. Dunnam

Council on Adult Ministry
Sybil Tucker, Chairman
Rubye Carlile
Margaret Colby
Robert E. Darmody
Hazel B. DeHaan
Miller Delgadillo
James Gordon

Ex Officio Staff
Marvin Budd
Rev. Earl A. Johnston

Council on Children's Ministry
Barbara Melton, Chairman
Lee Billings
Christy Brooks
JoAnn Grear
Christie Manuel
Liza Ozier
Carol Stricklin

Laura West
Linda Wright
Ann Zambetti

Ex Officio Staff
Patrick D. Whaley

Counseling and Family Life
Dr. Ken Robinson, Chairman
Shed Caffey
Raymond Cummins
Mary Ann Fisher
Judy Hogue
Diane Land
Paula Middleton
Courtney Sexton
Betty Shipmon

Ex Officio Staff
Dr. Maxie D. Dunnam
Rev. Fred C. Morton

Day School Board
Harry A. Johnson III, Chairman
Donald J. Helm
Scott Fleming
Rick Linder
John McCall
Debbie Miller
Janet Mitchell
H. Allen Whitsitt III

Ex Officio Staff
David W. Fox
Rev. James L. Loftin

Finance
John S. Wilson, Chairman

Phillip Brodnax III
Mary Condra
John DeCell
Orin R. Johnson
George P. Lewis
Jean Maier
Anita L. Ramsey
T. L. Smith Sr.
Bill Thompson
John Whitsitt Jr.
Dr. Phillip E. Wright

Ex Officio Staff
Don Bourland
Ben Carpenter
Kathy Clark
Dr. Maxie D. Dunnam
Dee Dyer
Bert Ferguson
Charles V. Holmes
Rev. Earl A. Johnston
Thomas P. Kelly III
Emmett Marston
P. D. Miller
Charles Parnell
Jamie Smith
Robin Taylor
Roy H. Thurmond Jr.
Liz Wagner
William Watkins Jr.

House and Grounds
Ben M. Carpenter, Chairman
Dud Curry
Ramona Jasper
James A. Massey Jr.
William P. Poole
Adair Rainey
Bill Smith
Roger D. Watson

Ex Officio Staff
Richard Boda
Rev. Earl A. Johnston

Insurance
Michael F. Sheahan,
    Chairman
Gene Bailey
Larry M. Bryant
Steve Mitchener
George T. Roberts
Paul Tuberville

Ex Officio Staff
Rev. Earl A. Johnston

Kitchen
Charles Parnell,
    Chairman
Margaret Colby
Virginia Darmody
Mary French
Eddins L. Hopps
Eloise Mays

Ex Officio Staff
Rev. Earl A. Johnston

Investment Committee
Donald A. Thomas,
    Chairman
Bill Thomspon
Gene C. Williams

Music
Betty Gossett,
    Chairman
Eddie Bobbitt
Jeff Capwell Jr.
Arrena Cheek
Margaret Colby
Cheryl Farnsworth

Karla Hefty
Chris Howdeshell
Colby S. Morgan Jr.
Betsy Peck
Jack W. Sanders
Phoebe Smith
Dee Wright
Joy Weisinger

Ex Officio Staff
Jack Hearn
Susie Hills
Emily McAllister

Nomination and Personnel
Dr. Maxie D. Dunnam,
    Chairman
Don Bourland
Nick Clark
Tom Dyer
Betty Harbison
Ray Healey
Karen Jetton
Rev. Earl A. Johnston
Anita Ramsey
Michael Sheahan
Suzanne Schaeffer

Pension and Trust Fund
Ernest A. Jetton,
    Chairman
Hazel DeHaan
Mark Medford
Preston McDaniel
H. Clay Shelton Jr.
Trudy Simpson

Planned Giving
Don W. Morgan,
    Chairman
Fannie Belle Burnett
Margaret Henrich

Lowell G. Hays Jr.
Mary Lou Medlin
Steve Mitchener
Frances Parsons
Edwin S. Roberson

Ex Officio Staff
Rev. Earl A. Johnston

Policy Committee
Dr. Maxie D. Dunnam,
    Chairman
Dr. Hal C. Brunt
Dee Dyer
Ted Medlin
P. D. Miller
John S. Wilson

Property Disposition
Minor Murrah,
    Chairman
Julia DeBardeleben
Betty Marston
Ed Meier
Bert McCool
Kitty Anderson Stepp

Ex Officio Staff
Rev. Earl A. Johnston

Property Use
Ted Medlin, Chairman
Dr. Hal C. Brunt
Ben Carpenter

Record and History
Louise Smith, Chairman
Gynette Bennett
Myrtle Curry
Patty Henson
Troy E. O'Brien
Ann Piper

Appendix: The Official Boards, Commissions, and Committees

James W. Sanders Jr.
Ramona Seabold
Frances Smith
Marsha Thompson

Ex Officio Staff
Dr. Maxie D. Dunnam
Rev. Earl A. Johnston
Jane Isbell Haynes

Recreation
Bill W. Patrick,
  Chairman
Richard C. Burt Jr.
Dick Cockrell
Kathy Farnsworth
Jennifer Hamilton
Alvin R. Hartman
Linda Hays
David R. Heckel
Jana L. Jones
Larry W. Karban
David Montague
Katherine W. Patrick
Calvin B. Ridenhour
Melissa Robinson
Mary Lynn Rote
Bettye Slappey

Ex Officio Staff
Jan Averwater

Staff-Parish Relations
John H. Morris III,
  Chairman
Thomas R. Dyer
Dr. James C. Eoff III
Anne Howdeshell
Burns Landess
Jack G. Moore
Warren L. Simpson
Mary Elizabeth Thomas
Carole West

Ex Officio Staff
Bert Ferguson
William H. Watkins Jr.

Trustees
P. D. Miller Jr.,
  Chairman
Susan Davis
Mary Lou Medlin
Jackson W. Moore
Randy Noel
George R. Roberts
Carolyn Rogers
Dick Ross
R. Keith Weisinger

*Work Area on
Assimilation*
Charles V. Holmes,
  Chairman
Amy Bowden
Larry O. Brooks
Margaret Carlson
Rick Carlson
Craig Cowles
Sharon Cowles
Arnold Cox
Mrs. Pat Ginn
Terry Hall
Robert L. Hardin
Mike Johnson
Kizer Jones
Larry W. Karban
Beverly Klenz
Rick Klenz
Chris Marshburn
Elizabeth Marshburn
Mark Medford
Suzanne Medford
Kathy Mitchener
Steven Mitchener
Julia Morrison

Gordon Morrow
Kay Morrow
Keith Parsons
Cindy Rapp
Roger Rapp
Marty Redding
Diana Reid
Frank Reid
Paul Rogers
Anthony Rutz
Marianne Rutz
Dennis Starr

Ex Officio Staff
Rev. Shirley G. Lynn

*Work Area on Church
and Society*
Chris Marshburn,
  Chairman
Mike Clark
Amy Ford
Mona Hoover
Tim Joyce
Carol Malone
Eloise Mays
Marie Roberson
Jane Sharp
Beth Whitsitt

Ex Officio Staff
Marvin H. Budd

*Work Area on
Discipleship and Small
Groups*
Robin Taylor, Chairman
Paula Bourland
Vickie Hall
Don Howdeshell
Leslie Morgan
Melissa Neyland

213

Lissa Noel
Mark Sistrunk
William Taylor
Terry Whitsitt

Ex Officio Staff
Rev. James L. Loftin

Work Area on Education
Dee Dyer, Chairman
Helen Boyd
Carmen Brown
Ken Draffin
Mark B. Guenther
Julie Holliday
Marilyn Holmes
Joy Jaqua
Barbara Melton
Clinton Stewart
Marylyn Walker
Dr. William H. West

Ex Officio Staff
Marvin H. Budd
Lynn Koeneman
Ben Landess
Barbara Melton
Sheila Moody
Carol Stricklin

Work Area on Evangelism
Harry Cost, Chairman
Rodney Greener
Cynthia Greener
C. S. Jasper
Ramona Jasper
Rob Keener
Tina Keener
Richard Klenz
Mickie Klenz
Connie McIntyre
Steve McIntyre

Paul McQuiston
D. J. Meyer
C. Edward Meyer
Philip E. Mischke
James R. Mulroy II
Nancy Mulroy
Ruth Mulroy
Amanda Perry
Beth Ramsey
John Seabold
Charlotte Snow

Ex Officio Staff
Rev. E. H. Barnes
Dr. James R. Mulroy

Work Area on Higher Education and Campus Ministry
Adam Webster, Chairman
Joyce Bittle
Carolyn Rogers
Richard T. Ross
Edward Rutz
Clinton F. Stewart
Donald W. Tucker

Ex Officio Staff
Rev. James L. Loftin

Work Area on Missions/Outreach
Don Bourland, Chairman
W. S. Beckwith III
Ed Bobbitt
Jewel Crowson
Ernest T. Felts
Chuck Gadd
Jenny Hammack
Marcia Kreunen

M. W. Lipscomb III
Kellie May
Betty Moore
Lily Rutledge
Bob Sharp
Brenda Sippel
Missy Sistrunk
Mary Elizabeth Thomas
Claudia Twardzik
Sara Williams

Ex Officio Staff
Dr. Maxie D. Dunnam
Rev. James L. Loftin

Work Area on Stewardship
Ed Roberson, Chairman
Robert A. Blackmon Jr.
J. E. Bobbitt
Russell Day
James Delgadillo
Paul Dorman
John Eubank Jr.
Ned M. French
Louis P. Goke
Mark N. Guam
Dr. Mack A. Land
George Lewis
Dr. J. H. McClain
Edwin S. Robinson
Ann Ross
William Taylor
Dr. Donald Tucker
Tom Watson

Ex Officio Staff
Rev. Earl A. Johnston
David Rogers

Work Area on Worship
Kathy Clark, Chairman
Jewel Crowson

Appendix: The Official Boards, Commissions, and Committees

Debbie Dorman
Dr. James C. Eoff III
Betty Harbison
Eddins Hopps
Tom Iverson
Bruce Loveless
Greene Mille

Virginia McClain
W. H. Meadows Jr.
Frances Parsons
Ramona Seabold
Trudy Simpson
Mimi Steepleton
Dr. Clinton F. Stewart

Ex Officio Staff
Dr. Maxie D. Dunnam
Jack Hearn
Emily McAllister

THE ADMINISTRATIVE BOARD
1992

William Watkins,
   Chairman
Bert Ferguson, Lay
   Leader
Dr. Hal C. Brunt
Mary Condra

Class of 1992
V. Hugo Akin
Larry M. Bryant
Fannie Belle Burnett
Mary Condra
John DeCell
William W. Dunlap Jr.
R. Byron Fisher
Evelyn Fondren
Jack W. Foster
Steve Fransioli Jr.
Ned M. French
Maggie Hollabaugh
Orin R. Johnson
Fran Lewis
Richard M. Marsh
Mark Medford
Arnie Miller
Steve Mitchener
Ray Moore
Dallas E. Nelson
R. Nash Neyland
Carla Parris
Paul Rogers
Roger Rutledge

Ramona Seabold
Janet N. Sheahan
Michael F. Sheahan
H. Clay Shelton Jr.
Henry C. Shelton III
Andrew A. Sippel Jr.
Tommy L. Smith Sr.
William Taylor
William V. Thompson
Dick Thompson Jr.
John C. Whitsitt Jr.
Dr. James L. Wiygul

Class of 1993
Bruce Berry
Betty Cook
Bill Crosby
Russell Day
Deborah Dorman
Jill Ellis
Dr. James C. Eoff III
Steve Farnsworth
Jay Ford
Chuck Gadd
Lewis Goke
James Gordon
Gary Grear
Betty Harbison
David Harris
Don Helm
Margaret Henrich
Linda Hubbard

Tom Iverson
Tom Kelly
Myra Barksdale Kelso
Cindy Lipscomb
Dr. Diane Long
D. J. Meyer
David Montague
Ed Mullikin
Cooper Robinson
Edward Rutz
Jim Sanders
Kay Sears
John Stone
Roy Thurmond
Paul Tuberville
John Walker
Dr. Mark Wiygul
Buddy Wright
Katherine Young

Class of 1994
Milton J. Bennett
Lee Billings
Horace B. Branch
Jack N. Brown
Billy G. Hall Jr.
Roger A. Hoover
John T. Hutton
Geneva Jackson
James A. Lee
George P. Lewis
Don W. Morgan

James R. Mulroy II
Doreen Neal
Ken W. Patton
George T. Roberts Sr.
Julia Sayle
Connie Stevens
Harold W. Ware

*Administrative Board
Officers and Ex Officio*
Jan Averwater
E. H. Barnes
Don Bourland
Paula Bourland
Dr. C. Hal Brunt
Kathy Clark
Dick Cockrell
Ellen Cockrell
David Compton
Harry Cost
Dr. Maxie D. Dunnam
John DeCell
Dee Dyer
Tom Dyer
Rev. Ray Fitzgerald
John C. Ford
David W. Fox
Dr. Charles W. Grant
Don Greene
Everett C. Handorf
Jay Harvill
Paul Jackson Hearn
Charles V. Holmes
Harry A. Johnson Jr.
Rev. Ron Johnson
Anita Jones
Rev. Rick Kirchoff
Helen Knepper
Dr. Wayne A. Lamb
Rev. James L. Loftin
Rev. Shirley G. Lynn

Thomas Marino
Chris Marshburn
Emmett Marston
Samuel H. Mays
Mark Medford
Lee B. McCormick
Barbara Melton
Dr. P. D. Miller
Don W. Morgan
Rev. Fred C. Morton
Dr. James R. Mulroy
Minor Murrah
Charles Farnell
Bill W. Patrick
Ken Patton
Betsy Peck
Wayne Pyeatt
Rev. Howard W. Rash
Ed Richmond
Edwin S. Roberson
Dr. Ken Robinson
Carolyn Rogers
David Rogers
James H. Seabrook Sr.
Janus Smith
Mimi Steepleton
Louise Smith
Phoebe Smith
Sybil Tucker
Bill Watkins
Carole West
Allen Whitsitt
Patrick D. Whaley

*Honorary Administrative
Board Members*
Bert Ferguson
Everett C. Handorf
Samuel H. Mays Sr.
Lee B. McCormick
Ed Richmond
James H. Seabrook Sr.

*Lay Delegates, Annual
Conference*
John C. Ford
Harry A. Johnson Jr.
Preston McDaniel
Philip Mischke
Jack Morris
Lou Payne
Flo Seward
Henry C. Shelton III
Phoebe Smith
Don Wood

*Reserves for Lay
Delegates, Annual
Conference*
Becky Ford
Penny Johnson
Charles H. Johnston
Martha Anne Johnston
Wayne Pyeatt
Ann Ross

Council on Ministries
Dr. Hal C. Brunt,
    Chairman
Ken Patton
John DeCell
Jay Harvill
Bill Patrick
Betsy Peck
Wayne Pyeatt
Mike Sheahan
Bill Watkins
Carole West

Work Area Chairpersons
Don Bourland
Paula Bourland
Kathy Clark
Harry Cost
Dee Dyer
Jay Harvill

Appendix: The Official Boards, Commissions, and Committees 217

Chris Marshburn
Ed Roberson

Age-Level Coordinators
Dick Cockrell
Ellen Cockrell
John Ford
Don Green
Charles V. Holmes
Helen Knepper
Barbara Melton
Steve Mitchener
Dr. Ken Robinson
Sybil Tucker

Ex Officio Staff
Jan Averwater
Dr. Maxie D. Dunnam
David W. Fox
Paul Jackson Hearn
Rev. James L. Loftin
Rev. Shirley G. Lynn
Thomas M. Marino
Rev. Fred C. Morton
Dr. James R. Mulroy
Patrick D. Whaley
Carolyn Rogers

Program Committees and Work Areas

Adult Ministry
Sybil Tucker, Chairman
Rubye Carlile
Margaret Colby
Miller Delgadillo
James Gordon

Ex Officio Staff
Pat Whaley

Older Adult Committee
John Ford, Chairman
Jean Branch

Suzanne Bratton
Rubye Carlile
Clarence Colby
Bob Darmody
Hazel DeHaan
Jim Duncan
Larry Hawkins
C. S. Jasper
Flo Seward
Mary Elizabeth Thomas

Assimilation
Charles V. Holmes, Chairman
Dr. Ken Caldwell
Carolyn Caldwell
Amy Bowden
Larry O. Brooks
Rick Carlson
Margaret Carlson
Craig Cowles
Sharon Cowles
Arnold Cox
Mona Evans
Terry Hall
Jan Hickey
John Hutton
Carol Hutton
Kizer Jones
Larry W. Karban
Beverly Klenz
Rick Klenz
Sandi Loftin
Kristen Lovan
Mark Lovan
Chris Marshburn
Elizabeth Marshburn
Amy McRae
Jerry Martin
Sue Martin
Kathy Mitchener
Steve Mitchener
Julia Morrison

Gordon Morrow
Kay Gordon
Sarah Norton
Keith Parsons
Helen Parsons
Mary Redding
Paul Rogers
Dennis Starr
Joann Wholley
Amy Wilson
Ralph Wilson
Paul Wisnewski

Ex Officio Staff
Rev. Shirley G. Lynn

Children's Ministry
Barbara Melton, Chairman
Melissa Bell
Lee Billings
Scotty Brafford
Christy Brooks
JoAnn Grear
Diane Hall
Christie Manuel
Lisa Mischke
Sheila Moody
Carol Stricklin
Nancy Thompson

Ex Officio Staff
Patrick D. Whaley

Child Care Committee
Lisa Ayerst, Chairman
Debbie Crom
Dee Dyer
Randy Gardner
Sallie Harris
Renee Karban
Helen Parsons

Kay Ryan
Robin Taylor
Terry Whitsitt

Ex Officio Staff
Barbara Melton
Lisa Mischke
Bettye Smith
Carole West
Pat Whaley
Debbie Wolters

Church and Society
Chris Marshburn,
   Chairman
Mike Clark
Ellen Gardner
David Harris
Mona Hoover
Tim Joyce
Eloise Mays
Jane Sharpe

Ex Officio Staff
Carolyn Rogers

Communications
Mike Sheahan,
   Chairman
Carol Coletta
Mary Lyn Davis
Mike Farnsworth
Ray Henley
Rob Manuel III
Elizabeth Marsburn
Richard Neal
Missy Sistrunk

Ex Officio Staff
Dr. Maxie D. Dunnam
Carolyn Rogers

Counseling and Family Life
Dr. Ken Robinson,
   Chairman
Dr. Shed Caffey
Mary Ann Fisher
Keith McCormick
Paula Middleton
Betty Shipmon
Roger Watson
Bill White

Ex Officio Staff
Dr. Maxie D. Dunnam
Rev. Fred C. Morton

Discipleship and Small Groups
Helen Knepper,
   Chairman
Paula Bourland
Horace Branch
Dot Brannen
Jack Brown
Carla Butler
Vickie Hall
Don Howdeshell
Melissa Neyland
Lissa Noel
Carla Parris
Janet N. Sheahan
Mark Sistrunk

Ex Officio Staff
Rev. James L. Loftin

Education
Dee Dyer, Chairman
Helen Boyd
Carmen Brown
Ken Draffin
David Harris
Jay Harvill

Julie Holliday
Marilyn Holmes
Arnold Lawing
Dan Norton
Clinton Stewart
Dr. William H. West

Ex Officio Staff
Barbara Melton
Sybil Tucker
Karen Jetton
Ben Landess
Lynn Koeneman
Sheila Moody
Carol Stricklin
Jeff Bigger
Debbie Kelly
Thomas Marino
Patrick Whaley

Evangelism
Harry Cost, Chairman
Rick Carlson
Rodney Greener
Cynthia Greener
Brenda Huffstutler
C. S. Jasper
Ramona Jasper
Rob Keener
Tina Keener
Richard Klenz
Mickie Klenz
D. J. Meyer
C. Edward Meyer
James R. Mulroy II
Ruth Mulroy
Amanda Perry
Judy Reed
Frank Reid
Beth Ramsey
John Seabold
Charlotte Snow
Phyllis Weems

Appendix: The Official Boards, Commissions, and Committees 219

Ex Officio Staff
Dr. James R. Mulroy

Higher Education and Campus Ministry
Jay Harvill, Chairman
Joyce Bittle
Shiree Charles
Molly Morgan
Howard Morrison
John Russell
Edward Rutz

Ex Officio Staff
Rev. James L. Loftin

Music
Betsy Peck, Chairman
Dwain Andereck
Eddie Bobbitt
Jeff Capwell Jr.
Cheryl Farnsworth
Colby S. Morgan Jr.
Martha Nicely
Keith Parsons
Lynne Patterson
Phoebe Smith
Joy Weisinger

Ex Officio Staff
Paul Jackson Hearn
Maggie Lee
Emily McAllister
Jennifer Ormon
Lois Parker
Jeremy Ramey
Jacqueline Smith

Missions/Outreach
Don Bourland, Chairman
Beck Beckwith III
John Brannen
Terry Brown
Larry Bryant
Debbie Dorman
Chuck Gadd
Jon Knepper
Marcia Kreunen
Donna Libby
Kellie May
Amy Melton
Dr. Bill Parris
Kenneth W. Rash
Lily Rutledge
Missy Sistrunk
Stephanie Tate
Roy Thurmond
Claudia Twardzik
Pam Vollmer

Ex Officio Staff
Dr. Maxie D. Dunnam
Rev. James L. Loftin

Recreation
Bill W. Patrick, Chairman
Jean Branch
Richard C. Burt Jr.
Jane Caffey
Dick Cockrell
Bill Crosby
Kathy Farnsworth
Jennifer Hamilton
Alvin R. Hartman
Debbie Miller
David Montague
Melissa Robinson
Mary Lynn Rote
Linda Smith
Ned Spangler
Don Thompson

Ex Officio Staff
Jan Averwater

Work Area on Stewardship
Ed Roberson, Chairman
Carol Adams
Russell Day
James Delgadillo
Paul Dorman
John Eubank Jr.
Ned M. French
Louis P. Goke
Dr. Mack A. Land
George Lewis
Dr. J. H. McClain
Richard Neal
Randy Noel
Melissa Robinson
Dr. Donald Tucker
Tom Watson

Ex Officio Staff
Rev. Rick Kirchoff
David Rogers

Work Area on Worship
Kathy Clark, Chairman
Jewel Crowson
Russell Day
Debbie Dorman
Dr. James C. Eoff III
Betty Harbison
Eddins Hopps
Tom Iverson
Bruce Loveless
Greene Miller
Bill Meadows Jr.
Frances Parsons
Ramona Seabold
Trudy Simpson
Mimi Steepleton
Dr. Clinton Stewart

Guild Chairpersons
Darilyn Christenberry, Chairman

Virginia Hollon
Jennifer Jones
Anne Miller
Eugenia Trousdale
Sugar Walker

Ex Officio Staff
Dr. Maxie D. Dunnam
Paul Jackson Hearn
Emily McAllister

Administrative Committees

Audit
Mark Medford, Chairman
Jerry Davis
Henry H. Harry

Budget
David Rogers, Chairman
Grace Hayden
Karen Jetton
Mat Lipscomb
Ted Medlin
Boyd Rhodes
Cooper Robinson
Lee Ann Walker

Capital Maintenance Endowment Trust
Ernest Felts, Chairman
Ed Richmond
David Rogers

Day School Board
Allen Whitsitt, Chairman
Pam Cianciolo
Scott Fleming
John McCall
Debbie Miller
Janet Mitchell
Ruthie Samaha
Cleo Stevenson
Tom White

Ex Officio Staff
David W. Fox
Rev. James L. Loftin

Finance
John DeCell, Chairman
Don Bourland
Philip Brodnax III
Dwight Clark
Dr. Charles E. Harbison
Orin R. Johnson
Debbie Kelly
Mark Medford
Anita L. Ramsey
Tom Shelton
Trudy Simpson
Bill Thompson
Jeannette Watkins
John Whitsitt Jr.
Tom Williams

Ex Officio
Dr. Hal C. Brunt
John C. Ford
Wayne Pyeatt
Ed Roberson
Jamie Smith
Bill Watkins

Ex Officio Staff
Dr. Maxie D. Dunnam
Rev. Rick Kirchoff
Rev. Fred C. Morton
Rev. Shirley G. Lynn
Rev. James L. Loftin

House and Grounds
Harry A. Johnson Jr., Chairman
Jack Allen
Dud Curry
Walter Hughes
Ramona Jasper
Art Massey Jr.
Greene Miller
Adair Rainey
Bill Smith

Ex Officio Staff
Richard Boda
Larry G. Pennington

Insurance
Paul Tuberville, Chairman
Larry M. Bryant
Steve Mitchener

Ex Officio Staff
Larry O. Pennington

Kitchen
Charles Parnell, Chairman
Margaret Colby
Virginia Darmody
Mary French
Mike Sheahan

Ex Officio Staff
Larry Pennington

Investment Committee
Donald A. Thomas, Chairman
Bill Thompson
John Whitsitt Sr.

Ex Officio Staff
Dr. Maxie D. Dunnam
Rev. Rick Kirchoff
Don Bourland

Appendix: The Official Boards, Commissions, and Committees

Tom Dyer
Steve Farnsworth
Betty Harbison
Karen Jetton
Richard Marsh
Larry G. Pennington
Suzanne Schaeffer
Mike Sheahan
Wally Simpson

Pension and Trust Fund
Ernest A. Jetton,
    Chairman
Burns Landess
Mark Medford
H. Clay Shelton Jr.
Trudy Simpson

Planned Giving
Don W. Morgan,
    Co-Chairman
Bob Sharpe,
    Co-Chairman
Fannie Belle Burnett
Margaret Henrich
Virginia Holland
Don Howdeshell
Virginia McClain
Steve Mitchener
Frances Parsons
Ed Roberson

Ex Officio Staff
Rev. Rick Kirchoff

Policy Committee
Dr. Maxie D. Dunnam,
    Chairman
Dr. Hal C. Brunt
John DeCell
Dee Dyer
Ted Medlin
P. D. Miller

Property Disposition
Minor Murrah,
    Chairman
Julia DeBardeleben
Ed Meier
Bert McCool
Kitty Stepp

Ex Officio Staff
Rev. Rick Kirchoff
Larry G. Pennington

Property Use
Ted Medlin, Chairman
Dr. Hal C. Brunt

Records and History
Louise Smith, Chairman
Gynette Bennett
Milton Bennett
Myrtle Curry
Patty Henson
Ann Piper
Ramona Seabold
Frances Smith
Marsha Thompson

Ex Officio Staff
Dr. Maxie D. Dunnam
Jane Isbell Haynes

Staff-Parish Relations
Tom Dyer, Chairman
Paula Bourland
Dr. James C. Eoff III
Anne Howdeshell
Burns Landess
Jack G. Moore
D. A. Noel
Mary Elizabeth Thomas
Gene Williams

Ex Officio
Wayne Pyeatt

Trustees
P. D. Miller Jr.,
    Chairman
Susan Davis
Mary Lou Medlin
Randy Noel
George R. Roberts
Dick Ross
Tommy Smith
Keith Weisinger

Ex Officio
Larry Pennington
Rick Kirchoff

THE ADMINISTRATIVE BOARD
1993

Dr. Richard Ross,
    Chairman
Wayne Pyeatt,
    Lay Leader

Class of 1993
Bruce Berry
Deborah Dorman
Jill Ellis

Dr. James C. Eoff III
Steve Farnsworth
Chuck Gadd
Lewis Goke

James Gordon
Gary Grear
Betty Harbison
David Harris
Dr. Fred Hatch
Don Helm
Linda Hubbard
Tom Kelly
Cindy Lipscomb
Dr. Diane Long
D. J. Meyer
David Montague
Ed Mullikin
Cooper Robinson
Jim Sanders
John Stone
Roy Thurmond
Paul Tuberville
John Walker
Dr. Mark Wiygul
Buddy Wright
Katherine Young

Class of 1994
Lee Billings
Horace Branch
Jack N. Brown
Billy G. Hall Jr.
Roger A. Hoover
John T. Hutton
Geneva Jackson
James A. Lee
George P. Lewis
Don W. Morgan
James P. Mulroy II
Doreen Neal
Ken W. Patton
George T. Roberts Sr.
Julia Sayle
Connie Stevens
Harold W. Ware
Lori Wisnewski

Class of 1995
Gene Bailey
Larry Brooks
Louise Clarke
Jimmy Grubbs
Jimmy Kelly
Donna Libby
Bruce Loveless
Amy Melton
Carl Rackley
Dean Scott
Trudy Simpson
Tom Watson
Pat Wilson
Beck Beckwith
Arrena Cheek
James Delgadillo
Renee Karban
Diane Latimer
Scott Linder
Donna Marsh
Layne Popernik
Dick Ross
Hunter Seabrook
Carlos Smith
Bill White

Honorary Administrative Board Members
Bert Ferguson
Everett C. Handorf
Samuel H. Mays Sr.
Lee B. McCormick
James H. Seabrook Sr.

Lay Delegates, Annual Conference
Mary Condra
Tom Dyer
Harry A. Johnson Jr.
Philip Mischke
Jack Morris
Lou Payne
Flo Seward
Suzanne Schaeffer
Henry C. Shelton III
Wally Simpson

Reserve Lay Delegates, Annual Conference
Becky Ford
Charles H. Johnston
Martha Anne Johnston
Wayne Pyeatt
Ann Ross

Administrative Board Program Council
Tom Kelly, Chairman

Finance
John DeCell

U.M.W. President
Jeanette Watkins

Program Council Work Area Chairpersons

Weekday Child Care Committee
Lisa Ayerst

Missions
Don Bourland
Kathy Clark

Education
David Harris, Chairman

Library Coordinator
Karen Jetton

Evangelism
Richard Klenz

Appendix: The Official Boards, Commissions, and Committees 223

Discipleship and Small Groups
Helen Knepper

Church and Society
Chris Marshburn

Music
Betsy Peck

Assimilation
Roger Rapp

Stewardship
Ed Roberson

Recreation
Melissa Robinson

Prayer Ministry
Janet N. Sheahan

Communion
Mike Sheahan

Stephen Ministry
Pam Vollmer

Age-Level Coordinators

Counseling and Family Life
Shed Caffey

Youth Age-Level Coordinator
Dick Cockrell
Ellen Cockrell

Older Adult
John S. Ford

Single Adult
Don Green

Young Adult Age-Level Coordinator
Steve Mitchener

College and Career
Tracy Wyatt

Ex Officio Staff
Jan Averwater
Gene Barnes
Skip Burzamato
Dr. Maxie D. Dunnam
David W. Fox
Linda Gabriel
Gail Gaddie
Paul Jackson Hearn
Leigh Hook
Matt Hook
Eddins Hopps
Rick Kirchoff
James Loftin
Thomas Marino
Emily McAllister
Fred Morton
Jim Mulroy
Lany Pennington
Carolyn Rogers
Patrick D. Whaley

Administrative Board, Ex Officio
David Compton
John DeCell
Rev. Ray Fitzgerald
Dr. Charles W. Grant
Anne Howdeshell
Nancy Hutcheson
Everett C. Handorf
Rev. Ron Johnson
Dr. Wayne A. Lamb
Emmett Marston
Samuel H. Mays Sr.
Lee R. McCormick

Don W. Morgan
Randy Noel
Charles Parnell
Wayne Pyeatt
Lois Sawyer
James H. Seabrook Sr.
Louise Smith
Allen Whitsitt

Executive Committee
Dr. Richard Ross, Chairman
Dr. Maxie D. Dunnam
Margaret Colby
John DeCell
Dr. Charles E. Harbison
Anne Howdeshell
Tom Kelly
Rick Kirchoff
George Lewis
Donna Libby
Randy Noel
Lany Pennington
Wayne Pyeatt
Mary Ann Thurmond
Jeanette Watkins

Other Adminstrative Committees

Finance
John DeCell, Chairman
Don Bourland
Phil Brodnax
Jack Brown
Dwight Clark
Gary Grear
Jimmy Grubbs
Dr. Charles E. Harbison
Debbie Kelly
Mark Medford
Nash Neyland
David Rogers

Tom Shelton
Trudy Simpson
Jeanette Watkins
Tom Williams

Ex Officio
Dr. Maxie D. Dunnam
Rev. Linda Gabriel
Nancy Hutcheson
Tom Kelly
Rev. Rick Kirchoff
Rev. James L. Loftin
Rev. Shirley G. Lynn
Rev. Fred C. Morton
Randy Noel
Larry Pennington
Wayne Pyeatt
Ed Roberson
Dick Ross

Nomination and Personnel
Dr. Maxie D. Dunnam, Chairman
Rev. Rick Kirchoff, Co-Chairman
Mary Condra
Steve Farnsworth
Chuck Gadd
Don Green
Betty Harbison
Richard Marsh
Suzanne Schaeffer
Mike Sheahan
Wally Simpson

Staff-Parish Relations
Anne Howdeshell, Chairman
Paula Bourland
Burns Landess
Mat Lipscomb
Phil Mischke

Jack G. Moore
D. A. Noel
Betty Shipmon
Gene Williams

Ex Officio
Dr. Maxie D. Dunnam
Wayne Pyeatt
Dick Ross

Trustees
Randy Noel, Chairman
Bill Crosby
Susan Davis
Ernest A. Jetton
Harry A. Johnson Jr.
Mark Melton
Tommy Smith
Carole West

Ex Officio
Richard Boda
Dr. Maxie D. Dunnam
Rick Kirchoff
Larry Pennington

Joel Committee
Dusty Rhodes, Chairman
Miller Delgadillo
Dr. Maxie D. Dunnam
Dr. James C. Eoff III
Chuck Gadd
Rick Kirchoff
Mat Lipscomb
Robbie McQuiston
Randy Noel
Robert Rogers
Dick Ross
Suzanne Schaeffer
Robin Taylor

Audit
Mark Medford, Chairman
Jerry Davis
Larry Pennington

Budget
Grace Hayden
Karen Jetton
Mat Lipscomb
Boyd Rhodes
Cooper Robinson
David Rogers

Capital Maintenance Endowment Trust
Ernest Felts
Larry Pennington

Day School Board
Allen Whitsitt, Chairman
Steve Brown
Scott Fleming
John McCall
Debbie Miller
Nash Neyland
Ruthie Samaha
Julie Sutch
Cleo Stevenson
Tom White

Ex Officio
David W. Fox
Rev. James L. Loftin

Insurance
Paul Tuberville
Larry M. Bryant

Ex Officio
Larry G. Pennington

Appendix: The Official Boards, Commissions, and Committees 225

Kitchen
Charles Parnell,
　Chairman
Margaret Colby
Mike Sheahan

Ex Officio
Larry Pennington

Investment Committee
Bill Thompson
John Whitsitt Sr.

Ex Officio
Larry G. Pennington

Pension and Trust Fund
Ernest A. Jetton,
　Chairman
Burns Landess
Larry Pennington
H. Clay Shelton Jr.

Planned Giving
Don W. Morgan,
　Chairman
Bob Sharpe
Don Howdeshell
Virginia McClain
Steve Mitchener
Frances Parsons

Ex Officio
Rev. Rick Kirchoff

Policy Committee
Dr. Maxie D. Dunnam,
　Chairman
John DeCell
Tom Kelly
Randy Noel
Dick Ross

Records and History
Louise Smith, Chairman
Milton Bennett
Sheila Grubbs
Patty Hansen
Virginia Norton
Ann Piper
Annette Sardwick
Ramona Seabold
Marsha Thompson

Ex Officio Staff
Dr. Maxie D. Dunnam
Jane Isbell Haynes

Committees and Work Areas
Sybil Tucker, Chairman
Jack Brown
Miller Delgadillo
Amy Doville
Dee Dyer
James Gordon
Don Green
Sarah Green
Mary Knepper
Cindy Lipscomb
Betsy Peck
Ken Robinson
Janet N. Sheahan
Henry C. Shelton III
Mark Sistrunk
Mary Ann Thurmond
Tom Twardzik
Betty Wilson

Ex Officio
Pat Whaley

Older Adult Committee
John S. Ford, Chairman
Jean Branch

Suzanne Bratton
Rubye Carlile
Clarence Colby
Bob Darmody
Hazel DeHaan
Jim Duncan
Larry Hawkins
C. S. Jasper
Flo Seward
Mary Elizabeth Thomas

Assimilation
Roger Rapp, Chairman
Keith Barger
Dr. Ken Caldwell
Carolyn Caldwell
Steve Childs
Linda Childs
Craig Cowles
Sharon Cowles
Arnold Cox
Russell Day
Sharon Day
Mona Evans
Sandi Green
Terry Hall
Bob Hardin
Dr. Fred Hatch
Donna Hickman
Lowell Hickman
Jan Hickey
John Hutton
Carol Hurron
Beverly Klenz
Rick Klenz
Dr. Tom Long
Mark Lovan
Kristen Lovan
Chris Marshburn
Elizabeth Marshburn
Amy McRae
Jerry Martin

Sue Martin
Dennis Norton
Sarah Norton
Keith Parsons
Helen Parsons
Cindy Rapp
Paul Rogers
Bill Tupis
Cindy Tupis
Joann Wholley
Amy Wilson
Ralph Wilson
Paul Wisnewski
Lori Wisnewski
Buddy Wright
Dee Wright

Ex Officio
Rev. Shirley G. Lynn
Rev. Gail Gaddie

Children's Ministry
Scotty Brafford,
  Chairman
Lee Ann Clark
Vickie Gandee
Diane Hall
Carol Malone
Sheila Moody
Diane Reed
Denise Rose
Mary Lynn Rote
Linda Smith

At-Large Members
Sara Adams
Joan DeTar
Patty Johnson
Pat Wegener

Ex Officio
Patrick D. Whaley

Child Care Committee
Lisa Ayerst, Chairman
Debbie Crom
Dee Dyer
Randy Gardner
Sallie Harris
Renee Karban
Helen Parsons
Kay Ryan
Robin Taylor
Terry Whitsitt

Ex Officio
Barbara Melton
Lisa Mischke
Bettye Smith
Carole West
Pat Whaley
Debbie Wolters

Church and Society
Chris Marshburn,
  Chairman
Mike Clark
Ellen Gardner
David Harris
Jane Sharpe

Ex Officio
Carolyn Rogers

Communications
Mike Sheahan,
  Chairman
Carol Coletta
Mary Lyn Davis
Mike Farnsworth
Ray Henley
Elizabeth Marshburn
Missy Sistrunk

Ex Officio
Dr. Maxie D. Dunnam
Carolyn Rogers

Counseling and Family Life
Dr. Shed Caffey,
  Chairman
Keith McCormick
Roger Watson
Bill White

Ex Officio
Dr. Maxie D. Dunnam
Rev. Fred C. Morton

Discipleship and Small Groups
Helen Knepper,
  Chairman
Paula Bourland
Horace Branch
Dot Brannen
Jack Brown
Carla Butler
Vickie Hall
Don Howdeshell
Carla Parris
Janet N. Sheahan

Ex Officio
Rev. James L. Loftin

Education
David Harris, Chairman
Jeff Bigger
Helen Boyd
Carla Butler
Mary Louise Caldwell
Dr. James C. Eoff III
Jimmy Grubbs
Chris Guenwald
Jay Harvill
Grant Houser
Karen Jetton
Penny Johnson
Arnold Lawing

Appendix: The Official Boards, Commissions, and Committees 227

Sam Mays
Paul Newman
Dan Norton
Clinton Stewart
Adam Webster
Ralph Wilson

Ex Officio
Jeff Bigger
Scottie Brafford
Barbara Draffin
Karen Jetton
Debbie Kelly
Tom Marina
Lisa Mischke
Carol Stricklin
Sybil Tucker
Patrick Whaley

Evangelism
Richard Klenz,
    Chairman
Mark Brown
Jim DeTar
Rodney Greener
Cynthia Greener
James Hester
Brenda Huffstutler
Mickie Klenz
James P. Mulroy II
Nancy Mulroy
Ruth Mulroy
Amanda Perry
Judy Reed
Frank Reid
Reba Robinson
John Seabold
Gene Shanks
Charlotte Snow
Debbie Smith
Phyllis Weems

Ex Officio
Dr. James R. Mulroy

Growth Group Bible Study
Jill Ellis
Jeanette Eppes
Linda Hays
Lowell Hays
Ellen Petrie

Higher Education and Campus Ministry
Tracy Wyatt,
    Chairman
Shiree Charles
Molly Morgan
Howard Morrison
John Russell

Ex Officio
Rev. James L. Loftin

Music
Betsy Peck, Chairman
Dwain Andereck
Dr. William Crom
Joan DeTar
Cheryl Farnsworth
Leigh Hobson
Scott Moore
Lady Nellis
Martha Nicely
Keith Parsons
Lyndell Patterson
Phoebe Smith

Ex Officio
Paul Jackson Hearn
J. J. Doughtie
Luanne Hearn
Emily McAllister
Jennifer Ormon
Jeremy Ramey
Jeanne Redding

Missions/Outreach
Don Bourland,
    Chairman
John Brannen
Terry Brown
Larry Bryant
Rachel Cook
Myrtle Curry
Debbie Dorman
Michael Farnsworth
Julie Ferrell
Chuck Gadd
Lisa Hays
John Knepper
Donna Libby
Amy Melton
Mark Melton
Bill Parris
Kenneth W. Rash
Reba Robinson
Cindy Stewart
Stephanie Tate
Roy Thurmond
Claudia Twardzik
Pam Vollmer
Adam Webster

Ex Officio
Dr. Maxie D. Dunnam
Rev. James L. Loftin

Prayer Ministry
Janet N. Sheahan,
    Chairman
Frances Crenshaw
Eleanor Eubank
Pauline Hord
Tonya McDonald
Paul McQuiston
Phil Mischke
Nelle Weddington

Recreation
Melissa Robinson,
　Chairman
Mike Andereck
Jean Branch
Jane Caffey
Dick Cockrell
Bill Crosby
Jennifer Hamilton
Scott Linder
Debbie Miller
David Montague
John Seabold
Jill Seabrook
Linda Smith
Ned Spangler
Don Thompson

Ex Officio
Jan Averwater

Stephen Ministries
Pam Vollmer, Chairman
Ellen Cockrell
Carroll Pinner
Melissa Robinson
Steve Vollmer

Ex Officio
Rev. Linda Gabriel

Work Area on Stewardship
Ed Roberson, Chairman
Carol Adams
Russell Day
James Delgadillo
Paul Dorman
Karla Grant
Syble Gwatney
Lynn Holloway
George Lewis
Don W. Morgan
Richard Neal
Andrew A. Sippel Jr.

Ex Officio
Rev. Rick Kirchoff
David Rogers

Work Area on Worship
Kathy Clark, Chairman
Bubba Clark
Jewel Crowson
Ken Draffin

Scott Little
Bruce Loveless
Frances Parsons
Betsy Peck
Ramona Seabold
Trudy Simpson

Guild Chairpersons
Dianne Latimer,
　Chairman
Janice Fly
Virginia Hollon
Bill Mainord
D. J. Meyer
Dean Scott
Eugenia Trousdale
Sugar Walker

Ex Officio
Dr. Maxie D. Dunnam
Paul Jackson Hearn
Emily McAllister

The Administrative Board
1994

Dr. Richard Ross,
　Chairman
Randall D. Noel,
　Lay Leader
Trudy Simpson

Class of 1994
J. Milton Bennett
Lee Billings
Horace B. Branch
Jack N. Brown
Billy B. Hall Jr.

Roger A. Hoover
John T. Hutton
Geneva Jackson
James A. Lee
George P. Lewis
Don W. Morgan
James R. Mulroy II
Doreen Neal
Ken W. Patton
George T. Roberts Sr.
Julia Sayle

Coni Stevens
Harold W. Ware

Class of 1995
Gerri Bailey
Beck Beckwith
Larry Brooks
Arrena Cheek
Louise Clarke
James Delgadillo
Jimmy Grubbs
Amy Harvill

Appendix: The Official Boards, Commissions, and Committees 229

Renee Karban
Jimmy Kelly
Diane Latimer
Donna Libby
Scott Linder
Bruce Loveless
Donna Marsh
Layne Popernik
Carl Rackley
Dick Ross
Dean Scott
Hunter Seabrook
Trudy Simpson
Carlos Smith
Tom Watson
Bill White
Pat Wilson

Class of 1996
Lynn Adkins
Jeff Bigger
Helen Boyd
Phil Brodnax
Larry Bryant
Michael Calhoun
Ben Carpenter
Craig Cowles
Warren Dinter
Byron Fisher
Alan Greer
Randy Jelinek
Dr. John Kakales
Rob Keener
Priscilla Little
Amy McRae
Howard McClain
Barbara Melton
Jack G. Moore
Nash Neyland
Bill Parris
Bob Rouse
Andrew A. Sippel Jr.
Cindy Stewart
Don Thompson

Scott Walker
Tommy Wammack

Honorary Administrative Board Members
Bert Ferguson
Everett C. Handorf
Samuel H. Mays Sr.
Lee McCormick
James H. Seabrook Sr.

Lay Delegates, Annual Conference
Tom Dyer
Harry A. Johnson Jr.
Jack Morris
Flo Seward
Suzanne Schaeffer
Henry C. Shelton III
Wally Simpson
Trudy Simpson
Phoebe Smith

Reserve Lay Delegates, Annual Conference
Mary Condra
Becky Ford
Charles H. Johnston
Martha Anne Johnston
Ann Ross

Adminstrative Board Program Council
Tom Kelly, Chairman
Tom Williams
Randy Noel
Dick Ross
Jeanette Watkins

Program Council Work Area Chairpersons
Lisa Ayerst
Jack Brown

Teny Brown
Tom Dyer
David Harris
Richard Klenz
Keith Parsons
Roger Rapp
Melissa Robinson
Janet N. Sheahan
Mike Sheahan
Trudy Simpson
Linda Smith
Sybil Tucker
Pam Vollmer

Age-Level Coordinators
Shed Caffey
Paul Dorman
Debby Dorman
Donna Hannon
Leigh Lawyer
Scott Martin
Sybil Tucker

Ex Officio Staff
Jan Averwater
Gene Barnes
Skip Burzamato
Rev. Don Burford
David W. Fox
Elaine Friedrich
Linda Gabriel
Bradley Gabriel
Don Green
Win Green
Paul Jackson Hearn
Donna Hickman
Leigh Hook
Matt Hook
Eddins Hopps
Karen Jetton
Rick Kirchoff
James Loftin
Thomas Marino

Janet Misner
Emily McAllister
Larry Pennington
Jim Mulroy
Carolyn Rogers
Patrick D. Whaley

Administrative Board,
Ex Officio
David Compton
Rev. Ray Fitzgerald
Dr. Charles W. Grant
Nancy Hutcheson
Everett C. Handorf
Rev. Ron Johnson
Dr. Wayne Lamb
Emmett Marston
Samuel H. Mays
Lee B. McCormick
Don W. Morgan
Randy Noel
James H. Seabrook Sr.
Mike Sheahan
Louise Smith
Tommy Smith
Julie Sutch
Gene Williams
Tom Williams

Executive Committee
Dr. Richard Ross,
    Chairman
Arrena Cheek
Margaret Colby
Dr. Charles E. Harbison
Tom Kelly
Rick Kirchoff
George Lewis
Randy Noel
Larry Pennington
Janet N. Sheahan
Tommy Smith
Jeanette Watkins

Tom Williams
Gene Williams

Other Administrative
Committees

Finance
Tom Williams,
    Chairman
Don Bourland
Kirk Baillie
Phil Brodnax
Jack Brown
Dwight Clark
Jimmy Grubbs
Dr. Charles E. Harbison
Debbie Kelly
Amy Lincer
Mark Medford
Nash Neyland
Tom Shelton
Trudy Simpson
Jeanette Watkins

Ex Officio
Jack Brown
Rev. Linda Gabriel
Nancy Hutcheson
Tom Kelly
Rev. Rick Kirchoff
Rev. James L. Loftin
Rev. Fred C. Morton
Randy Noel
Larry Pennington
Dick Ross
Tommy Smith

Nomination and
Personnel
Ben Carpenter
Mary Condra
Steve Farnsworth
Chuck Gadd

Martha Anne Johnston
Rev. Rick Kirchoff
Wally Simpson
Carlos Smith

Staff-Parish Relations
Gene Williams,
    Chairman
Paula Bourland
Mat Lipscomb
Phil Mischke
D. A. Noel
Ed Roberson
Betty Shipmon
Mary Ann Thurmond
John Whitsitt

Ex Officio
Randy Noel
Dick Ross
Rick Kirchoff

Trustees
Tommy Smith
Bill Crosby
Ernest A. Jetton
Orin R. Johnson
Mark Melton
Jane Sharpe
Bill Watkins
Carole West

Property Committee
Harry A. Johnson Jr.,
    Chairman

Architectural
Bill Crosby

Fine Arts
Eugenia Trousdale

Grounds
Jack Allen

Appendix: The Official Boards, Commissions, and Committees 231

Interior Design
Virginia Rippee

Maintenance
Wally Simpson

Property Disposition
David J. Harris

Property Use
Ted Medlin

Security
Art Massey

Ex Officio
Richard Boda
Rick Kirchoff
Larry Pennington

Joel Committee
Boyd Rhodes, Chairman
Kathy Clark
Miller Delgadillo
Chuck Gadd
Charles Johnston
Rick Kirchoff
Helen Knepper
Mat Lipscomb
Robbie McQuiston
Rich Neal
Noel Randy
Val Reed
Taylor Robin
Robert Rogers
Dick Ross
Andrew Schaeffer
Suzanne Schaeffer
David Tichenor

Audit
Mark Medford,
    Chairman

Jerry Davis
Larry Pennington

Capital Maintenance Endowment Fund
Ernest Felts, Chairman
Larry Pennington

Day School Board
Julie Sutch, Chairman
Steve Brown
Amy Kuerz
Nash Neyland
Harry Orr
Ruthie Samaha
Cleo Stevenson
Tom White
Katherine Young

Ex Officio
David W. Fox
Rev. James L. Loftin

Insurance
Paul Tuberville,
    Chairman
Larry M. Bryant

Ex Officio
Larry G. Pennington

Kitchen
Mike Sheahan,
    Chairman

Ex Officio
Larry G. Pennington

Pension and Trust
Burns Landess,
    Chairman
David Rogers
Bill Thompson

Policy Committee
John DeCell, Chairman
Tom Kelly
Randy Noel
Dick Ross

Records and History
Louise Smith, Chairman
Betty Pyeatt
Sheila Grubbs
Annette H. Lott
Virginia Norton
Annie Paden
Frances Sturdyvin

Ex Officio Staff
Jane Isbell Haynes

Committees and Work Areas
Sybil Tucker, Chairman

Adult Ministry
Jack Brown
Miller Delgadillo
Amy Doville
Dee Dyer
James Gordon
Don Green
Sarah Green
Mary Knepper
Cindy Lipscomb
Betsy Peck
Ken Robinson
Janet N. Sheahan
Henry C. Shelton III
Mark Sistrunk
Mary Ann Thurmond
Tom Twardzik
Betty Wilson

Ex Officio
Pat Whaley

Older Adult Committee
John S. Ford, Chairman
Jean Branch
Suzanne Bratton
Rubye Carlile
Clarence Colby
Bob Darmody
Hazel DeHaan
Jim Duncan
Larry Hawkins
C. S. Jasper
Flo Seward
Mary Elizabeth Thomas

Assimilation
Roger Rapp, Chairman
Ellen Arterbum
Keith Barter
Dr. Ken Caldwell
Carolyn Caldwell
Steve Childs
Laura Childs
Dr. Troy Cole
Craig Cowles
Sharon Cowles
Russell Day
Sharon Day
Mona Evans
Sandi Green
Page Gregory
Annie Gregory
Bob Hardin
Dr. Fred Hatch
Donna Hickman
Loel Hickman
Jan Hicky
John Hutton
Carol Hutton
Dr. Tom Long
Mark Lovan
Kristen Lovan
Amy McRae

Elizabeth Marshburn
Jerry Martin
Sue Martin
Dennis Norton
Sarah Norton
Steve Popernik
Layne Popernik
Ann Jo Price
Cindy Rapp
Karel Saalwaechter
Bill Tupis
Cindy Tupis
Joann Wholley
Lee Ann Walker
Ralph Wilson
Amy Wilson
Buddy Wright
Dee Wright

Ex Officio
Rev. Bradley Gabriel

Children's Ministry
Leigh Lawyer, Chairman
Linda Smith
Donna Marsh
Carla Parris
Denise Rose
Kay Ryan

At-Large Members
Sara Adams
Joan DeTar
Patty Johnson
Pat Wegener

Ex Officio
Elaine Friedrich
Vicki Gandee
Bettye Smith
Carole West
Debbie Wolters

Church and Society
Tom Dyer, Chairman
Kirk Bailey
Mike Clark
Ellen Gardner
David Harris
Jane Sharpe

Ex Officio
Carolyn Rogers

Communications
Mike Sheahan,
    Chairman
Phil Brodnax
Jo Ellen Druelinger
Ray Henley
Jimmy Rowland
Andrew A. Sippel Jr.

Ex Officio
Dr. Maxie D. Dunnam
Janet Misner

Counseling and Family Life
Dr. Shed Caffey,
    Chairman
John Allen
Carolyn Garner
Keith McCormick
Karel Saalwaechter
Betty Shipmon
Bill White

Ex Officio
Rev. Fred C. Morton

Discipleship and Small Groups
Helen Knepper,
    Chairman

Appendix: The Official Boards, Commissions, and Committees

Paula Bourland
Horace Branch
Dot Brannen
Jack Brown
Carla Butler
Vickie Hall
Don Howdeshell
Carla Parris
Janet N. Sheahan

Ex Officio
Pat Whaley

Education
Kathy Tuberville,
  Chairman
Jeff Bigger
Helen Boyd
Carla Butler
Mary Louise Caldwell
Dr. James C. Eoff III
Jimmy Grubbs
Chris Gruenwald
Jay Harvill
Grant Houser
Karen Jetton
Penny Johnson
Arnold Lawing
Sam Mays
Paul Newman
Dan Norton
Clinton Stewart
Adam Webster
Ralph Wilson

Ex Officio
Jeff Bigger
Barbara Draffin
Karen Jetton
Debbie Kelly
Tom Mann
Lisa Mischke
Carol Stricklin

Sybil Tucker
Patrick Whaley

Evangelism
Richard Klenz,
  Chairman
Mark Brown
Jim DeTar
Mike Feehan
Amy Feehan
James Hester
Brenda Huffstutler
Steve Popernik
Judy Reed
Frank Reid
Gene Shanks
Debbie Smith
Virginia Weakes
Martin Zumack

Ex Officio
Dr. James R. Mulroy

Growth Group Bible Study
Jill Ellis
Jeanette Eppes
Linda Hays
Lowell Hays

Higher Education and Campus Ministry
Shiree Charles,
  Chairman
Molly Morgan
Howard Morrison
John Russell

Ex Officio
Rev. James L. Loftin

Music
Keith Parsons,
  Chairman

Dwain Andereck
Dr. William Crom
Joan DeTar
Cheryl Farnsworth
Leigh Hobson
Scott Moore
Lady Nellis
Martha Nicely
Keith Parsons
Lyndell Patterson
Phoebe Smith

Ex Officio
J. J. Doughtie
Luanne Hearn
Paul Jackson Hearn
Emily McAllister
Jennifer Ormon
Jeremy Ramey
Jeanne Redding

Missions/Outreach
David Harris, Chairman
John Brannen
Terry Brown
Lany Bryant
Louise Clark
Barbara Dodge
Jim Dodge
Debbie Dorman
Michael Farnsworth
Julie Ferrell
Mark Forrester
Lucy Forrester
Bill Hall
Amy Harvill
Jay Harvill
Lisa Hays
John Knepper
Donna Libby
Mark Melton
Bill Parris
Reba Robinson

Cindy Stewart
Stephanie Tate
Roy Thurmond
Pam Vollmer
Adam Webster
Rachel Wise

Ex Officio
Rev. James L. Loftin

Prayer Ministry
Janet N. Sheahan,
    Chairman
Jan Campbell
Frances Crenshaw
Pauline Hord
Harriet McClendon
Tonya McDonald
Paul McQuiston
Phil Mischke
Nelle Weddington

Recreation
Melissa Robinson,
    Chairman
Mick Andereck
Jean Branch
Jane Caffey
Philip Cantrell
Kay Clark
Bill Crosby
Julia DeBardeleben
Scott Linder
Debbie Miller
John Seabold
Jill Seabold
Linda Smith
Ned Spangler
Don Thompson
Tim Wise

Ex Officio
Jan Averwater

Stephen Ministries
Pam Vollmer, Chairman
Ellen Cockrell
Carroll Pinner
Melissa Robinson
Steve Vollmer

Ex Officio
Linda Gabriel

Work Area on Stewardship
Jack Brown, Chairman
Carol Adams
James Delgadillo
Mark Forrester
Karla Grant
Syble Gwatney
Lynn Holloway
Brad Koeneman
Don W. Morgan
Richard Neal
Andrew A. Sippel Jr.

Ex Officio
Bradley Gabriel
Rev. Rick Kirchoff
David Rogers

Volunteer Ministry Advisory Group
Terry Brown, Chairman
Lisa Ayerst
Paula Bourland
J. J. Doughtie
Sallie Harris
Meade Moore
Don Thompson
Mary Ann Thurmond

Work Area on Worship
Trudy Simpson,
    Chairman

Jack Brown
Bubba Clark
Jewel Crowson
Ken Draffin
Scott Little
Bruce Loveless
Barbara Melton
Keith Parsons

Guild Chairpersons
Diane Latimer,
    Chairman
Lorraine Bradford
Jean Branch
Christie Clark
Mim Duncan
Janice Fly
Virginia Hollon
Bill Mainord
Eugenia Trousdale
Carole Watson

Ex Officio
Dr. Maxie D. Dunnam
Paul Jackson Hearn
Matt Hook
Emily McAllister

At-Large Members
Jewel Crowson
Bruce Loveless

Joel Committee
Dusty Rhodes,
    Chairman
Kathy Clark
Miller Delgadillo
Chuck Gadd
Charles Johnston
Rick Kirchoff
Helen Knepper
Mat Lipscomb

Appendix: The Official Boards, Commissions, and Committees

Robbie McQuiston
Rich Neal
Randy Noel
Val Reed

Robert Rogers
Dick Ross
Andrew Schaeffer
Suzanne Schaeffer

Robin Taylor
David Tichenor

INDEX

Adams, Aileen, 1221
Adams, Barry, 85
Adams, Carol, 85
Adkins, Caryline, 74
Administrative Board, 17–19, 35, 38, 42, 92, 94, 104, 165
Alive in Christ, 11, 30, 32–33
Allen, Avis Davidson, 48, 54
Allen, John, 21
Altar Guild, 122
Anderson, Anthony, 165
Anderson, Jesse Andrew, 121, 159
Anderson, Jesse, family, 119–20
Anderson, Kitty, 121
Annual Conference, 28, 54–65, 116–17, 132; See also Memphis Annual Conference
Archive Room, 47–51
Armstrong, Bishop, 28
Asbury Theological Seminary, Wilmore, Ky., 6, 11, 14–15
Ashworth, Virginia S. "Genie," 74
Atkinson, George, 20
Atkinson, Julia, 20, 70
Averwater, C. J., 87
Ayerst, Lisa, 85
Ayerst, Rob, 85

Bagley, Charles, 16, 101
Bailey, Father Doug, 31
Bailey, Rev. Gene, 85
Bailey, Marion, 74
Bailey, William P., Jr., 56
Barclay, William, 9
Barefoot Days of the Soul, 1
Barksdale, Myra (Mrs. Jack C.), 119, 128
Barnes, Rev. Gene, 16
Barta, Gary, 56, 58, 62–63
Be Your Whole Self, 8
Beasley, Nancy, 105
Beaty, J. Harold, xi, 11, 16, 25, 30, 95, 119, 159, 162
Beaty Activities Building, 53, 104–05
Beck, Melissa, 87
Beckham, Lori, 85
Beckwith, Beck, 70
Beeson, Nettie, 7

Beeson, Ralph Waldo, 15
Bennett, Gynette O. (Mrs. J. Milton), 48, 162
Bennett, J. Milton, 48, 57, 125, 162
Bigger, James F., Jr., vi
Bigger, Mrs. James F., Jr., 108–10
Billings, Dorothy, vi
Black, Sarah (Mrs. Robert C.), 129
Blessed to be a Blessing, 10
Bloom, Anthony, 10
Board of Directors, 89
Board of Discipleship, 8, 29
Board of Pensions, 58
Board of Trustees, 37–38, 92–94, 97, 99–100, 103, 122
Bobango, John, 85
Boda, Richard, 63, 87
Boone, Howard, 24
Boone, Virginia, 24
Born of Conviction, 7
Bouknight, Bill, 13, 165
Bourland, Don, 85, 105
Bradford, Lorraine Brown, 48
Brady, Dale, 162
Brady, Sandra, 31, 33, 162
Branch, Horace, 21
Branch, Jean (Mrs. Horace), 85, 107, 162
Brasfield, Karen, vi
Brewster, Harold, 69
Brewster, Mrs. Harold, 69
Brewster, Julie (Mrs. Michael), 132
Brewster, Michael, 132, 162
Bride's Room, 62
Brindley, Barry, 92
Brooks, Christy, 85
Brooks, Larry, 85
Brouland, Paula, 85
Brown, Jack, 85
Brown, Terry, 85
Brunt, Francie, 58, 62–64
Bryant, Shirley, 85
Budd, Marvin H., 16, 28, 54, 66, 70, 97, 128, 162
Burford, Rev. Don, 16, 89, 164
Burnett, Susan, 85
Burzumato, Skip, 75, 77, 85, 87
Cabbage, Richard, 69
Cabbage, Mrs. Richard, 69

Caldwell, Mary Louise, 54, 57, 70, 115–16
Callahan, Kim, 162
Calvary Episcopal Church, 31, 33, 118
Candler School of Theology, Emory University, xi, 4
Capital Property Maintenance Endowment Trust, 93, 99, 100–02
Carder, Bishop Kenneth, 14
Carlile, Rubye, **x**
Carnes, Kim, 85
Carpenter, Ben M., vi, 24, 48, **ix**
Carpenter, Lillie (Mrs. Ben M.), vi, 24, 107
Carruth, Tom, 7, 10
Carver, Estelle, 7
Cassibry, John, 138
Central Church, 25, 45, 83
Chambliss, Walter, 85
Channels of Challenge, 4
Charge Conference, 18, 94, 99–100, 115, 117, 120
Charismatic Movement, 32
Charles, Shiree, 162
Cherry Road, 92
Chickasaw Country Club, 11–12
Chitagwa, New York, 10
Christ Church, 45
Christ Church Chancel Choir, 56
Christian Church Committees, Evergreen, Ala., 6
Christ Methodist Day School, 244
Christ United Methodist Church Foundation, 101
Church School, 28, 66
Church Women United, 114
Clark, Kathryn S. "Kathy" (Mrs. Dwight A.), 105, 107, 119, 122, 158, 161, **109**
Clark, Louise, 111
Clarke, John, 58
Clayton, Paul W., 16
Cochran, Nell, vi
Cockerham, Indie, 138
Cokesbury, 56
Colby, Clarence, 24, 119
Colby, Margaret, 24, 54–55

236

Comes, Rev. George, 56
Commercial Appeal, 11
Commission on Education, 52, 243
Committees
  Advisory, 21
  Assimilation, 41–43
  Bar-B-Q, 64
  Budget, 64, 94
  Building Planning, 53
  Building, 48, 50–51, 98, 104–05, 121, 243–44
  Church School, 243
  Conference, 59
  Curriculum, 25, 28
  Evangelism, 43, 46
  Executive, iv, 17–18, 40, 42, 104
  Finance, 42–44, 94
  Flower Distribution, 128
  Host, 1991 Memphis Annual Conference, 56, 58–59, 62, 64–65
  Joel, 35–46
  Library, 52–53
  Missions, 44, 46, 69, 165
  Nominations, 18, 42, 45–46, 94, 244
  Pastor-Parish Relations, 24–29
  Planned Giving, 98
  Program, 28
  Projects Policy, 93
  Property, 103–04, 121
  Property Disposition, 93
  Records and History, 48–51
  Staff-Parish Relations, 39, 41–42, 45–46, 162–63
  Steering, 12
  Stewardship, 43–44
  Surplus Funds, 113
  Worship, 38, 121, 164
Communicator's Commentary on Galations, The, 30
Communicator's Commentary, The, 13, 32–33
Compton, David, 62
Conder, Brad, 56
Conder, Jan, 162
Condra, Mary (Mrs. Robert), 24, 55, 107, 109
Conference Council on Ministries (CCOM), 62
Cook, Betty, 85
Cook, George, 85
Cook, Michael, 87
Cook, Rich, 87
Cordova, 13
Corlew, Rev. Jerry F., 16, 28, 105
Council on Ministries, 25, 28, 97, 121
Counseling Center, 20–21
  Al-Anon, 20–21
  Alcoholics Anonymous (AA), 20–21
  Career Suport Ministry, 20–21
  Christian Parenting, 20
  Christians in Recovery, 21
  Divorce Care Workshop, 21
  Lay Chaplains' Ministry to the Homebound, 20
  Marriage Enrichment, 20
  Preparation for Marriage Workshops, 20
Courier, 62, 95
Craig, Mrs. W. H., 107
Crisologo, Dorothy (Mrs. Loreto), 69
Crisologo, Loreto, 69
Crizzard, Carolyn, 66
Crosby, Bill, 86
Crosby, William J., 105
Crosby, William J., family, 119
Crowder, Douglas, 70
Crowder, Mrs. Douglas, 70
Crowson, Jewel (Mrs. William N.), 119, 122, 162
Crump, Rev. Robert "Bob," 56, 58–59, 63–64
Cruser, Sharon, 103
Cummins, Ray, 93
Curry, Anne, 112
Curry, Dud, 70
Curtis, Dana, 138

Daily Devotional Guide, 9
Dancing at My Funeral, 8, 12
Daniel, Faye, 24
Daniel, Jennifer, 87
Daniel, Skip, 24
Darmody, Virginia, 112
Davenport, Howard, 12
Davenport, James A., vi
Davenport, Kate (Mrs. Charlie), vi, 54–55
Davenport, Mary, vi, 12
Davis, Jeff, 85
Davis, Mary Lynn, 85
Davis, Rubye, vi
Day, Russell, 85
Day, Sharon, 85, 111
Day School, 66
Dayview Association, 11
Delgadillo, Miller, 35, 58–59, 62–63
Delta Realty Investment Company, 87
Denman Papers, 10
Department of Human Services, 90
Dewire, Norman E., 56
Dickinson, Buford, 4
Dickinson, Jean (Mrs. Buford), 14
Dike, Jane, 85
Direction and Destiny, 8
Doddsville United Methodist Church, 119
Donalds, Charles, 115
Dorman, Debbie, 85
Dorman, Lashlee, 85
Doughtie, J. J. (Mrs. Dick, III), 24, 54–55, 57, 121
Douglas Street lecture, 11
Dowling, Eugenia (Mrs. Forrest, Jr.), 120–21
Dowling, Forrest, Jr., 120–21
Downen, Clara, x
Draffin, Barbara, 85
Draffin, Ken, 85
Drash, Sam, 66, 162
Druelinger, JoEllen, 85
Druelinger, Steve, 85–86
Dunkin, Sewell, 24, 105
Dunnam, Cora, 1, 7, **3–4**
Dunnam, Dr. Maxie D., xi, 1–16, 20–21, 24–27, 32, 34–35, 37–38, 44–45, 48, 56, 64, 87–89, 97, 100–04, 115, 117, 119–22, 137, 158, 162–64, **xii**, **3–4, 9, 12–14**
Dunnam, Edgar, **3–4**
Dunnam, Irma, **4**
Dunnam, Jerry (Morris), 5–6, 8–9, 11–14, 56, 59, 75, 77–80, 93, 163, **6, 13–14**
Dunnam, Kerry, 9, **6**
Dunnam, Kevin, 9, **6**
Dunnam, Kim, 6, 9, **6**
Dunnam, Lloyd, **3–4**
Dunnam, Lois, **3–4**
Dunnam, Murdock "Mut", 1, **3–4**
Dunnam Building, 47, 53, 104–05
Durham, Durelle, 13
Dyer, Thomas R. "Tom," 54–55, 120, **168**

Earle, Ann, 86
East Side Baptist Church, 2
Echols, Linda, 85
Echolston, Louise, 7
Ecumenical Institute of Spirituality, 10
Edwards, Mrs. Robert, 107
Edwards, Scott, 87
Elijah, 132
Emmaus movement, 9, 27
Emmaus Walk, 25, 34
Eoff, James "Jim," III, 35
Eoff, Virginia (Mrs. James, III), 52
Esperian, Kallen, 14, 132
Eubank, Ellen, 87
Evangelism Training Day, 118
Evans, Betty, 63
Evans, Rev. Albert M., 16
Everett, Janet, 87
Executive Committee of the World Methodist Council, 12, 28

Faith at Work Movement, 8
Farnsworth, Cheryl, 74
Farras, JoAnn, 85
Favazza, Debby, 87
Fellowship Hall Building, 52, 104
Ferguson, Bert, 54, 57, **169**
Ferrell, Julie, 73–74
Ferrell, Thad, 74
Finger, Bishop Ellis, 28
First Evangelical Church, 25
Fisher, Byron, 54, 63–64
Fisher, Dorothy, vi
Fisher, Frank, vi
Floyd, Kay, 85
Floyd, Tommy, 85
Fones, William H. D., vi
Ford, Becky, 55
Ford, John S., 55, 85
Ford, Mrs. John S., 108
Foster, Allison, 159
Foster, Angelique, 159
Foster, Holt, 159
Foster, Joseph Holt, Jr., 159
Fournier, Norman, 74
Fox, David, 66
Fox, Dr. Eddie, 14, **9**
Fox, Mrs. Eddie, **9**
Foy, Ben, 85
Foy, Terry, 85
Frazer, Mary Ann, 117
French, Mrs. Ned, 107–09
Friedrich, Elaine, 16
Fulmer, Alice (Mrs. J. Albert, Jr.), vi
Fulmer, J. Albert, Jr., vi
Funds
　Building, 94
　Communion, 94
　General, 93
　Minister's Discretionary, 94
　Mission, 94
　Music, 94
　Pension, 94
　Single Purpose Project, 94
　Youth, 94
　"Up with Christ" Capital Funds Program, 164

Gabriel, Rev. Bradley W., 16, 43
Gabriel, Rev. Linda, 16, 21–22
Gadd, Chuck, 35
Gaddie, Rev. B. L., 16
Galloway, Ira, 8
Gamble, Jane, 131
Garrett, Chris (Mrs. H. Edward), 108–09, 129, **110**
Gattas, Leslie, 66
Gedney, Millie, 117
General Board of Missions, 67, 70
General Conference, 29, 32
Gilliam, Lisa, 85
Godbold, Laura, 85

Godbold, Mark, 85
Gossett, Bill, 85
Grant, Charles W., xi, 16, 159, 244
Grant, Sallie Simmons (Mrs. David), 52–53, 107–08
Gravely, Ila, 69
Gravely, Jim, 69
Greathouse, Gordon, 70
Greathouse, Teca, 70
Green, Don, 75–81
Green, Sandi, 75, 77–81
Green, Sarah, 74
Green, Rev. Win, 16
Grissam, "Brother," 2
Group Life, 41–42
Gruenwald, Chris, 85
Gruenwald, Leanne, 85
Gwatney Chevrolet, 87

Habitat for Humanity, 70
Hackett, Richard "Dick," 59
Hall, Billy G., Jr., 74, 85
Hall, Diane, 85
Hall, Mandy, 85
Hall, Mark, 85
Hampshire, Peggy, 111
Hampton, Clarence, 24, 54
Hampton, Denice, 162
Handorf, E. C., 55
Harrington, Barbara, 74
Harrington, O. B., 74
Harris, David, 85
Harris, Sallie, 85
Harsh, Pam, 70
Harvill, Jay, 87
Hawkins, Julie, 73
Hawkins, Larry, 54
Hawkins, Sam, 73
Hawkins, Wilma, 53
Haynes, Jane Isbell, 47–51, 54–55
Hays, Drew, 87
Hays, Lisa, 75, 78–79
Hays, Lowell G., Jr., family, 119
Hearn, Jack, 121, 132, 158
Hearn, Luanne, 132
Hearn, Margaret, 132
Hearn, Paul, 132
Heartsong Church, 13
Hendricks, Abel, 10
Hendricks, Freida, 10
Henrich, Erie Sanson, 20, 53, 159
Henrich, Margaret Y. (Mrs. Erie Sanson), 52–53, 106, 113, 159, **108**
Henricks, Abel, 116
Henricks, Freida, 116
Heyer, Edward, 69
Heyer, Jane, 69
Hickey, Thomas, 87
Hollabaugh, Maggie, 58–59, 62–63, 65

Hollabaugh, Robert S. "Bob," 74, 73
Hollon, Virginia, 24
Holloway, Lynn (Mrs. David), 110, 158, **111**
Holmes, Jim, 64
Homesick for a Future, 9
Hook, Rev. Matt, 16, 40
Hoover, C. Winston, Jr., 105, 159
Hoover, Mrs. C. Winston, Jr., 159
Hopps, Eddins, 87, 92
Horton, Rev. W. Edward, 12, 16, 20
Howdeshell, Anne, 54
Howdeshell, Don, 20, 54, 57
Hudsmith, Pam, 86
Hudsmith, Stuart, 86
Huerta-Mendez, José, 74
Huggins, John, 86
Huggins, Lynn, 86
Humphreys, Sonny, 86
Hurdle, Betty (Mrs. William L.), vi, 108
Hurdle, William L., vi

Ingram, Al, 58, 62–63
Ingram, James C., Jr., vi
Ingram, June, vi

Jackson, Alvin, 14
Jackson, Rev. Billy Joe, 70
Jayroe, Mrs. Jack C., Jr., 107
Jelinek, Patti, 86
Jelinek, Randy, 86
Jesus Claims Our Promises, 137
Jetton, Karen Henrich (Mrs. Ernest A.), 52–53, 106–07, 109–10, 121, **110**
John Gaston Hospital Maternity Ward, 114
Johnson, Bob, 86
Johnson, Carol, 86
Johnson, Harry A., Jr., vi, 11–12, 24–26, 34, 54–56, 58–59, 62–63, 65–66, 92, 95, 98, 100–03, 243–44, **243**
Johnson, Harry, III, 244
Johnson, Kelly, 244
Johnson, McKenzie, 244
Johnson, Mrs. Orin, 106
Johnson, Orin, 20
Johnson, Patty, 244
Johnson, Penny (Mrs. Harry A.), vi, 11–13, 55, 112, 243–44, **243**
Johnson, Tim, 71–72
Johnston, Charles H., 55, 105
Johnston, Rev. Earl A., 16, 48, 57–58, 66, 97–98, 101, 103, 162
Johnston, Jerry, 12
Johnston, Jerry (Mrs. Earl A.), 20
Johnston, Martha Anne, vi, 24, 54–55, 57

Jones, E. Stanley, 7, 10
Jones, Randy, 93
Jordan, Dr. G. Ray, 4–5
Joyner, Kate, 54
Jubilee Ministry, 115
Juvenile Court, 90

Kane, Sara, 52
Karban, Larry, 86
Karban, Renee, 86
Keesler Air Force Base, 7
Kelley, Carolyn (Mrs. B. J.), 129
Kelley, David L., vi
Kelley, Mary (Mrs. D. Keith), vi, 119
Kelly, Delaine (Mrs. Jimmy M.), 129
Kelly, Tom, 121
Kemmons Wilson family, 105
Kennedy, Bishop James, 7
Kentucky Conference, xi
King, Gail (Mrs. W. Scott), 124, 128–29
Kirby, David, 86
Kirby, Elizabeth, 86
Kirchoff, Rev. Rick, 16, 35, 88
Klenz, Richard "Dick," 83–86
Knepper, Helen, 86
Knepper, John G., 74, 85
Koon, Alexander, 10
Lamb, Susan Ruby Breland (Mrs. Wayne A.), 48, 54, 108–10, 115
Lamb, Rev. Wayne A., 16, 118
Lamplighters Sunday school class, 20
Lamppost Library & Resource Center, 53; *See also* Library
Lance Webb lectures, 11
Landess, Burns, 21
Lange, Eva, 86
Larson, Bruce, 8
Laubach, Frank, 7
Laurence, C. Z., 142
Laverty, John, 71–72
Leathers, Leann, 58–59, 63–64
Ledbetter, Burgess, 104
Leuze, Steve, 85
Lewis, David, 59
Libby, David, 86, 158
Libby, Donna, 86
Libby, Margaret, 85
Library, 52–53, **52**; *See also* Lamppost Library & Resource Center
God's Little Lambs & Ewe, 53
Keys to Summer Reading program, 53
Library Week, 53
Life Focus '93, 89
Limin, Mary Lou, 86
Linder, Amy, 86
Linder, Scott, 86

Lipscomb, Cindy, 158
Lipscomb, Mat, 35, 158
Lloyd, Dr. Larry, 89
Loftin, Ashley, 86–87, 162
Loftin, Carolyn, 74–75, 79, 86–87, 117, 162
Loftin, Rev. James L., 16, 67–68, 70, 74–75, 77–79, 87–88, 162, **74**
Loftin, Jonathan, 162
Long, Diane, 74
Long, Tom, 73–74, **74**
Louisville Art Glass Studio, 138, 158
Lyles, Elva, 53
Lynn, Rev. Charles H., 16
Lynn, Rev. Shirley G., 16, 54, 118, 162
Lyon, Sanford, 86

MacGruder, Harris, 87
Machen, Tom, 131–32
Madden, Ben, 93
Madden, Mary, 86
Madden, Pat, 86
Madison Heights Methodist Church, xi
Maintenance Building, 104
Manipulator in the Church, The, 8
Manning, Trudy (Mrs. Warren L.), 48
Man the Manipulator, 8
Manuel, Martha, 62
Marcum, Ray, 71
Marino, Frank, 85
Marino, Jana, 162
Marino, Mary Knapp (Mrs. Michael A.), 48, 85
Marino, Tom, 63–64, 87, 162–64
Markum, Barbara, 71
Markwell, Helen (Mrs. Kenneth, Jr.), 108, 118, **109**
Markwell, Kenneth, Jr., 105
Marsh, Dayle, 86
Marsh, Donna, 86
Marsh, Richard, 86
Marshall, Elizabeth, 86
Marshall, Jerry, 86
Marston, Ann, 20
Marston, Betty, 24
Marston, Emmett, 24
Martin, Jean, 57
Martin, Lou, 20
Massey, Art, 58, 62–63
Massey, Mary Glen (Mrs. Art), 93
Maughlin, Joanne, 69
Maughlin, Stanley, 69
Mays, Chris, 131
Mays, Eloise (Mrs. Samuel), vi, 24
Mays, Samuel, 24
McAllister, Emily, 131–32, 158

McAllister, J. W., 93
McBain, Bob, 132
McCarty, Lee, 138
McCarty, Mickael, 158
McCarty, Pup, 138
McClain, Howard, **168**
McClain, Virginia, 111
McCormick, Lee B., 24, 98, 101
McCrary, Yvonne (Mrs. Conrad), 107–09, 117, **109**
McDaniel, Rev. Pamela, 16
McDaniel, Preston, 55
McDavid, Bishop Joel, 56
McDonald, Emily, 87
McGee, Lisa, 87
McGehee, Nickolson, and Burke architectural firm, 97
McKee, Evelyn, 116
McKeithen, David, 2
McKenna, David, 15
McKenzie, Mrs. S. K., **52**
McKingh, Mary Clyde, 48
McMullen, Jane, 86
McNatt, Sandy, 86
McQuiston, Robbie, 35, 118
McVean, Ella, 24, 121
McVean, Linda, **ix**
Meador, Marguerite Murphy, 119
Medford, Mark, 86
Medford, Suzanne, 74, 86
Mediation and Reconciliation Ministry (MARM), 89–90
Mediation and Restitution/Reconciliation Services (MARRS), 44, 68, 88
Medlin, Mary Lou (Mrs. Theodore W.), 129
Medlin, Ted, 20
"Meeting Tree, The," 10
Meierhofer, Kurt, 24
Meierhofer, Ruth, 24
Meisterman, Georg, 142
Melton, Amy, 75, 77, 82
Melton, Barbara, 86, **ix**
Melton, Mark, 86
Memphis Annual Conference Journals, 19
Memphis Annual Conference, 20, 56–57, 113, **60–61**; *See Also* Annual Conference
Memphis Leadership Foundation (MLF), 89–91
Memphis Press Scimitar, 52
Men's Bible Class, 70
Methodist
Central Hospital, 59, 62, 112
Hospital Auxiliary, 106
North Hospital, 112
Publishing House, xi
School of Nursing, 112
South Hospital, 112

Metropolitan Inter-Faith
  Association (MIFA), 67, 70,
  115, 118
Middlecoff, Edith (Mrs. Carey), 119
Miles, Gordon A., vi
Miles, Tennie, vi
Miller, Anne, 24, 121
Miller, Herb, 39
Miller, Jackie, 24, 57
Miller, Keith, 8
Miller, Mrs. Greene, vi
Miller, P. D., vi, 103
Ministries
  Adult Group, 45
  Adult, 45
  Bethany Home, 70
  Children's, 45
  Prison Fellowship, 70
  Service Over Self (SOS), 68
  Youth, 45
Mischke, Lisa, 86
Mischke, Philip, 55, 59
Missions Ministry, 74
Missions, 67–91
  Africa, 69
  Atlixco, Mexico, 67, 71–72
  Bambelar, 73
  Brazil, 69–70, 164
  Congo (Zaire), 69
  Costa Rica, 164
  Czechoslovakia, 70, 164
  Dominican Republic, 164
  El Salvador, 164
  Fiji Islands, 69
  MiHaiti, 69
  Iglesia Nazaret Church, 73
  India, 69
  Jamaica, 69
  Japan, 69–70
  Korea, 69–70
  LoveLink ministry, 73
  Memphis, 70
  Morocco, 68
  Russia, 68, 75–78, 80–82, 164
  San Salvador, El Salvador,
    67–68, 73–75, **73–74**
  Sarawak, Borneo, 69
  Sierra Leone, 69
  Southern Rhodesia, 69
  Tapaluacha, 73
  Zaire, Africa, 67, 70
Mississippi Boulevard Christian
  Church, 45, 83, 90
Mississippi Conference, 7
Mitchener, Steve, 86
Montgomery, John A., vi
Moore, Beth, 24, 86
Moore, Betty, 14
Moore, Bob, 85–86
Moore, Jack, 24
Moore, Meade, 24, 86

Moore, Nancy, 24
Moore, Raymond E., vi
Morgan, Leslie, 53
Morris, Jack, 54–55, 57, **168**
Morris, Louise, 69
Morris, Rev. Marshall, 16
Morris, William, 59
Morrison, Mary Ward, 48
Morrison, Warren, 20
Morton, Rev. Fred C., 16, 20–21
Mott, Richard A., 70
Mott, Mrs. Richard A., 70
Mt. Vernon Baptist Church, 45, 83,
  90
Mulroy, Rev. Jim, 16
Mulroy, Paul, 71–72
Mungen, Thomas, 66, 162
Murchison, Harry, 86

Nashville, Tenn., 8–9
Neal, Doreen, 75
Neighborhood Center Thrift Store,
  116
Neighborhood Centers, 63, 67 70,
  106, 114
New Room, 10
Newman, Bishop Ernest W., 56
Newman, Mrs. Charles W., 107
Neyland, Melissa, 87
Neyland, Nash, 85
Noel, D. A., 24–27, 47, 50–51, 98,
  104–05, ix
Noel, Mrs. D. A., 107
Noel, Randall D. "Randy," 35, 55,
  169
North Shaba Conference,
  Lubumbashi, Zaire, 70
Nowlin, Virginia, vi, 130

Oak Court Mall, 63
Ochs, Matthew, 75
Official Board, 25, 93, 113, 243–44
Ogilvie, Lloyd John, 13, 163
Oldham, Ray, 86
Orr, Ann (Mrs. Alton G.), 24,
  54–55, 57, 86, 108–09
Orr, Harry, 24, 86
Ostner, Jim, 86
Ozier, Liza, 24

Page, Anne, 24
Page, Jonathan, 24, 86
Parham, Curt, 75
Parks, Roylyn, x
Parry, Sherman, 70
Parry, Virginia, 70
Parson, Keith, 86
Parsons, Frances, 57
Parsons, Frank, 159
Parsons, John Alden, 159
Parsons, Mrs. John A., 159

Parsons, Keith, 86
"Pastor Willy," 5
Patton, Charles, 93
Payne, George R., vi
Payne, Lou, vi, 55
Peel, Dorothy, 118
Pennington, Larry, 43, 87
Perceptions, 13–14
Perrine, Lauren, 86
Perrine, Nancy, 86
Perry, Franklin, 70
Pevahouse, Joe, 58
Pierce, Andy, 87
Pipher, Helen, vi
Pollock, Sean, 132
Poole, Elizabeth, vi, 24
Poole, William, vi
Popernik, Steve, 86
Poplar Avenue, 20, 165
Positive Christian Singles (POS),
  70
Pouco, Marvin, 69
Powell, Father John, 10
Program Committee for the World
  Methodist Conference, 12
Program Council, 40–42, 45
Programs
  Parents' Day Out, 66
  Willing Workers, 70
Purinton, Helen, 53
Pyeatt, Wayne, 55, **169**

Quarterly Conference, 28
Quiet Day, 114
Quinlan, Jack, 21

Rackley, Carl, 86
Rackley, Paige, 86
Ragland, Glenn, ix
Raley, Karen, 75
Rambo, Andy, 85, 87
Ramey, Jeremy, 164
Ramsey, Anita Lotz, 86
Ramsey, Beth, 86
Ramsey, George, 85
Rash Building, 52
Rash, Rev. Howard W., 16, 119, 159
Rauscher, Melinda, 24
Ray, Amy, 87
Redfearn, Perry, 132
Reeves Chapel, 119
Renshaw, Jack, 24, 105, 159
Renshaw, Mrs. Jack, 159
Requiem, 132
Rhodes, Boyd, 86, **35**
Rhodes, Trudy, 86
Riberts, Vikki, 110
Richmond, Edward R., 103–05
Ridolphi, Fred Miller, 159
Ridolphi, Mrs. Fred Miller, 159
Robert E. Brown Construction

Company, 105
Roberts, Bob, 24, 86
Roberts, Frances (Mrs. George T.), 119
Roberts, Irma, 53
Roberts, Mrs. R. H., 110
Roberts, Vikki, 24, 86
Robinson, Jim, 75
Rogers, Carolyn, 112
Rogers, David, 103
Rogers, Robert, 35
Rogers Youth Center, 104–05, 163
Roma, Charles, 119, 159
Rone, Gene, 121
Ross, Ann, 55
Ross, Richard "Dick" T., 35, 54–55, **168**
Ross, Todd, 86–87
Rote, Kyle, 14
Rucker, Charlene, 86
Rucker, Drew, 86
Rugh, Donald E., 69
Rugh, Mrs. Donald E., 69
Ryan, Elizabeth, 87
Ryan, Tom, 87

Samaha, Ruthie, 53
San Clemente, Calif., 6, 8–9
Sanders, Beth, **x**
Sanford, Donald L., 16, 131
Saudners, Sherry, 75
Sayle, Julia, 86
Schadt, Deborah, 21
Schaeffer, Suzanne, 35, 55
Scherr, Helen, 86
Scherr, Ralph, 86
School of Mission, Lambuth, 116
Schowengerdt, Dean Louis, 69–70
Schowengerdt, Mrs. Dean Louis, 69–70
Scott, Dan, 24
Scott, Sara Jane, 24
Seabold, Jeff, 85, 87
Seabold, Ramona, 112
Seabrook Hall, 21, 38, 58, 103–05
Segner, Ed P., Jr., 57
Semrau, Larry, 21
Service Over Self (SOS), 83–84, 87–88
Seward, Flo, 55, 132
Shafley, Sarah Allison, 87
Sharpe, Robert "Bob," 98, 101
Sheahan, Mike, 21, 70
Shelby County Interfaith, 89
Shelton, H. Clay, Jr., vi, 54–55, **52**
Shelton, Harriet (Mrs. H. Clay, Jr.), vi, 107, 110–12, **108**
Shelton, Henry C. "Hank," III, 54–55, 57
Shipmon, Tom, 20
Shostrum, Everett, 8

Shular, Steve, 57
Shumaker, Samuel, 8
Simmons, Whit, 86
Simpson, Trudy (Mrs. Warren L.), 55, 105–07, 109–10, 115, 121–22, **108**
Simpson, Wally, 55
Sippel, Brenda, 86
Sister Lelia, 7
Sistrunk, Mark, 86
Sistrunk, Missy, 86
Slappey, Bettye, 24
Slappey, Gordon, Jr., 24, 54–55
Smith, Carlos, 24
Smith, Debbie, 86
Smith, Dorree Jane, 16
Smith, Dorris, 20, 24
Smith, Eldon, 4
Smith, Jamie, 103
Smith, Linda, 111–12
Smith, Lynda, 53
Smith, Nancy, 111
Smith, Nell Carolyn (Mrs. Thomas W.), vi
Smith, Phoebe, 55
Smith, Thomas Wade, vi
Smith, Vince, 86
Smith, Mrs. William C., 108
Snow, Charlotte, 24
Snowden, Lita, 10
South Claybrook, 112
Southern Mississippi College, Hattiesburg, 2
Spangler, Mary, 86
Spangler, Ned, 86
Special Funds, 93
Spore, Richard, 86
Spore, Trish, 86
St. Columba Episcopal Conference Center, 116–17
St. Luke's Methodist choir, 132
Stafford, Dorothy (Mrs. Noel), 119
Stanley, Pat, 21
Steere, Douglas, 10
Stephen Ministry, 21–23
Stevens, Amy, 86
Stevens, Laura, 86
Stewart, Alcidean, 110
Stewart, Clinton, 86
Stewart, Mrs. Harold W., 110
Stewart, James, 9
Stires, Kartha, 53
Stolte, Alice B., vi
Stone, Jane (Mrs. John), vi
Stone, Steve, 13
Stream I: A Vision, 89
Stroud, Rev. Joe, II, 69–70
Stroud, Mrs. Joe, II, 69–70
Stubblefield, Ernest, 66
Studstill, John O., 69
Sullivan, Jane, 86

Sullivan, Jewell, vi
Summers, Mary (Mrs. J. A.), vi
Summit Club, 12
Sutch, Dan, 24
Sutch, Julie, 24, 57

Tanner, Ann, 71
Tanner, Tommy, 71
Tate, Charles Robert, 159
Tate, Eloise Garrison, 159
Taylor, Jane A., vi
Taylor, Lias, 86
Taylor, Robin, 35
Thomas, Agnes, 24
Thomas, Donald A., vi, 95, 100–01
Thomas, Donna, 162
Thomas, Mary Elizabeth, 54
Thomas, Saralene, vi
Thompson, Don, 87
Thompson, Gary, 86
Thompson, Marsha, 86
Thompson, Melanie, 86
Thompson, Nancy, 111
Thompson's Creek, 2, 6, **6**
Thorn, Ed, 105
Thorn, Howe, Stratton, and Strong, 105
Thurmon, Roy, 87
Thurmond, Mary Ann, 162
Timothy House, 163
Trinity Church, Gulfport, Miss., 6–7
Trousdale, Eugenia, 130
Trueblood, D. Elton, 22
Trust Agreement, 100
Tuberville, Kathy, 86
Tuberville, Paul, 86
Tucker, J. P., 24
Tucker, Jean, 24
Tullis, Bishop Edward, 10–11
Turner, Bart, 75
Turner, Kenneth, 89
Turpin, Tom, 244
Turpin, Janet, 12, 244
Turpin, Jay, 244
Turpin, Lauren, 244
Turpin, Mary Kate, 244
Twardzik, Tom, 86

United Methodist Women, 106–118
 Adventures in Prayer, 117
 Auxiliary Christmas Bazaar, 118
 Centennial Era Celebration, 115
 Church Women United, 115
 Circle 11, 118
 Circle 12 (Church Service Group), 116–18
 Circle 13 (Neighborhood Center Group), 118

Circle 14 (Membership and Visitation Group), 118
Circle 17, 115
Circle 18, 115
EWHA University in Korea, 115
Hospital Auxiliary, 112–14
Into the Future by Faith, 118
Ministries
  Bread of Life, 118
  Church Women United, 116, 118
  Dial-A-Prayer, 112
  Love Ward, The, 112
  Meals on Wheels, 118
  Memphis City Jail, 114, 116, 118
  Methodist Hospital Auxiliary, 116–18
  Neighborhood Center Church, 117
  Neighborhood Center Thrift Store, 118
  Neighborhood Seniors, 118
  Reelfoot Rural, 114, 116, 118
  RIF, LaRose School, 116, 118
  St. John's Soup Kitchen, 115
  Sunshine Home, 114, 116, 118
  UNICEF, 117
  United Methodist Adoption Agency, 115
  United Methodist Hospital, 115
  United Methodist Neighborhood Center, 115
  USO, 114, 116, 118
  Vacation Bible School, 118
  Wesley Foundation, 114–16, 118
  Wesley Highland Manor, 116, 118
Natives of North America, 116
Neighborhood Center Arts Festival, 115
Neighborhood Center, 116
Outside the Gate—Hebrews, 113
People of the Silver Sea, 113
Pink Lady Volunteers, 113
Quiet Day, 116–17
Toward Wholeneess-Forgiveness, 116
Wesley Highland Manor, 114–15
Winning with Prayer, 117
"Uncle Walt," 2, 4
United Methodist Church
  Board of Discipleship, 33
  Board of Evangelism, 8
  Discipleship Resources, 29

General Council on Ministries, 56
United Methodist Renewal Services Fellowship, 29, 32
University of Memphis, 20
Upper Room, The, xi, 8–11, 27–29, 33–34, 112, 116

Vandervoort, Martha, 20, 116
Van Hoose, Jilll, 87
VanSteenburg, Judy, 105
Vestol, Mimi, 118
Vickers, Nash, 67, 70, 75–77, 79
Visitors and Conventions Bureau, 62
Vital Congregation, The, 39
Volunteer Ministry, 42
Volunteers in Mission (VIM), 71–73, 164

Wadsworth, Amy, 87
Walker, David, 86
Walker, Jeff, 70
Walker, Mrs. John R., III, 161
Walker, Paige, 86
Walker, Scott, 87
Walker, Sugar (Mrs. John, III), 122
Walk to Emmaus, 33
Walton, Rev. Edward W., 16
Waston, Roger, 21
Watkins, Jeanette (Mrs. William), 58–59, 63, 111–12, **111**
Watkins, William, **169**
Weber, Henry, 54, 57
Weber, Martha, 54
Webster, Adam, 87
Weeden, John, 87
Weldon, Wilson, 8
Wertz, Bishop Frederick, 28
Wesley, John, 10
Wesleyan Fellowship, 58
West, Carole (Mrs. William), 110–11, **111**
Whaley, Rev. Patrick, 16, 63, 66
White, Deborah, 86
White, Mike, 86
Whitney, Ron, 86
Whitsitt, Mrs. H. Allen, III, 107
Whitsitt, John, 54
Whitsitt, Terry, 87
Wilder, Ann, 118
Williams, Deborah L., 75, 86, 162
Williams, Gene, 100–01, 103
Williams, John, 54
Wilroy, Sid, 75
Wilson Chapel, 12, 104–05, 121, 137–161, 164

Wilson, Amy, 86
Wilson, Dorothy, 121
Wilson, Kemmons, 121, **137**
Wilson, Mrs. Kemmons, **137**
Wilson, Pat (Mrs. John S.), 109, **110**
Wiseman, Chris, 87
Witt, Ben, 86
Witt, Stephanie, 86
Wittenberg, Jim, 87
Wood, Bob, 33
Wood, Rev. Catherine, 16
Wood, Don, 55
Wood, Rev. Robert H., 16
Woodard, C. Lasseter, 48
Woodard, Ruth Green (Mrs. C. Lasseter), 48
Word Books, 30
Work Area
  Communications, 43–44
  Education, 25, 28
  Evangelism, 44–45
workbooks
  Workbook of Coping as Christians, The, 10
  Workbook of Intercessory Prayer, The, 10
  Workbook of Spiritual Disciplines, The, 10
  Workbook on Being Alive in Christ, The, 10
  Workbook on Christians Under Construction and in Recovery, The, 10
  Workbook on Living Prayer, The, 10
  Workbook on the Christian Walk, The, 10
World Council, **9**
World Evangelism, 12
World Thanks Offering, 114
Wright, Ervin H. (Buddy), **x**
Wright, Jack, vi
Wright, Martha, vi
Wyatt, James R., vi
Wyatt, Mary Kate, vi
Wyont, Denise, 86

You Can Preach, 4
Young, Katherine, 86
Young, Terry, 86
Young Life, 162

Zachery, David, 87
Zambetti, Ann, 85, 162
Zambetti, Ellen, 86
Zambetti, Richard, 85, 162
Zambetti, Wade, 86

ABOUT THE AUTHOR

Harry A. Johnson Jr. and Penny Johnson have been married for fifty-eight years. She has supported him through thick and thin in all of life. She has given as much, if not more, of herself to Christ Church as he has, but has always listened and given her support to him.

Harry retired as a colonel, United States Marine Corps, after forty years of regular and reserve service. He was awarded fourteen medals and ribbons with four battle stars for his participation in the amphibious attack on Tarawa in the Gilbert Islands and the first landing in the Philippines, on the Island of Leyte, to occupy the Philippine Islands.

He completed a year at a naval academy preparatory school in Silver Springs, Maryland, and courses in English and analytical geometry at Siena College before entering the Marine Corps in 1941.

He was an honor student at the Naval War College and the Industrial College of the Armed Forces. He was a graduate of the Marine Corps and Army's Field Artillery Schools, the Command and Staff School at Quantico, Virginia, the Amphibious Warfare Schools at Little Creek, Virginia, and Coronado, California, and he served as commanding officer of reserve units in Memphis for eighteen years, including a Russian intelligence unit.

He was with Seabrook's for twelve years, president of Harry Johnson, Inc., for eleven years, president of Shelby-Skipwith, Inc., for fifteen years, and vice president of Woodson & Bozeman, Inc., for seven years.

In 1991, he organized Commercial and Military Computers, Inc., to sell computer equipment to the United States government worldwide and served as its president for over ten years.

Harry was chairman of the Commission on Education, chairman of the Building Committee, vice chairman of the Official Board, and helped organize and was the first president and a teacher of the Jack Hayes Class at Madison Heights Methodist Church.

He was chairman of the Church School Committee for the Steering Committee that organized Christ Methodist Church. A charter member, he served as the first church school superintendent, and on the first Building Committee, the Nominating Committee, and the Official Board. With Dr. Charles Grant, he established Christ Methodist Day School.

He served as chairman of the Host Committee when the Memphis Annual Conference was held at Christ Church in 1986, 1991, and 1996.

Penny and Harry have traveled extensively in all fifty states, all seven provinces of Canada, and in twenty-three countries in Europe and Asia. Most of the travel was done without reservations in order to enjoy the people and the countries without time constraints. Their pride and joy has been their son Harry III, his wife Patty, their children McKenzie and Kelly; and their daughter Janet and her husband, Dr. Tom Turpin, and their children Mary Kate, Lauren, and Jay.